DATE DUE

DEC 1 1 1987			
NOV 1 9 1992			

D1154357

DEMCO NO. 38-298

The Institute of Social Sciences
Seoul National University

International Studies Series No. 8

Seoul National University Press

☐ International Studies Series ☐

No 1. Maoism and Development

Chong-Wook Chung

No 2. Soviet Deterrence Doctrine

Young-Hoon Kang

No 3. Social Development and Political Violence

Chung-Si Ahn

No 4. Nuclear Proliferation, World Order and Korea

Young-Sun Ha

No 5. East Asia and the Law of the Sea

Choon-Ho Park

No 6. The Political Character of the Japanese Press

Jung-Bock Lee

No 7. Asian Perspectives in Social Science

Edited by W.R. Geddes

No 8. Asian Peoples and Their Cultures

Sang-Bok Han

SNU PRESS

ASIAN PEOPLES
AND THEIR CULTURES

Continuity and Change

Edited by SANG-BOK HAN

Seoul National University Press

ASIAN PEOPLES AND THEIR CULTURES
Continuity and Change

PREFACE

This is a collection of papers submitted before the First International Conference on "Asian Peoples and Their Cultures: Continuity and Change" held in Seoul, Korea from December 8 to 10, 1980. The conference was designed and organized by the Korean Society for Cultural Anthropology with a view to promote mutual cooperation and to share common problems and anthropological knowledge among Asian anthropologists.

Most Asian anthropologists seem to have had few opportunities so far to communicate with each other beyond their national boundaries. They know much more about anthropologists in Europe and North America and they are more in contact with Western anthropologists than they do know about and contact those who live and work across the national frontiers of their own continent. It is also true that due to the shortage of professional anthropologists and financial difficulties, most Asian anthropologists have concentrated their research on their own peoples and cultures alone, and have rarely conducted anthropological fieldwork in neighboring countries. Also they have published their research findings in their own languages. Thus, their knowledge about neighboring peoples and cultures has mostly been derived from works done by Western or native scholars who wrote in Western languages.

However, anthropology in Asia, though only recently developed, has gained firm ground as will be seen in the papers presented in this volume. There is in evidence a growing demand for anthropology in all the countries in Asia. Not only has it been regarded as academically important, its role in the solutions of practical socio-cultural problems has also been acknowledged. The fact that the anthropologists of the region have become concerned about policy relative to the growth of anthropology is a sure enough indicator of the coming of age of the discipline. What is needed now is a forum for the exchange of ideas and cooperative research activities.

For the first time in the history of Asian anthropology, twenty odd anthropologists from eight countries including Thailand, Malaysia, Indonesia, the Philippines, Hong Kong, the Republic of China, Japan, and Korea spent three days together to discuss various problems under two broad themes, "anthropological studies in Asian countries" and "continuity and change in Asian peoples and their cultures." Fourteen papers were presented and discussed at the conference. Our acknowledgement must be given to the primary contributors: Chi-Lu Chen, National Taiwan University; Chien Chiao, Chinese University of Hong Kong; Oak-La Cho, Sokang University; F. Landa Jocano, University of the Philippine System; Shin--Pyo Kang, Academy of Korean Studies (at present Hanyang University); Koentjaraningrat, University of Indonesia; Kwang-Kyu Lee, Seoul National University; Hood Salleh, University of Kebangsaan Malaysia; Takao Sofue, National Museum of Ethnology (at present University of Air); Michio Suenari, University of the Sacred Heart; Srisakra Vallibhotama, Silpakorn University; and Sung-Hsing Wang, Chinese University of Hong Kong.

To the chairpersons, co-chairpersons, and discussants of the conference sessions: Hyup Choi, Chonnam University; Cha-Whan Chung, Sacred Heart College for Women; Joo-Hee Kim, Songshin University; Kwang-Ok Kim, Seoul National University; Yi-Gu Kwon, Yeungnam University; Du-Hyun Lee, Seoul National University; Mun-Woong Lee, Seoul National University; Eun-Kyung Park, Ewha Women's University; Joong-Chul Yeo, Yeungnam University; Suk-Jay Yim, Korean Society for Cultural Anthropology; and all the contributors who chaired and discussed at the sessions, substantial thanks are also due for their critical insight, valuable comments, and suggestions. Koentjaraningrat and Vallibhotama submitted two papers respectively. Yih-Yuan Li of Academia Sinica, Republic of China was expected to present a paper which was to be a general assessment of anthropological studies on Taiwanese aborigines but he could not attend the conference for personal reasons and was not able to send us the expected paper until the last stage of the editorial process.

Representing the Korean Society for Cultural Anthropology, I would like to express appreciation for the patience and sincerity of the participants and the invaluable help of students of the Department of Anthropology at Seoul National University. I am indebted to my former graduate students Myeong-Seok Oh for his secretarial work for the conference and Ik-Joo Hwang for the final proofreading and indexing of this book. A special word of gratitude should go to my two colleagues at Seoul National University. Mun-Woong Lee played a critical role as the Executive Secretary who was responsible for the administrative work of the conference. Kwang-Ok Kim, on his return from Oxford, joined in the preparation of the conference and helped in editing the present volume. My special thanks are due to the Ministry of Education of the Republic of Korea which provided generous financial support for the conference. I also convey my thanks to Dr. Kyong-Dong Kim, Director of the Institute of Social Sciences, and Professor Jong-Chul Lim, Director of the University Press, of Seoul National University for making this publication possible.

With my sincere apologies for the delay of publication, I hope the second conference of this kind will be duly held under the initiative of the Republic of China or the Federation of Malaysia as it was unanimously decided at the end of the first conference.

Sang-Bok Han

Seoul, Korea.
March, 1986

CONTRIBUTORS

Chen, Chi-Lu   Born 1923, Taiwan, China. Educated at St. John's University, Shanghai, B.A.; University of New Mexico, M.A.; University of Tokyo, Ph.D. Has done fieldwork among various aboriginal groups in Taiwan and Chinese communities. Currently professor of Anthropology, National Taiwan University; Member of Academia Sinica. Visiting Scholar at School of Oriental and African Studies, University of London; Visitng Professor at Michigan State University (1969-70). Director, Institute of American Culture, Academia Sinica. Dean of College of Liberal Arts, National Taiwan University. Author of *Woodcarving of the Paiwan Group of Taiwan; Social Organization of the Sun-Moon Lake Thas; Material Culture of the Formosan Aborigines,* and over 90 articles.

Chiao, Chien   Born 1935, China. Educated at National Taiwan University, B.A., M.A.; Cornell University, Ph.D. Has done Fieldwork among aborigines in Taiwan, and Navajo. Lecturer, Assistant Professor, and Associate Prfessor of Anthropology, Indiana University (1966-76); Visiting Lecturer, Hofstra University (1967); Associate Research Fellow, Insititute of Ethnology, Academia Sinica (1970-71); Lecturer, Senior Lecturer and Chairman, Department of Anthropology, The Chinese University of Hong Kong (1973-) Author of *Continuation of Tradition in Navajo Society* (1971); Co-author of *A First Course in Literary Chinese* (1968); and many other articles in Chinese and English.

Cho, Oak-La   Born 1950, Korea. Educated at Seoul National University, B.A., M.A.; State University of New York at Stony Brook, Ph.D. Has done fieldwork in rural villages in Korea. Instructor, Seoul National University (1980); Instructor, Assistant Professor since 1981 at Sogang University. Author of 'Peasant Society and Yang-Ban' *Chintan Hakpo* (in Korean, 1981); 'A Study on Korean Rural Villages from Anthropological Perspectives' *Korean Cultural Anthropology* (in Korean, 1981); and other papers.

Han, Sang-Bok   Born 1935, Korea. Educated at Seoul National University, B.A., M.A.; Michigan State University, Ph.D. Has done fieldwork mainly in farming and fishing villages in Korea and Japan. Instructor, Hanshin University (1962-64); Instructor, Fulltime Lecturer, Assistant Professor, Associate Professor and Professor since 1964 at Seoul National University. Director of the Population and Development Studies Center, at the same University since 1982. President of Korean Society for Cultural Anthropology (1978-1980). Author of *Life in Urban Korea* (1970); *Socio-Economic Organization and Change in Korean Fishing Villages* (1972); *Korean Fishermen* (1977); *Continuity and Change in Korean Culture* (in Korean, co-author, 1980); *Koreans and Korean Culture* (in Korean, editor, 1982); and numerous books and articles.

Jocano, F. Landa   Born in the Philippines. Educated at University of Philippines, B.A.; University of Chicago, M.A., Ph.D. Has done studies on various Philippine subcultural groups and fieldwork among ethnic groups in the Philippines and American Indians in New Mexico. Curreutly Professor of Anthropology and Dean of the Institute of Philipine Studies at the Philippine Center for Advanced Studies, University of the Philippines System. Held various positions including Senior Anthropologist at the National Museum in Manila; Research Associate of the University of Chicago, and Professorial Lecturer at Centro Escolar University. Author of *Sulod Society* (1968); *Tuburan* (1976); *Outline of Philippine Mythology* (1969); *Philippine Prehistory* (1975); *Folk Medicine in a Philippine Municipality* (1978). Co-author of *San Antonio* (1976); *The Filipino Family in Its Rural and Urban Orientation* (1974); and numerous books and articles.

Kang, Shin-Pyo   Born 1936, Korea. Educated at Seoul National University, B.A., M.A.; University of Hawaii, Ph.D. Has done fieldwork in Hawaii and in various subcultural sectors in Korea. Instructor, Seoul Women's College (1962-65); Fulltime Lecturer, Seoul Teacher's College (1965-67); Assistant Professor, Yeongnam University (1973-1977); Associate Professor, Ewha Women's University (1977-1980); Professor, Academy of Korean Studies (1980-82); Presently Professor at Hanyang University since 1983. President of Korean Society for Cultural Anthropology (1980-82). Author of *The East Asian Culture and Its Transformation in the West* (1973); *Korean Immigrants in Tansan* (in Korean, 1980); 'The Structural Principle of Chinese Worldview' *The Unconscious in Culture: Strcuturalism of Lévi-Strauss in Perspective,* ed. by I, Rossi (1974); and numerous books and articles.

Koentjaraningrat   Born 1923, Indonesia. Educated at the University of Indonesia, B.A.; Yale University, M.A., University of Indonesia, Ph.D. Has done filedwork among Central Javanese Peasants, West New Guinea sago gatherers, and Dutch fishermen. Deputy Chairman of the Indonesian Institute for Sciences (1968-77), Guest Professor at the University of Utrecht (1966-1968), Columbia University (Summer 1967), University of Illinois

(Winter 1968), Ohio State University (1972), and University of Wisconsin (1980). Presently Professor of Anthropology and Assistant Director of the Central Ecological Studies and Human Resources of the University of Indonesia. Author of 15 books including *Villages in Indonesia* (1967); *Social Sciences in Indoensia* (1975); *Anthropology in Indonesia* (1976); and over 60 articles in Indonesian, English, and Dutch.

Lee, Kwang-Kyu   Born 1932, Korea. Educated at Seoul National University, B.A.; Vienna Universität, Ph.D. Instructor, Vienna Universität (1964-66); Instructor, Assistant Professor, Associate Professor, and Professor since 1967 at Seoul National University; Visiting Professor at Plymouth University (1973-74); Visiting Professor at the University of California, Berkley (1979-80). President of Korean Society for Cultural Anthropology (1976-78). Author of *Kinship System in Korea* (1975); *Historical Study of Korean Family System* (in Korean 1977); *Study on the Structure of Korean Family* (in Korean 1975); and many other books and articles.

Salleh, Hood   Born 1942, Malaysia. Educated at University of Western Australia, B.A.; University of Oxford, Diploma, B. Litt., D. Phil. Has done fieldwork among the Malay. Tutor (1970-1973), Lecturer (1973-1975), Head of the Department (1975-76, 1979-1982), of Social Anthropology, University of Kebangsaan; Currently Senior Lecturer of Social Anthropology, and Fellow at the Institute of Malay Language, Literature and Culture, University of Kebangsaan. Main research efforts have been on the *Semelai* principally on their oral history (*Akademika,* 1975), morality (*Monograph 3,* UKM. 1976), and healing rites (Seminar paper, UKM. 1976). (Mainly in Malay and English).

Sofue, Takao   Born 1926, Japan. Educated at the University of Tokyo, B.Sc(Anthropology). Has done fieldwork among Alaskan Eskimo, and various Japanese communities. Professor of Anthropology and Sociology, Meiji University (1966-74); Professor of East Asian Studies and Psychological Anthropology, National Museum of Ethnology, Osaka (1974-1984); Professor of Anthropology, Hoso University, Tokyo (1984-); President, Japanese Ethnological Association 1969-72. Author of *Prefectural Personalities* (in Japanese, 1970); *Culture and Personality* (in Japanese, 1976); *Introduction to Cultural Anthropology* (in Japanese, 1979); 'Aspects of the Personality of Japanese, Americans, Italians and Eskimos: Comparisons Using the Sentence Completion Test' *Journal of Psychological Anthropology* Vol. 2, No. 1, 1979; and many other books and articles.

Suenari, Michio   Born 1938, Japan. Educated at University of Tokyo, B.A., M.A., Ph.D. Has done fieldwork in various farm villages in Japan, Korea, and Taiwan. Studied at University of Chicago (1965-66). Professor of Social Anthropology, University of the Sacred Heart, Japan since 1972. Author of 'First Child Inheritance in Japan' *Ethnology* (1972); 'Family and the First Child Inheritance among the Paiwan' *The Memoirs of the Institute of Oriental Culture* (in Japanese, 1973); 'The Cult of the Ancestors in Taiwan' *Seishin Studies* (in Japanese, 1977); 'The Cult of the Dead at the Grave in Andong District of Korea' *The Journal of the Institute for Shilla Kaya Culture* (in Korean, 1978); and other papers.

Vallibhotama, Srisakra   Born 1938, Thailand. Educated at Chulalongkorn University, B.A.; University of Western Australia, M.A. Has done fieldwork in various Thai communities. Lecturer in Thai History, Silpakorn University (1961-71); Visiting Lecturer of Anthropology, Chiengmai University (1971-72); Lecturer in Thai Studies, Silpakorn University (1972-77); Head of Department of Anthropology, Silpakorn University (1977-1980); Visiting Professor, Cornell University (1980); Associate Professor of Anthropology, Silpakorn University (1980-). Author of 'The Kingdom of Haripunjaya' *Art and Archaeology in Thailand* (1974); 'The Need for an Inventory of Ancient Sites for Anthropological Research in Northeastern Thailand' *Tonan Ajia Kenkyu* (1972); 'Thai Studies in Transition: Report on Origins, Problems, and Trends' *East Asian Cultural Studies* (1980); and other papers.

Wang, Sung-Hsing   Born 1935, Taiwan, China. Educated at National Taiwan University, B.A.; London School of Economics and Political Sciences, M.A.; University of Tokyo, Ph.D. Has done fieldwork in various Chinese societies. Research Fellow at the Institute of Ethnology, Academia Sinica 1965-1976. Has taught at the Department of Anthropology, the Chinese University of Hongkong since 1976. Author of *Kuei-Shan Tao: A Study of a Chinese Fishing Community in Formosa* (1967); co-author of *Rice Farming-Taiwan* (1974); and many other articles.

CONTENTS

Editor's Preface   v

Contributors   ix

1. Introduction: Anthropological Studies on
   Asian Peoples and Their Cultures   Sang-Bok Han   1

Part I. Anthropological Studies in Asian Countries

2. Status of Anthropological Studies
   on the Philippine Society and Culture   F.L. Jocano   15

3. Anthropological Research on Aboriginal
   Groups of the Malay Peninsula   Hood Salleh   29

4. Anthropology and Sociology in Indonesia
                                            Koentjaraningrat   45

5. Anthropological Studies in the Republic
   of China during the Last Three Decades   Chi-Lu Chen   89

6. Sinology and Sino-anthropology :
   Family Study as an Example   Sung-Hsing Wang   105

7. Anthropological Studies in Korea   Kwang-Kyu Lee   117

8. Thai Studies in Transition : A Report
   on Origins, Problems and Trends   Srisakra Vallibhotama   139

Part II. Asian Peoples and Their Cultures

9. Continuity and Change of Ancestor
   Worship in East Asia : A Comparative Study of Memorial Tablet
                                             Michio Suenari   167

10. The System of Belief in Korean
    Rural Communities   Oak-La Cho   185

11. Meru : A Symbol of Continuity
    and Change in Thai Society   *Srisakra Vallibhotama*   201
12. Spiritual Movements in Javanese Culture   *Koentjaraningrat*   221
13. Games Are Forever : A Preliminary
    Discussion on Continuity and Change
    in Manipulative Behavior of the Chinese   *Chien Chiao*   241
14. Continuity and Change in the Japanese
    Personality   *Takao Sofue*   259
15. A Buddhist Approaches in Anthropology:
    An Understanding of Margaret Mead   *Shin-Pyo Kang*   277

    Index   283

1 Introduction : Anthropological Studies on Asian Peoples and Their Cultures

The papers brought together in this volume cover so wide and various a range that it is almost impossible to draw up a bird's-eye picture for an over-all evaluation. Therefore, for convenience of presentation, they are divided into two parts according to the nature of contents: (1) anthropological studies in Asian countries and (2) Asian peoples and their cultures.

Anthropological Studies in Asian Countries

The papers in the first half of the book are devoted to a general review of the trends in anthropology in some countries such as the Philippines, Malaysia, Indonesia, Republic of China, Korea, and Thailand. Seven papers are classified as belonging to this category; two papers concerning China and one for each of the rest. From the outset, however, we find ourselves in deep water since it appears that the style and contents of the papers are different, and the contributors also differ in their scope and the concept of anthropology they have adopted. For example, whilst Lee of Korea deals with only the field of cultural anthropology in which he includes studies made in the field of folklore, material culture, and oral tradition but excludes those carried out in the field of physical anthropology and archaeology, Jocano of the Philippines gives more weight to archaeological studies in his review of anthropology in his country. Chen from Taiwan confines his review to the studies of minority groups by Japanese and Chinese anthropologists of the prewar generation whilst other contributors such as Salleh from Malaysia and Koentjaraningrat from

Indonesia introduce researches conducted mainly by contemporary Western anthropologists and sociologists. In contrast to the above contributors, Vallibhotama of Thailand reviews current problems and trends in archaeological, historical, sociological, and anthropological studies of the country by both native and foreign scholars.

This variety in the style and content of presentation reflects not only personal points of view but also, and perhaps more significantly, the condition of the discipline in their respective countries. Despite the variety, it is still considered worthwhile publishing these papers in their original form. By doing so, we may overcome the irony that we are ignorant of our neighbors whereas we know a great deal more about anthropology in other countries such as U.S.A. and the U.K. or even those in the African continent.

In fact, the conference provided the participants with the first opportunity of its kind to meet each other and to learn from each other. So seldom had contact been made that during the conference each participant acted in relation to each other as though they were dealing with some native informants during fieldwork. An anthropologist from Thailand, for example, spent considerable time exchanging ideas with his counterpart from Malaysia, and a Chinese anthropologist expressed great interest in what had been going on in the field of anthropology in Japan.

Each paper has its own flavour reflecting the specific nature of anthropological study in each country. Jocano discusses three fields in anthropology: archaeology, ethnology, and culture change in his brief assessment of the status of the discipline in the Philippines. According to Jocano, as a consequence of the growing national consciousness for a redefinition of Filipino national identity, archaeological researches are funded and supported by the government and private organizations more than any other field in anthropology. Linguistic categories and genetic studies as well as prehistoric archaeological studies are actively carried out among contemporary anthropologists in order to trace the ethno-cultural origin and the route of Filipino migratory movement. Recently, studies on socio-cultural change have also become dominant in anthropological research in connection with government projects for socio-economic development.

The study of cultural origin is also one of the main themes in Malaysia but in this case it is the domain of social anthropology. Salleh reports that most anthropologists specializing in Malay society are engaged in the study of orang asli, the aborigines of the society. With a brief review of the history of anthropological study about the indigenous people he illustrates some ethnographical researches conducted by contemporary anthropologists. He also stresses the need for a linguistic approach in the study of continuity and change of the culture of *orang asli* which is undergoing drastic changes as a result of contact with outside elements such as people of the Chinese and Malay origins. He also introduces some studies concerning these changes with regard to their world view, concepts of economic value, political structure, and the process of economic exploitation by the Chinese and the Malay.

Such studies with reference to ethno-cultural origins and culture change seem to have been more emphasized in polygenous societies. In addition to the Philippines and Malaysia, those ethnically heterogeneous countries like Indonesia and Taiwan also emphasize the importance and value of the study of ethnicity. Koentjaraningrat in his over-all historical review of anthropological studies in Indonesia emphasizes the contribution of anthropology to national reconstruction through the pursuit of cultural heritage and the way to solve the ethnic problems. As the title of his paper suggests, anthropology and sociology have developed side by side and there has been a close relationship between the two disciplines, though the former is more inclined toward the study of cultural tradition and diversity, ethnic problems, and socio-cultural dynamics whilst the latter mainly concerns itself with rural development projects and social improvement studies.

Chen's historical review of anthropological studies in the Republic of China begins with a brief summary of studies on minority groups in the mainland by Chinese ethnologists before 1945. Then he shifts his eye to Taiwan and looks at ethnological investigations on aborigines conducted by Japanese scholars during the period of the Second World War, and those by Chinese anthropologists since 1945. Along with the traditional researches on the aborigines, young anthropologists recently began studies of their own society and culture which in the past have been studied mainly by American students. At the same time, it is noted that the nature of anthropology is changing from that of a humanity to that of a social science with an orientation toward behavioural science and the study of current social problems. Anthropologists are also expected to contribute in their reconstruction of local social history. Chen draws our attention to the fact that there are, apart from the Chinese, more than nine ethnic groups which are culturally distinct from each other, and he emphasizes the urgent need for more systematic and ethnographic studies about these groups which are undergoing drastic change.

We could have learned more about these Taiwanese aborigines, had we got Professor Yih-Yuan Li's paper as it was expected to deal with anthropological studies on them.

Criticizing the so-called 'worm's-eye-view' of village studies, Wang suggests, in accordance with B. Ward and M. Freedman, the importance of collaboration of sinology and anthropology in the study of China which has such complicated cultural settings and a long history. To support his ideas, he draws some examples of Japanese sinologists who used historical records in their study of the Chinese family system. It is regrettable that further discussion on his paper was aborted due to his absence. I would like to mention here that many anthropologists have already recognized the usefulness of historical materials and the importance of an interdisciplinary approach for the study of a society which has a long cultural tradition. We see examples of this kind of work even in this volume where Chen and Suenari emphasize the importance of cooperation between anthropology and history, and Chiao and Vallibhotama use historical data and many other materials in order to understand Chinese political behavior and the symbolic meaning of funeral processes in Thailand respectively.

Lee's review of Korean anthropology reveals a slightly different picture. Since Korea is an ethnically and culturally homogeneous society, the studies on ethnic groups and their cultural origins are not so popular in the field of cultural anthropology today though some historians and archaeologists have shown interest in such studies. Within the field of cultural anthropology of his own definition, Lee attempts a general description of works in such subjects as folklore, material culture, social anthropology, and religion. His statistical tabulation indicates that family, kinship, marriage, and lineage are predominant in the field of social anthropology. At the same time, the study of religion, especially shamanism, has been the most popular subject among students of all generations. He also points out that the folklorist tradition of anthropology is being replaced by a social science orientation by young anthropology students who try to diversify not only in their study area but also in theory and methodology as well.

Finally Vallibhotama's paper concerning the condition of Thai studies is included. Though it was originally published elsewhere the editor decided to put it in the present edition because it provides a clear picture of the trends and overall nature of anthropology in Thailand. The writer maintains that studies on Thai society and culture in the sense of social science began with the introduction of anthropology into that country during the 1960s. Since then, new theories and methodology are expected to overcome the previous trend of study marked by 'nationalistic overtones'. However, as Vallibhotama points out, heavy teaching loads, limited research funds, most of which are being allocated to problem-oriented governmental projects, and an academic generation gap are the main obstacles against development of the discipline. Despite these problems, the Thai studies have reached a transitional stage through the establishment of anthropological approaches.

The status quo of anthropology in Thailand is characterized by two main features. One is what Vallibhotama terms 'a cultural lag'; whilst intellectuals of the younger generation insist anthropology be most useful for the study of their culture in social context and dynamic aspects as well, traditional elites and older generation scholars are much more interested in history and old fashioned archaeology The other is an overemphasis on an interdisciplinary approach among the new intellectual groups for applied purposes. Hence, they often overlook the differences in the frames of reference and tend to rely on one or two social theories, i.e. the Marxist approach. Vallibhotama's realistic assessment of the situation in Thailand may be applied to most Asian countries to varying degrees.

All in all, anthropology in the countries mentioned above appears to have some common features. First, the developmental process of the discipline is very similar in each country: anthropology, whether accorded the name of ethnology or folklore, was introduced by foreign elements such as Western scholars and missionaries or colonial administrators through their research and establishment of educational institutions. So-called native anthropologists began to be produced mostly after the Second World War as young students were given more opportunities to be trained in Western countries with advanced theories and methodology. As a consequence, the folklorist tradition is replaced by modern anthropology and the 'butterfly collecting' of old-generation anthropologists is replaced by the systematic research of new-generation anthropologists. It has also been noted that along with the tradition of Asian anthropologists engaged in studying their own culture, studies of other cultures have recently increased.

Second, anthropology in Asian countries in general is in a transitional period: the nature of the discipline is moving from the pole of the humanities to that of the social sciences. The role of anthropology is stressed in dealing with national reconstruction and social development projects. It is also expected to take the lead in the pursuit of an interdisciplinary approach which is strongly recommended within the field of social sciences.

Third, topics of anthropological research are very much diversified as the number of anthropologists increases and newly developed theories are introduced from Western countries. Not only the study of ethno-cultural origin and its transformation, but also modernization processes and even medical anthropology are dealt with by anthropologists. Also new perspectives, i.e. symbolism, structuralism, and cultural ecology are introduced and theory-building work is paralleled with those in applied fields.

It is hoped that the continuation of this kind of conference will facilitate the mechanisms for more systematic assessment and conclusive accumulation of knowledge focussing on a single subject and thus, comparative studies will be possible. I would note with regret that in this conference we could not get papers on the status of anthropological studies in other countries in Asia including Japan and mainland China, though they are considered to have a relatively long tradition of anthropology. Fortunately, however, the reports on the status of anthropology in the following Asian countries are available in other sources: Bangladesh (Afsaruddin 1985), People's Republic of China (Rossi 1985), India (Vidyarthi and Rai 1985), Japan (Terada 1975), Nepal (Manandhar 1985), Pakistan (Dani 1985), Singapore (Clammer 1985), Sri Lanka (Pieris 1985), and Turkey (Magnarella and Turkdogan 1976). As we continue and expand this kind of meeting, we sincerely hope that we may have more opportunities in the future to know more about each other and also to include other Asian countries which were not able to participate in this conference.

Asian Peoples and Their Cultures

The second half of the book is devoted to the proceedings of various topics under the common subject of the conference "Asian Peoples and Their Cultures: Continuity and Change". This part begins with Suenari's paper 'Continuity and Change of Ancestor Worship in East Asia' based on the result of his fieldwork carried out in Taiwan, Korea, and Japan. It is a comparative study of the relationship between kinship ideology and the form of ancestor worship ceremony focussing on memorial tablets. His findings are as follows. Korean memorial tablet-worship seems to be based on a strict patrilineal principle, to be comparatively uniform, and to be coloured with Confucian formalism. Among the Chinese in Taiwan, especially those of Fukien origin, the patrilineal principle is somewhat attenuated in order to permit a range of deviation whilst a strong sense of reciprocity between the ancestors and descendants can be observed. In Japan, however, tablet-worship is closely related with the *ie* system and thus, it has greater variety and non-kin members are included more widely than in the case of the Chinese in Taiwan. Faced with the sharp contrast of Korean formalism and Japanese looseness in the ancestor worship ceremony, Suenari suggests that in Japan only the material element in the custom of ancestral tablet was introduced while dropping the patrilineal element and Confucian ritualism. Then he attempts to develop a model for understanding the historical process by analyzing the process of culture change with special reference to the form of ancestor worship among the Puyuma, a tribe of Taiwanese aborigines. Pointing out the similarity of the ritual with the Chinese, although the lineage regulation is different, he concludes that the Puyuma have been able to worship their ancestors in the Chinese manner using their own principles of descent. He infers this as a result of the elasticity of the native kinship system. In the same way, he proposes a hypothesis that a similar process might have occurred when the Chinese tablet system was introduced into Japan due to the elasticity of the *ie* system.

Continuity of traditional culture is also examined by Cho. In her much revised paper, Cho describes belief systems among the rural people of Korea which she classifies into two broad categories; ancestral worship and folk religion expressed in the form of animism and shamanism. Her departing point is that ancestral worship which is based on Confucian ethics hardly encourages the worship of spiritual beings but people still adhere to the folk religion which concerns the relationship between man and supernatural beings. She argues that folk religion in fact does not cause conflict directly with Confucianism, because its emphasis on the power of the dead person's spirit provides the common ground for the ancestor worship ceremonies which are the core of Confucian rituals. As a result, peasant rituals for the relationship between man and nature take the same formality as Confucian rituals. She maintains that ancestral worship is observed mainly by the upper class whilst other folk religions such as animism and shamanism are the domain of the commoner and womenfolk. She points out that traditional belief systems have undergone very little change and a new religion such as Christianity does not enjoy influence, and attributes the fact to the rigidity of the traditional social class system. It may be the case in her own village but local variations should be examined before attempting a generalization. It is interesting that she tries to understand different forms of religion in relation to social strata. As far as the belief system is concerned, however, we should be careful not to confuse the form of expression with the underlying system of ideas.

An interesting case of a materialist approach to symbolism is seen in Vallibhotama's interpretation of symbolic meaning in a continuing structure of funeral rites focussing on the cremation on the pyre called *Meru* in Thailand. Symbolizing the pillar of the universe according to Hindu-Buddhist conception, the *Meru*, a rectangular platform constructed in the temple for cremation, was monopolized by the king and royal family members in the past. Though not in the same way, high ranking officials were also allowed by the king to use the structure. Therefore, cremation on the *Meru* was the symbol of the sacred, the highest social status of the royal family, and as well, that of the socio-political prestige of the bureaucracy. Vallibhotama notes that despite the end of the absolute monarchy and the development of an open society which facilitates easier social mobility, the cremation on the *Meru* becomes more and more popular only among the previously mentioned sector of the population and its permanent construction can be seen nowadays in almost all temples in Bangkok. The writer interprets this phenomenon as an expression of class consciousness among the upper class who would otherwise lose their distinctiveness because other material objects including television sets, cars, houses which had hitherto served as a class indicator, are now shared with the whole of the population as a result of the general socio-economic development of Thai society. At the same time, common people also use the pyre in order to earn new social prestige and to share the traditional symbolic meanings which were not allowed to them in the past. As a consequence, the cremation fees have now become one of the major income sources of temples, and construction of the pyre has become widespread in the rural areas as well. Vallibhotama concludes that this proliferation of the past installment for cremation implies continuity and change of traditonal culture: continuity of its symbol and form of practice, and change in its function.

Koentjaraningrat deals with religious movements in Indonesia through the analysis of spiritual movements within the Javanese Islamic circles. This movement is divided into two categories: *kebatinan* movement and *santri* movement. The *kebatinan* movement is characterized as being fundamentally a self-innovation movement to strengthen and to purify the individual's religious mind and life whilst the *santri* movement is a puritanical movement toward the return to pristine Islamic religious beliefs and practices. Both movements emphasize the adherence to the traditional Islamic religious beliefs and practices.

Observing the rapid spread and proliferation of such spiritual movements among the population, Koentjaraningrat seeks the causes from 'the increasingly rapid socio-cultural changes which have occurred in the period of transformation, the extreme hardships, poverty, and insecurity suffered by the people during the period of the Pacific War, the Japanese occupation, the Indonesian Revolution, and the unsettled conditions during the first decades of Indonesia's independence'. Therefore, in both sections of the movement, mysticism and magic along with ethical movements for the purification of the soul and messianic movements are common and predominant.

His paper, being concerned mainly with a general description of organizations and doctrines for the movement, leaves us with hope for a more detailed analysis of his data in relation to mysticism and magic in other opportunity.

Apart from those papers on religion, Chiao attempts a study on politics. He emphasizes continuity rather than changing aspects of a culture in dealing with the principles of political behavior which he hypothesizes as being an important aspect of traditional Chinese culture. On the premise that social and political strategies form a highly sophisticated, extensive and uninterrupted tradition in Chinese culture, he argues that what is manifested by the contemporary Chinese in their manipulative behavior is basically the continuation of the old tradition. Then he selects thirty basic principles of political behavior as expressed by Chinese characters of phrases to examine.

It is a very interesting study but whether these principles can be labelled 'Chinese' may be questioned especially when these manipulative behaviors are supposed to be found in any society. At the same time, a question about the degree of social recognition as principle among the Chinese population was raised during the discussion session.

However, a study of this kind is significant in that it helps us understand the dynamics of Chinese society and the true face of its social mobility. Chiao emphasizes that contrary to the stereotyped description of the Chinese society as a highly rigid system in which each individual is fixed to a specific status, it contains more alternatives for its members to maneuver and optimize than any of the other traditional societies.

While Chiao concerns himself with the continuity of tradition in Chinese political behavior, Sofue deals with the changing aspects of Japanese culture, especially in the field of personality as manifested in the behavior and psychology of the young generation. While stressing that most of the typical personality features are maintained in their traditional form, Sofue selects some aspects which are distinctive among contemporary young people to observe the dynamic aspects of a changing Japanese society.

His analysis is as follows. Vertical relationships are changing greatly and this aspect may be illustrated by the fact that compulsive obedience and the honorific use of terms have greatly diminished among the young people. Heterosexual relationships based on Confucian ideology are also changing toward more equal and free relationships and this is expressed by the prevalence of love marriages and the increasing voice of women in political and social life. The collateral relationship which has been very prominant among the Japanese as a whole is changing as a result of ever increasing opportunities for international communication. As a result, the so-called 'we-japanese-feeling' is relatively weak among the young generation. Achievement aspiration which is the label of Japanese work ethics developed during the *Tokugawa* period and encouraged by the *Meiji* imperial government is now differently valued between the old and the young generations. Those of the latter group are oriented more to individualism and enjoy their economic prosperity enough to support leisure time and recreation. On the other hand, the compromise and group orientation, though changing, are still sustained because they are deeply rooted in their lack of self-confidence in the face of an uncertain future. Lastly, views concerning nature are considered. The Japanese attitude toward nature is termed 'harmony with nature', as seen in their arrangement of garden or house decoration which symbolizes a continuity between the interior living space and the outside, and in the flavour for raw food. Sofue goes on; despite the high development of technology and successful industralization, this does not give the Japanese a real experience of the development of a scientific tradition which attempts to understand natural phenomena through observation. The traditional 'man in nature' orientation, therefore, may continue.

Finally, the volume should conclude with Kang's paper which equates anthropologists' experiences to those of Buddhist priests. Comparing Margaret Mead to a Buddhist monk, he asserts that the anthropological tradition in Asian countries reflects certain aspects of Mahayana Buddhism, and attempts a possible junction between this Asian philosophical tradition and the Western anthropological methodology. His paper which sounded like a Margaret Mead memorial lecture delivered by a Buddhist monk was bombarded with many questions from the participants of the conference. To pick up only one, the question was why Mead should be compared with a Buddhist monk and what is the criteria, if there is any, which distinguish anthropologists from Buddhist monks or any one in the street who is interested in the meaning of life and ready for adventure? I requested a revision of the paper with more detailed explanations, but Kang responded by sending the original paper without a single alteration. Therefore, it had to be included in its original form with all the questions raised during the discussion unanswered. Anyway, it would be interesting if he would develop his idea to the extent that there could be a comparison between the Western and the Asian anthropologists' attitudes toward the meaning of human life, provided it can be empirically substantiated.

As we have reviewed, the themes and contents of the papers are so varied that they cannot be fully covered by one conference of three days. More constructive arguments beyond mere introductory presentations were painstakingly attempted since participants had not sufficient knowledge to lead full discussions on those proceedings which were extremely specialized. Nonetheless, it is believed that the present publication of the proceedings may contribute towards mutual cooperation among Asian anthropologists in the future and widen the scope of anthropological horizons. This volume is only the first step toward this ultimate goal.

References

Afsaruddin Mohammad
  1985 "Sociology and Social Anthropology in Bangladesh," *In* UNESCO
      1985, pp. 388-409.
Clammer, John
  1985 "Sociology and Social Anthropology in Singapore," *In* UNESCO 1985,
      pp. 265-310.
Dani, Ahmad Hasan
  1985 "Sociology and Social Anthropology in Pakistan," *In* UNESCO 1985,
      pp. 361-387.
Geddes, W.R. (ed.)
  1985 *Asian Perspectives in Social Science.* Seoul: Seoul National University
      Press.
Magnarella, P.J. and O. Turkdogan
  1976 "The Development of Turkish Social Anthropology," *Current Anthro-
      pology,* Vol. 17, No. 2, pp. 263-274.
Manandhar, M.S.
  1985 "Social Science Development in Nepal," *In* Geddes (ed.) 1985, pp.
      69-73.
Pieris, Ralph
  1985 "Social Science Development in Sri Lanka," *In* Geddes (ed.) 1985, pp.
      99-116.
Rossi, Alice S. (ed.)
  1985 *Sociology and Anthropology in the Peoples' Republic of China.*
      Washingron D.C.: National Academy Press.
Terada, Gasuo
  1975 *Nihonno Jinruigaku* (Japanese Anthropology). Tokyo: Shisakushia.
UNESCO
  1985 *Sociology and Social Anthropology in Asia and the Pacific.* New Delhi:
      Wiley Eastern
Vidyarthi, L.P. and B.K. Rai
  1985 "History of Indian Anthropology," *In* Vidyarthi and Rai, *The Tribal
      Culture of India* (2nd ed.). New Delhi: Concept, pp. 3-24.

Part I

Anthropological Studies in Asian Countries

2   Status of Anthropological Studies on the Philippine Society and Culture

F. LANDA JOCANO

Introduction

In this paper, I shall present a brief historical assessment of the status of anthropological research in the Philippines. A detailed one would require a volume. As a discipline, anthropology is new in the country, although what might be considered anthropological writing has a long tradition. Scholars still find valid many of the observations which the early Spanish chroniclers observed during the contact period which dates back to 1521. Systematic research, however, is a post-Second World War phenomena. Attempts at systematic work began earlier, especially during the early American occupation of the archipelago at the turn of the 20th century. Much of what we know of the Philippines today is largely due to the works of such early pioneers as Dean Worcester, David Burrows, Frederick Starr, Fay Cooper-Cole, Alfred Kroeber, R. F. Barton, H. O. Beyer, and Fred Eggan. In order to put the present paper into proper perspective, I shall limit my presentation to the following: archaeology, ethnography, and culture change. I shall touch on previous accomplishments, problems encountered, and the future of the discipline as a research tool in advancing our knowledge of Filipino society and culture.

Archaeological Research

Archaeological research in the country did not receive the attention it deserved until the late 1960's and through the 1970's. Today it is the only area of anthropological research which is fully funded by the government and enthusiastically supported by the private sector. This is largely due to the growing national consciousness of Filipino national identity and pride. Nationalism has given it a very strong boost and today we have more jobs open to young archaeologists than in any other area of anthropology.

Systematic archaeology is a recent phenomena. Before 1920, there were only two important archaeological undertakings in the Philippines. The first one was by Alfred Marche, a Frenchman, in 1881. Marche worked in the island of Marinduque and explored other sites in central Philippines. Most of his collections were surface finds and are now with the *Musee de l'homme in Paris;* some found their way to Madrid. Of course, even earlier, sporadic finds and pot-hunting activities took place, and Feodor Jagor reported encountering a priest in Naga, Camarines Sur who collected artifacts from ancient graveyards.

The second systematic work in prehistoric archaeology was conducted by Carl Guthe of the University of Michigan between 1922 and 1925. It was carried out by Carl Guthe of the University of Michigan. The purpose of the Michigan archaeological expedition was to collect Chinese ceramics exported to the Philippines from China "that would aid in the reconstruction of the Philippine-Chinese relationship." In addition, however, Guthe collected locally-made earthenwares and other artifacts. His team likewise conducted several test-digs in Palawan, Bohol, northern Mindanao and other places in central Philippines. The collection, resulting from the trip, consisted of more than 30 cubic tons of prehistoric artifacts. These are now kept at the University of Michigan in the United States.

From 1926 to the outbreak of the Second World War, much of what was archaeologically known was the result of the pioneering work of the late H.O. Beyer. In fact, it can be said that early Philippine prehistoric research was largely built upon his works. Other workers during this time included Olay R. T. Janse, a Swedish-American archaeologist, who conducted a survey of porcelain sites in Calatagan in 1940, and Larry Wilson, a mining prospector, who assisted Beyer in the exploration of numerous Pleistocene sites in northern Luzon.

The years following the Second World War were characterized by an increased interest in the prehistoric beginnings of Philippine society and culture. As such, systematic archaeology was later on introduced as part of the curriculum at the University of the Philippines.

The first post-war excavations were conducted by Wilhelm Solheim II in Masbate island from 1951 to 1953. He was assisted by Alfredo Evangelista and E. Arsenio Manuel. In 1956, Robert B. Fox and Alfredo Evangelista, both working for the National Museum of the Philippines, under took a series of excavations in the caves of Cagraray, Albay, Bato, Sorsogon. Also in 1956, M. Sullivan explored several sites and reported on the status of archaeological research in the country. The first extensive post-war archaeological work to be undertaken, however, was the Calatagan diggings conducted by the archaeologists of the National Museum from 1958 to 1962. E. Arsenio Manuel of the University of the Philippines likewise conducted excavations in Marinduque and other parts of the country during the middle of the 1950's. Results of these diggings, however, are not yet available in print as of 1974.

Other minor diggings and explorations followed in the 1960's especially in the southern regions of the Bisayas and Mindanao. These were led by the anthropologists of the University of San Carlos and Siliman University. In 1963-64, for example, Marcelino Maceda of San Carlos University, technically assisted by the National Museum, conducted excavations in Kulaman Plateau and recovered a number of limestone burial jars. North of this place, Samuel Briones, then a graduate student at Siliman University, reported the presence of limestone burial jars in several caves he visited in 1966 while doing ethnographic work. This led to an organization of a team in 1967, headed by Edward B. Kurjak and Craig T. Sheldon, also graduate students, who excavated the area and recovered a number of artifacts.

Also in 1967, Alexander Spoehr of the University of Pittsburgh carried out an archaeological research in Sanga-Sanga in Tawi-Tawi, Sulu archipelago. In Cebu, Karl Hutterer and Rosa Tenazas of San Carlos University did salvage archaeology right in the middle of Cebu City and recovered prehistoric artifacts. Tenazas also dug in the Laguna Area and recovered valuable materials, mostly 10th and 14th century artifacts in 1968-69. In Palawan, Jonathan Kress of Yale University worked in the Tabon cave for his doctoral dissertation. Also in the same year, Warren and Jean Peterson carried out extensive work in northern Luzon for their doctoral dissertations. Warren did excavations in Pintu Rock Shelter, Nueva Ecija with the assistance of Israel Cabanilla, while Jean did ethnographic work among the Agta in Isabela province. In Lemery, Batangas a team of students from Ateneo de Manila carried out archaeological excavations from 1968 to 1970. The group was composed of Cecilia Y. Locsin,

Maria-Isabel Ongpin, and Socorro P. Paterno. The year 1970 saw two things: the shifting of the National Museum of its archaeological research in Cagayan Valley and a preliminary reconnaisance work in Panay and Guimaras Island for possible Pleistocene sites by a team from the University of the Philippines.

In 1971, Karl Hutterer returned to the site he previously discovered in Basey River in southern Samar. In conjunction with his project, the University of Hawaii conducted a summer field school in the area headed by David Tuggle. The result of this fieldwork has already been published in a local journal. The following year, Wilhelm Solheim II and Avelino Legaspi conducted a series of excavations in Davao del Sur. They found a shell-using culture which made tools from large shells through a flaking technique similar to that used in making stone tools.

In 1973, Robert Maher of the University of Western Michigan at Kalamazoo returned to Ifugao and did further archaeological work. The purpose of his work was to document the dates the scholars gave to the rice terraces. Radiocarbon-14 tests performed on the site revealed a date between 800 to 1000 ± 250BP. Felix Keesing's suggestion that the peoples of Central Cordillera moved into the interior as a result of Spanish pressure is challenged by Maher's data as untenable; this also challenges Beyer's conclusion that the rice terraces were constructed about 3000 B.C.

Perhaps the most dramatic among these archaeological diggings were the ones done by the archaeologists of the National Museum in Tabon and other caves in Palawan. It was in one of the trenches in Tabon cave, in a disturbed section, that fragments of fossilized human bones, including the frontal piece of a skull, were recovered. Also recovered were fossilized bones of small animals. Charcoal materials analyzed by carbon-14 technique revealed the presence of man in the area between 22,000 to 30,000 years ago.

Other than Tabon cave, the most promising archaeological sites today are those found in Cagayan Valley. As of 1971 fifty-four sites have been reported to be relatively rich in terms of additional information concerning the complex problem on Philippine prehistory. Data from three sites excavated indicate, at least tentatively, close association of fossil remains of ancient animals (like elephas and stegodons) and stone tools fashioned by prehistoric men. This suggests the possibility, though not definitely, that ancient men and animals were present in the area, perhaps contemporaneously, with the former hunting, the latter for food or vice-versa. The term "contemporaneous" does not mean "occurring precisely at the same time." Rather, the occurrence could possibly had been within a given time horizon ——a chronological span perhaps of hundred of years. There were places where animal fossils are found in strata which predate the appearance of man in the archipelago. It is hoped that one day the fossil bones of prehistoric men will be found in any of the Cagayan Valley sites. When such an event happens much of what took place in our country during prehistoric times will be clarified and our understanding of the past will be broader than what we know today.

Ethnographic Research

Ethnographic research in the Philippines has a long history. It began when the Spaniards came in the 16th century. The observations recorded by the friar-scholars are today the only source of materials for reconstructing the nature of Filipino society and culture during the contact period. Most of these materials were on native material culture, economic activities, and religious rituals. The documents contain very little materials on social structure (e. g. kinship data) and on value orientation.

Systematic work began when the Americans took over the political administration of the archipelago at the turn of the century. Between 1900 and 1910, the American Expeditionary Government established the Office of the Ethnological Survey, the unit tasked to conduct detailed study of the Filipino ethnic groups, particularly the mountain tribes. American scholars like Fay Cooper-Cole, C. R. Moss and others were employed to undertake the job. Cole came out with classic works on the Igorots, Tinggian, and the "Wild Tribes of Davao District, Mindanao."

Between 1910 and 1920, the professional workers were joined by non-anthropologists, mostly educators who came to teach in the Philippines. Outstanding among these fieldworkers are R. F. Barton, David Barrows, and H. O. Beyer. Barton produced classic works on Ifugao and Kalinga. H. O. Beyer became the "dean of anthropology" in the country. Most of the research work during this decade, however, were on the so-called non-Christians which included the Muslims in southern Philippines. A bureau known as the Bureau of Non-Christians was established to take care of the welfare of the pagans. The structure and function of this office followed the Bureau of American Indian Affairs in the United States.

Among the well-known anthropologists who wrote about the Philippines was Alfred Kroeber. He worte a series of monographs on Filipino society and culture, among which are *Peoples of the Philippines, Kinship in the Philippines* and *History of Philippine Civilization as Reflected in Religious Nomenclature*. Incidentally, Kroeber never did fieldwork in the country; he wrote his monographs on the basis of materials available at the American Museum of Natural History.

Between 1920 and 1940, most of excellent ethnographic work were done by missionaries. Among the outstanding workers at the time are Francis Lambrecht and Morris Vanoverberg. Lambrecht was stationed in the Ifugao and, particularly in Mayawyaw and he wrote excellent ethnography on the Mayawyaw and later on the Ifugao. Vanoverberg, on the other hand, worked among the Isneg and northern Luzon negritos and also produced excellent monographs on them.

The decade of the thirties was also productive. Most of the work done in the country, however, revolved around H. O. Beyer who, almost single-handedly collected massive data on the various aspects of Filipino society and culture —— from prehistory to culture change. By 1940 he had put together a 20 volume collection entitled *Philippine Folklore, Customs and Beliefs*. Unfortunately, the manuscript(my friend was librarian at Univ. of San Carlos and was sent to Austrailia to microfilm the collection. USC has now a copy on microfilm from National University in Austrailia) never saw publication and these are not even in the country today.

During the war years no field studies were done. However, with the cooperation of some Japanese scholars, Professor Beyer was able to preserve his pre-war ethnographic and archaeological collection. These materials became the base-line data on which many fieldworks in the decade of 1950s were based. The years following 1950 saw the active participation of Filipinos in anthropological research. During the prewar days only three Filipinos conducted fieldwork: Ricardo Galang, Marcelino Maceda, and Marcelo Tangco. In 1950 Professor Fred Eggan and Professor Evette Hester organized the Philippine Studies Program of the University of Chicago. Eggan trained a number of students ——Americans and Filipinos —whom he sent to the field. Among these students were Robert Fox, Frank Lynch, Jacques Amyot, Melvin Mednick, Charles Warren, Willis Sibley, Charles Kaut and George Smith. Except for Smith, these students did excellent work in various areas of Philippine society and culture. Among the Filipinos who were trained by Eggan in the 1950s were Alfredo

Pacyaya, Timoteo Oracion, Fred Evangelista, Moises Bellox, and Gudual-
do Reyes. These group of American and Filipino students constituted the
team which put out the *Chicago Handbook for the Human Area Relations
File.*

More and more Filipinos acquired training in anthropology in the
decade between 1960 and 1970. This group of professionally trained researchers included Mario Zamora, F. Landa Jocano, David Barada, Jesus
Peralta, Willy Arce, Jesuscita Sodusta, Realidad Santico-Rolda, Eric Casiño
and many others. Young Americans who made the Philippines their area
of research interests included David Szanton, James Anderson, Thomas
Keiffer, James Stewart, Stuart Schlegel, Harry Nimruo, among others.

Culture Change

The problem of change has recently become the dominant theme of
anthropological research in the Philippines. More funds are available, particularly projects enjoying UN or USAID funding as in population change,
technology transfer and agricultural innovations. Even labor has started to
utilize the services of the anthropologists in their industrial relations training
program.

Urbanization, as a critical area in change, has likewise gained con-
siderable attention. The Institute of Philippine Culture of the Ateneo de
Manila University, has done a marvelous job in the slums of Tondo. Mary
Hollingteine and her team have made valuable contributions to the growing
knowledge of city life in the country. In the University of the Philippines, F.
Landa Jocano has done extensive ethnography of slums as a way of life,
as well as detailed studies of the family in a government housing project in
Metro Manila. Realidad Rolda, also of U.P., has reexamined the impact of
congestion upon urban housing projects in Quezon City, Metro Manila.

Current Trends

The field of anthropology appears to be promising in the Philippines
in terms of job placements and research support.

This is very true in the field of archaeology, which three decades ago
was not even in the priority list of government funding. Today, the Philip-

pine National Museum alone has more than ten vacant positions, and more money for archaeological research. The growing national conscious-ness, demanding a redefinition of Filipino national identity, underlies the current prospect of anthropology in the country. This is reinforced by the greater emphasis placed by the government in the building of infrastructure in rural development.

Through these researches we now know more about the nuances of Filipino society and culture than we did three decades ago.

Anthropological Theories

The most exciting, if not currently the most controversial, contribution of anthropology to Philippine studies is in the field of prehistoric archaeolo-gy. In social anthropology, most of the research outputs are descriptive and, if analytical, are concerned with specific problems in such areas as ecological adaptation, law and order, kinship and social organization, values and value orientation and so forth. No attempt has so far been made to develop anthropological theories out of Philippine materials. The Philippine data are often used to validate, amplify, and demonstrate the workability of existing theories developed out of studies done elsewhere. This is understandable since most of the published works are originally graduate theses and dissertations.

This is not the case in prehistoric archaeology. During the last fifty years, research has been consistently focused on one problem: the recon-struction of Philippine prehistoric cultures. This continuity in research objective unearthed a massive amount of data which requires interpreta-tion. The archaeologists have, in other words, no other choice but to be creatively active; they came out with a number of theories concerning the development of local patterns.

One of these creative fieldworkers was the late H. O. Beyer. Our current knowledge of Philippine prehistoric culture is largely derived from his works. He presented several postulates concerning the development of Philippine past culture and society. These included the peopling of the archipelago through several waves of migrations, the classification of Filipi-nos under the Malay stocks and the almost perpetual tracing of Filipino cultural roots to Asia mainland and neighboring groups.

I stated that it is in the field of prehistory that anthropology in the

Philippines has exciting contribution because today Professor Beyer's ideas are challenged by younger scholars and tenaciously upheld by the older ones. There are also those researchers who take the middle ground. And this is what makes it the more exciting, especially today when the rising national consciousness has demanded a reexamination of the prehistoric base of contemporary institutions.

Migration Theory

In a number of publications, Beyer postulated several prehistoric waves of migration of people from Asia mainland and other parts of Southeast Asia which caused the population of the archipelago now identified as the Philippines. However, it was not in until 1947 that he crystalized his views on this matter and narrowed down the numerable speculations into six main "waves" of immigrants, namely:

(1) the primitive human type which was similar to the Java men (in Indonesia) of 250,000 years ago;

(2) the Australoid-Sakai type which represented the earliest pygmoid group together with the latter arrivals, the proto-Malays, and came between 25,000 to 30,000 years ago;

(3) the sea-faring, stone-tool using Indonesian "A" who came about 5,000 to 6,000 years ago;

(4) the bark-cloth wearing Indonesian "B" from Indo-China who came about 1,500 BC;

(5) the terrace-building group who came from Central Asia and arrived here between 800 and 500 BC; and

(6) the metal-using civilized Malays who came via Borneo, Palawqn, and Mindoro.

Each of these migrating groups were described as having distinctive cultural and physical characteristics. Their coming also represented the different evolutionary stages of Philippine society and culture. For example, the first migrants were said to be hunters and food-gatherers who subsisted on such raw foods as they were able to wrest from their surroundings by means of primitive stone tools which were their only artifactual possessions. By anthropological standards, this is a sound 19th century reconstruction. However, when the arguments shifted from cultural adaptation to human types, the reconstruction becomes highly suspect. The differentation between the "primitive human type",. the "Australoid-Sakai" and the "proto-Malays" are prehistoric characteristics which can never be reconstructed by whatever stretch of imagination one resorts to. So far we have no archaeological or paleontological evidences to show how the Australoid-Sakai or the proto-Malays looked like.

The same problem confronts us as soon as we examine the cultural (especially technological) competence of these immigrants. For example, following the Australoid-Sakai and the proto-Malays, we are told that the next to come were the Indonesian "A" groups. They were said to have advanced technology and they travelled in rafts and plank-built boats. They lived in grass-covered houses with wooden frames, having rounded roofs much like a modern *Quonset* hut, built directly on the ground or over a pit dug a meter or more below the surface. Moreover, they practiced agriculture, growing millet and yams. Their clothing consisted of dried skins of animals and barks of trees. These people came about 5,000 to 6,000 years ago.

Following the Indonesian "A" were the Indonesian "B". This group of people was said to have more advanced culture than their predecessors. They lived in houses with pyramidal roofs raised above the ground, on posts. We are further told that the Indonesian B groups had advanced woodworking tools made of very hard stones, such as nephrite or ancient jade, which were rectangular or trapezoidal in cross-section. They practiced extensive dry agriculture and introduced upland rice, taro (*gabi*), new varieties of cultivated yams, and other valuable crops. Their clothing, it has been further speculated, was made of beaten barkcloth, often intricately decorated with fine designs, printed in clothing with stone or wooden blocks. This group of people came about 1,500 BC.

The fifth group to come were the central Asians. They were said to be remarkably more advanced than the earlier groups and they introduced the rice-terracing complex in northern Luzon. They came about 800 to 500 BC. As in the previous events, the rice-terracing groups were followed by the last immigrants —— the so-called civilized Malays. The latter entered the archipelago by way of Borneo sometime about the 12th century AD. They were the ones who introduced into the new homeland four kinds of industries: (a) the smelting, forging, and manufacturing of tools, weapons, utensils and ornaments of iron and other metal products; (b) the manufacture of a great variety of turned-and-decorated pottery; (c) the art of weaving cloth on a handloom; and (d) the manufacture of beads, bracelets and other ornaments of green and blue glass.

Current Reactions

These reconstructions are lucid and convincing but they lack solid evidence to support them; not even ethnographic data. It is in the area of data-support and in the use of diffusionist models that younger scholars are challenging the migration theory. They argued that early scholars, particularly Beyer, had not apparently made use of materials ethnographers have gathered in order to reinforce their archaeological inferences. Most of the meager materials on which the theory was inferred were not systematically dug so that there was no room for further verification of "hunches" or hypotheses against raw data. What this shortcoming did give rise to, according to the critics, was armchair scholarship, speculations, and wholesale application of diffusionist model of cultural sequences established in other parts of the world, including Europe, to Philippine materials. The resulting picture has been that there is "nothing ancient peoples in the Philippines did but borrow from the outside; everything was brought by several migrating people." The hard reality of adaptation to new frontiers was never part of the neat speculation.

There is no doubt that inter-island movements of people had taken place during prehistoric times, even as early as perhaps the middle of the Pleistocene, some 500,000 years ago. But whether these early people came in waves, as described, and at specific time-intervals and historical sequence, is another matter. How big was one wave of immigrants so as to be able to reproduce the original culture they had in a new frontier? How do we determine the regularity of the time-sequence of their coming as to be able to express the "intrusion" of each "wave" into the archipelago in specific historical period? So far archaeology has not yet developed a technique by which this is possible; moreover, archaeological materials dealing with this problem are not sufficient to establish definitive correlations between migration and cultural developments. The descriptive tone of movements of people in terms of "waves" has to be revised, the critics insist, to allow for further corrections as archaeological materials accumulate.

As a working hypothesis, the critics further argue, the theory of migration has doubtful usefulness to current understanding of Philippine prehis-

toric cultures as these emerged in different island ecological niches. Its
inadequacy lies on several grounds. First, it is too simplistic to be useful in
explaining the complex problem of cultural development. Second, it is
quite unrealistic to assume that the physical characterisitcs of prehistoric
migrating peoples can still be categorically defined today after several
thousands of years of racial and cultural developments. Third, it is doubtful
whether the "immigrants" always arrived in periodic sequences and with a
foreknowledge of destination as implied by the term "migration." There
are no definitive data to show, moreover, that each "wave" of migrants
really constituted a culturally and racially homogeneous group. Fourth, it is
quite difficult, the critics further point out, to accept however one stretches
the imagination that small boatloads of people, coming at a certain
periodic time-sequence reducible only in terms of hundreds or thousands
of years, would be capable of maintaining large-scale community patterns
in a new land under pioneer conditions. It is likewise difficult to assume
that prehistoric population did not yield to such hazards of infant mortality,
epidemic of diseases, malnutrition, and others, which even until very recently, were considered serious problems, so as to enable them to maintain a stable population that is identifiable even today. And fifth, the theory
does not allow for variant social and cultural developments to take place in
response to local ecological and historical situations. Instead, it impresses
an orientation that all culture traits and physical types, as well, have been
brought to the country "ready-made" which is unlikely.

Alternative theoretical models have been presented to replace the
"migration theory." The logical consequence of ecological adaptation and
historical modification of exogenous cultural traits is what is now being
pursued by younger scholars. Ethnographic materials are currently being
brought to bear upon the reconstruction of past cultural complexes. It is
hoped that this new approach would clarify many of the interesting facets
of indigenous developments.

Supportive of the current approach to the idea that indigenous developments, instead of migration, had given rise to the present cul-
ture-complexes in the Philippines is the attempt to examine the social
organizations of the living population, especially the pagan minority
groups, in terms of levels of sociocultural integration which each attained.
There are five such types of integration, namely:

(1) *Band organization.* Groups organized in small, highly mobile bands

composed of one or two related families, with the oldest member as the head. Sociocultural integration is at the family level and there is no social class stratification. The family head is at once the political, economic, and religious leader. He leads the hunting and gathering activities. Sometimes he also functions as a herbalist or medicine-man. Interfamilial forms of cooperation characterize social and economic activities. Included in this type of social organization are the Tasaday, Tao't Bato, Agta, Pinatubo, Batak, Ati, and Mamanuwa.

(2) *Kindred organization.* Groups organized in semi-sedentary but scattered settlements or neighborhoods composed of two to five related families, with the oldest and influential member of the founding family as the head. For lack of better term, kindred is used to emphasize the cohesive force of kinship and neighborhood in cooperative work. Sociocultural integration is at the settlement or neighborhood level with an emerging, but not dominant, social class stratification based mainly on the personal abilities and affluence of the head of the family. Interfamilial form of cooperation characterize important social and economic activities. The leader is also a religious functionary, interpreter of customary laws, and defender of the group. In carrying out his duties, he generaly consults an informal group of elders who represent their respective families within the settlement. Groups with this type of social integration include the Tingguian, Ilongot, the Mangyans of Mindoro, Sulod, Tagbanua, Magahats, Tiruray, and the Subanon.

(3) *Ward organization.* Groups organized in compact villages composed of several families which may or may not be related to each other, with groups of influential men serving as a "council" of elders who function as decision-makers for the group and as mediators in cases involving group conflicts. Political leadership is by consensus among the members of the council. Religious functions are vested in the office of the *bailan* or the *pangat*. Village-wide religious ceremonies are obseved. Sociocultural integration is at the village level with distinct social class stratification based on economic affluence and good knowledge of the traditional lore. Included in this category are the Ifugao, Bontok, Kalinga, Ibaloi, Sagada, and the Arumanen Manobos of Cotabato.

(4) *Warrior organization.* Groups organized in composite villages made of several families which may or may not be related to each other,

with the most influential among the warrior families as the head. Political integration is represented by the authority of the *bagani* (among the Mindanao· groups) or the *mengal* (among the Luzon groups). Included in this category are the Apayao-Isneg, northern Kalinga, Gaddang, Ibanag, Mandaya Bilaan, and Agusan Bagobo.

(5) *Datu organization.* Groups organized in large communities made up of several villages composed of several related and unrelated families, with the influential member of the dominant families or ruling class as the head. He is known as the *datu.* Included in this type of social organization are the Higaonon, Cotabato Manobo, Bilaan, Upland Bagobo (Manuvu) and also the Mandaya.

This new approach has not yet been subjected to critical discussion although it is becoming one of the dominant approaches in studying peoples of the Philippines. It is hoped that as the data become more and more available, new ways of looking at the Philippine materials in terms of anthropological theory can shed new light in our current attempt to understand our society and culture.

3 Anthropological Research on Aboriginal Groups of the Malay Peninsula

HOOD SALLEH

The Orang Asli in Malaysian History

Historical writings on the peoples of the Malay peninsula appear to lack any positive references to its aboriginal population despite the fact that the latter have inhabited the country for thousands of years.[1] Considered today in a popular sense as *orang asli* ('original peoples') they still appear to be as obscure a minority group as if they were predestined to remain so. Administrators, researchers and individuals who are in close contact with them, however, object strongly to calling them by the term *orang asli* as it evokes images of backwardness ('aboriginality'), of distinct separateness from the larger ethnic majorities in the country and does not help to reflect in any way their social and cultural diversity. The question of diversity again is additionally influenced by their contiguity to the present urban environment which functions in many cases to underplay the sense of 'differentness' which they feel from the rest of the Malaysian population.

One plausible reasons for the lack of historical interest for the *orang asli* may be the thought that at the present time their influence on the broad sweep of events is completely peripheral, i. e. that their role in contemporary political life is hardly worth mentioning. Another possible reason might be that their very existence hardly raises any problems relating to the historicity of other peoples on the peninsula, although in fact it does. Thirdly, a point of general but primary importance a fault may lie in the outmoded method of conceiving history as that which is only concerned with the history of dominant groups within a country. These reasons among others are certainly responsible for the minimal attention given to many aboriginal population today.

Early Studies

The earliest attempts to study the *orang asli* began sometime in the 19th century but these were essentially unreliable by modern anthropological standards. The first efforts came in the form of missionary attempts to find out whether as a people they were susceptible to being converted to Christianity. As was fashionable during that era the aboriginal groups met come to be known by the convenient and universal term 'Indian'. Just as there were Indians of one sort or another on the American continents so the *orang asli* were also thought to be of similar kind. Thus after meeting with some Jakun *orang asli* in the 1940s the French Roman Catholic missionary P. Favre wrote[2]

> "The Jakuns, by their nature and their peculiar qualities offer the most encouraging hopes to the Missionaries who will be employed in their amelioration. Few Indians present such good dispositions to embrace the Gospel" (Favre 1865: 75).

Favre estimated that the total number of Jakun at that time was "five thousand at the most" and he himself confessed to have encountered about a thousand (ibid, p. 42). Unlike others, who thought of the *orang asli* as being either "wild" or "pagan" or both (e.g. Bourien 1865; Skeat and Blagden 1966), Favre was of the opinion that aboriginals had the potential and the propensity to be the same as any European he had known, given the means to develop their intelligence.

During the colonial period before the turn of the 20th century studies on the *orang asli* were not among the more popular concerns. This was apparent in Frank Swettenham's and Hugh Clifford's writings, two prolific writers among the colonial servants. As Signe Howell wrote, the latter scholars

> "... largely ignored the Orang Asli and did not appear to find them and their customs of much interest. Apart from one chapter on the Orang Laut in which Clifford says, "Beliefs and superstitions of the Fisher Folk would fill many volumes" (1897: 147) — a task which he refrains from without apparent difficulty — the Orang Asli only appear in their writings, which are of an ancedotal nature, as icidental characters who for one reason or another

enter and exist without notice being taken. Swettenham seems almost una-
ware of their existence......"   (Howell 1977: 4-5).

In contrast to the dismal indifference shown by the above scholars,
colonial researchers who came after this period made the *orang asli* a focal
point of their research activity. Furthermore, they were more scientifical-
ly-oriented in a comparative anthropological sense. This trend was clearly
shown in Skeat and Blagden's two monumental volumes, *Pagan Races of
the Malay Peninsula* (1906) which contains several chapters on physical
measurements and detailed information on such aspects as the *orang asli*
eyesight, their sense of balance, the speed with which they climb a tree,
etc. (Skeat 1906I: part I). Although Skeat and Blagden's survey was extensive, the material presented were of uneven and often unreliable quality.
Howell noted how they collected all available material, most of which,
though voluminous, was written by "travellers without any scientific training, and at the same time without any local knowledge". Blagden's contribution to the work is contained in the second half of volume two and
deals solely with language. He tries to identify the various language groups
and their distribution and gives a "comparative vocabulary of aboriginal
dialects" which covers 160 pages. His analysis is based on glossaries collected by earlier writers who did not speak any of the dialects themselves
and, in most cases, not even Malay. Hence one is left in considerable
doubt regarding the accuracy of many of the translations. However, one
significant achievement by Blagden is that he established the existence of
the three major linguistic groups in Malaysia, recognizing the affiliation of
the Negrito and Senoi dialects with the Mon-Khmer group of languages
and that of the Proto-Malay dialects with the Malayo-Polynesian group.
Other researches conducted during this period which deserves mention were by I.H.N. Evans, curator of the famous Taiping museum, who
had the distinction of being the first administrator to do extensive field
research among a wide range of groups. His interests encompassed studies
on the Proto-Malays in the southern part of the peninsula as well as the
Negritos in the north (Evans 1927; 1937). During 1910 and 1932 he
concentrated a great deal on groups in the lake of Perak, but occasionally
visited (for short periods mainly) groups in Selangor and northern Pahang.
As an administrator he could not engage as a 'participant observer', not
having the time to do so, and consequently had to depend a great deal on
interpreters. An examination of his publications reveal his interest to lie
mainly in the field of religions beliefs and practices, and omitting much that

should have been recorded in the field of economics, politics, and social organisation. By today's standards his descriptions appear to be rather patchy, but considering the administrative burdens he had to shoulder then, it may be said that he managed to record some interesting and very useful material which enable modern researchers to carry out comparative studies of the *orang asli*.

The German Catholic missionary Paul Schebesta, a subscriber to the *Kulturkreislehre* school began work among the *orang asli* in 1924. Financed by Pope Pius XI, he began research with the main aim of showing how Negritos of the peninsula worshipped one Supreme Being. Negritos were thought to belong to the most primitive cultures of the world and together with their 'food-gathering' ideology was seen to represent an earlier stage of human development. Because of this, it was thought that they should retain traces of man's earliest religion. Schebesta's ideas paved the way for some more interesting and illuminating work which was later taken up by K.M. Endicott nearly 50 years later. Endicott[2] later refined his ideas by more thorough and meticulous research on the Negritos, finally presenting his findings in an excellent monograph *Batek Negrito Religion* (Endicott 1979). One significant contribution which Schebesta made in the study of negrito social behaviour was that he corrected the view that the negrito mode of existence was not dominated by one single subsistence method. Though they were hunters and gatherers, they can turn their attention to whatever is available. Their social structure is well adapted by its simplicity to avail itself of any opportunity. Endicott in his study of the economy of the Batek Negritos (1973) substantiates this, finding this to be the same amongst eastern groups which Schebesta had not visited" (see Howell op. cit., p. 12).

Between 1930 and the '50s two researchers left an indelible mark in *orang asli* administrative history, H.D. Noone (Pat Noone) and P.D.R. Williams-Hunt. Noone was perhaps the first real anthropologist in the sense that his involvement in *orang asli* social life was total and he was extremely committed to their welfare, an involvement which led to a tragic end (Holman 1958). Noone published several papers, but his main contribution was in his description and recommendations in relation to the Temiar (Noone 1936). Although a substantial part of his research notes were lost in an unfortunate incident, his fellow researcher Kilton Stewart, a psychologist from the London School of Economics, managed to construct an interesting version of the use of dreams in Temiar social life. Noone's

researches were interrupted by the Japanese occupation and his own premature death but the dedication he exhibited in the conduct of his work
(and his style of administration) has become legend in *orang asli* history.
After Noone's efforts at research and his revelations in regard to the plight
of the *orang asli,* a Department of Aborigines was established with Williams-Hunt as its first Adviser. Willams-Hunt spent most of his time doing
field trips in Perak, mainly among the Semai. His *An Introduction to the
Malayan Aborigines* (1952) is a useful and practical guide-book on how to
survive among *orang asli* in Malaysian forest, including some useful
(though sometimes inaccurate statistical) information on many different
groups.

After Williams-Hunt whose career as Adviser ended tragically also the
Malaysian government appointed a career anthropologist-administrator
whose status was defined as Commisioner of Aboriginal Affairs, Iskander
Carey. Carey had the job of administering the *orang asli* in order to
suggest ways of improving their situation. *Orang asli* who lived in the deep
forest were occupying strategic positions and during the Malayan Emergency of 1948-1960 it was important to gain their support against insurgents
who exploited them to fight for their cause, either directly or indirectly.
Carey's position was a difficult one and the efforts he put in for research
on *orang asli* societies and cultures suffered from superficiality from an
ethnographic standpoint. This is reflected in his book (Carey 1976) which
consists of anthropological material of varying degrees of reliability. The
better part of his contribution lies in his accounts of the Temiar and the
Mah Meri (Ma Betisek).

Ever since the early '60s research on the *orang asli* was conducted
mainly by students working for their postgraduate degrees, starting with
Dentan (1962-63), Benjamin (1964-66), Endicott (1970-1973; 1975-76),
Hood (1972-1977), Wazir Karim (1973-1975), Laird (1973-1976),
Knud-Jensen (1975-1976), and Howell (1977-1979) among others. Each
concentrated their fieldwork on a group different from the others. Of these
little in the way of publication can be boasted of, although different aspects
relating to the different societies are dealt with in articles appearing in
various journals. Communication of research findings on the *orang asli* was
a problem for the reason that there were no occasions during which these
researchers could get together. A national seminar organized by the Malaysian Society for Asian Studies on 1st and 2nd October 1977 brought
together some local scholars but did not produce as much as was desirable

in the way of discussion on ethnographical matters (see *Federation Museums Journal,* Vol. 24, New Series, 1979). One outcome of the seminar was that it showed the need for more field research on the *orang asli,* either those of an in-depth anthropological nature or those which are multi-disciplinary in approach.

Research on Languages

Although within the last 30 years it can be said that anthropological research on *orang asli* has seen a sustained resurgence this is unfortunately not the case with the study of their languages. The main reason which can account for this is perhaps that researchers who have come to do anthropological research — with one or two exceptions — have not been trained in the field of linguistics or had not specifically come with the intention of researching on the anthropological linguistics of the area. It is therefore not surprising that in most theses, books, or articles concerned with the *orang asli* the same researchers who had done some kind of research on the languages continue to be quoted as authorities in the field. It is not an exaggeration to say that at the present time there remains a paucity of work in the field and that more can and should be done to improve the situation.

The research into the language situation among the *orang asli* got off to a difficult start before the turn of the 20th century. The first laudable attempt was made by Blagden who collected words from a variety of *orang asli* languages and classified them according to criteria ill-suited for a scientific study of the various characteristics of the languages. As a result there was little progress in this section. Later in 1910 Wilkinson collected several 200 word-lists from a selected sample of *orang asli* languages and divided these according to the anthropological material available then.

After the First International Conference on Austroasiatic Linguistics in Honolulu in January 1973 the Malaysian languages of the Austroasiatic family became known as *Aslian* languages, a term which connotes the "historical" or the "original" aspects of the people referred to, excluding the languages spoken by later, migrant groups such as the Jakun and the Belandas.

Benjamin divides the Aslian languages into three major subfamilies: Northern Aslian, Central Aslian, and Southern Aslian. The Northern Aslian subfamily consists of eight languages, namely, Kensiu, Kentakbong, Jehai, Mendriq, Badeg Deq, Mintil, Bateg Nong, and Che' Wong. The Central Aslian subfamily also has eight members and they are Semnam, Sabum, Lanoh Jengjeng, Lanoh Yir, Temiar, Semai I, Semai II, and Jah Hut. The smallest subfamily, the Southern Aslian, consists of only four members and they are Mah Meri, Semaq Beri, Semelai, and Temoq.

In terms of what has been said earlier about research in *orang asli* languages the outstanding problem is that little time and effort has really gone into this field. To the Malaysian Department of Aboriginal Affairs (J.H.E.O.A.) research into languages is not and has never been a priority area. This has something to do perhaps with the modern development-oriented programmes which emphasizes the desirability of rapid social integration with the national Malaysian system, a course of action which might inadvertently result in the lack of time and resources necessary to develop or even the record studies of a linguistic nature. This is certainly one field which deserves urgent anthropological attention.

Continuity and Change

What kinds of changes are *orang asli* societies undergoing now? What are some of the challenges which they have to face in the foreseeable future? Many interesting views have emerged from researches done so far.

The Issue of Exploitation

Each thesis or monograph on the *orang asli* has not failed to reveal the kinds of pressures which their society has been continually subjected to, especially within the last 20 to 30 years. I have argued in the same way as Carey (1977) and Baharon (1972) that the kinds of pressures that are being imposed on all aboriginal groups on the peninsula are slowly bringing about the transformation of their society from being basically tradition-oriented to a type which is peasantized, a situation which is not any different from that experienced by very rural upland Malays over the last 200 years. The case of exploitation of the *orang asli* stands out as a very prominent feature of their social condition. Baharon, the present Director-General of Aboriginal Affairs explains that the major source of exploitation is the ubiquitous "middleman", who may be either Malay, Chinese or any other ethnic type who are economically more advanced. When *orang asli* gather large amounts of jungle-produce such as rattan, resin and fruits they have the problem of marketing these items because they have to depend very heavily, or almost entirely, on outsiders. They are grossly handicapped by the lack of transport and communication facilities, a situation which is not alleviated by their relative illiteracy or semi-illiteracy, their ignorance of market prices and their lack of expertise in dealing with the sophisticated methods of the outsiders.

For exemplification Baharon mentions two typical situations, one involving rural-dwelling *orang asli* and the other deep-jungle dwellers. Both groups are vulnerable, deep-jungle dwellers perhaps more so than rural dwellers. Among rural dwelling *orang asli,* especially among Proto-Malay groups in Negri Sembilan and Johore, the situation appears to be a little different from that which obtains in Kelantan or Pahang, although the long term effects of the exploitation is the same in that the handicapped community is left in the lurch. In Negri Sembilan research by Baharon reveals that *orang asli* owning rubber small-holdings and *dusun* (orchards) lease out their land to traders for a relatively small amount of cash. The situation of exploitation is created when an *orang asli* is unable to pay back his debts. The shopkeeper suggests that they enter into an agreement whereby he is given the right to tap the latter's rubber or to collect fruits from his *dusun* for a number of years. The duration of bondage can last for a long time as the debt is compounded. In some cases, to bind the *orang asli,* agreements of this type are made in black and white and are duly stamped in order to give a semblence of legality. In time the amount owed to the shopkeeper becomes larger as more goods keep being purchased. One big-spending *orang asli* may be involved with many creditors at once. The situation is not easily controlled although the Department of Aboriginal Affairs try their best to do so.

In the case of jungle dwellers the mode of exploiting is basically similar: a businessman (usually Chinese) will first provide credit to a whole group of *orang asli* from one or many villages and the latter are obliged to supply him rattan, resin and other produce from the jungle. In this way extremely cheap labour and produce are obtained. Often the *orang asli* will involve not only himself in supplying the produce but also his wife, children and relatives. Work on swiddens is often ignored or totally abandoned for a little amount of quick cash.

On one level of analysis the evolution of typically peasant modes of obtaining credit and of fostering patron-client relationships have been generated by the increasing wants of the *orang asli*. The phenomenon is part of a wider historical trend, making the move to peasantry a logical development of continuous exploitation of weaker groups by unscrupulous more advanced "outsiders". What anthropological studies have been revealing so far is that the economy of the *orang asli* has been in a state of transition whereby the forces bringing about the transition get its main impetus from the wider capitalist market. This has made the demand for jobs and consumer goods even more acute for many groups. Carey gives some convincing examples from the case of the Temiar and the Mah Meri (Carey, op. cit.).

Changing Perceptions towards the Malay World

Another product of continuing anthropological research on the *orang asli* lies in observations pertaining to their perceptions of people who are identified as their administrators i.e. the Malays. Perceptions which are fast changing are those in the realm of culture, politics and economics. Culturally, *orang asli* picture themselves as being patronised by the Malays. They are thought to be 'pagan' and suitable objects of conversion to Islam. But it is also quite apparent that *orang asli* consider Malays as upstarts who are insensitive to the cultures and religious values of other peoples. The situation is aggravated by differences in language and traditions, including the magical. As a result of these factors, it is hardly suprising for instance, that *orang asli* reject the new values that have been offered to them.[3] The conflict of values is well described in the Negrito example encountered by Endicott. He says

> Most of the children...have gone to school only a few months, if at all. Their parents give several reasons for this state of affairs. One is that they would miss the children because they would have to board at the school for months at a time. Also, they do not see very much value in education for their children. But, the most important reason is that they are afraid the teachers will try to turn their children into Malays.

The conflict in values is usually aggravated by religious differences. Endicott writes

> ...some teachers (showed) lack of respect for the Batek and for their customs, especially when they contravene the teachings of Islam. The students

have been told, for example, that it is evil for them to eat pork. Sometimes they have been called "stupid savages" when slow at their lessons and at least one teacher gave the students Arabic style names and forbade them to use their Batek names in school. Although the intentions of these teachers may be good — to share what they regard as their superior civilisation with the Batek — such acts and attitudes are strongly resented by Batek parents and children. The parents say they would be willing to send their children to school if they were taught only reading, writing and mathematics, but they do not want their children to be taught to reject the way of life of their parents (ibid, p. 180-81).

The example from the Negrito case cites deep differences in values in the perception of the relative advantages to be derived from education and Islam. It may be argued that historically Negritos represent the most isolated of *orang asli* groups and to this day the majority of them still lead (and prefer) a nomadic way of life. But in the case of *orang asli* who live towards the southern part of the peninsula conflict of the type found among the northern groups are not as apparent. Instead social perceptions of the Malay world may be said to be more accommodating. One (though extreme) example is provided by Baharon (op. cit., p. 287) when he speaks of the existence of "a considerable degree of amity and mutual respect" between the Temuans and their Malay neighbours. We are told that the earlier *batin* (headmen) of Parit Gong were all close (*rapat*) with the contemporary Undangs of Jelebu. Malays on their part join in celebrating important events in Temuan community life such as the installation ceremony of the *batin* and other events. Temuans visit their Malay friends at Hari Raya (end of the fasting month celebration), and other occasions where they know they would be welcome. But Temuan are friendly and accommodating as they are discriminating towards Malays, people who they realise have heterogeneous origins. Like the Temiar, who distinguish between original Malay settlers (*gob asal*) and later Malay migrants of settlers (*gob mun*), the Temuans tend to have a low opinion of Malays depending on ancestry.

Politically *orang asli* recognize the state of affairs which have placed them in the present situation to be the outcome of their small numbers and their relative lack of economic power. Because they have no real economic power based on ownership of land (as a general rule) they are conscious of the remoteness of achieving meaningful political participation for themselves, that is until such time in the future when they will be given such opportunity as a group. Until then they would begrudge the Malays for the extensive power which the latter have in the conduct of their day-to-day affairs. The legitimate question to ask at this juncture is not so much the reasons for the lack of political power of the *orang asli* but whether the political values of the wider social system of which they form a part recognise their need for political participation. In traditional times *orang asli* perceptions of political leadership was not based on the same system as that of the Malays, indeed for many of them notions of rank and chieftainship were generally conspicuous by their absence. Benjamin speaks of an alien system of leadership and headmanship evolving in the Temiar situation in Kelantan beginning some time before the middle of the 19th century with the entrenchment of the Mikong (Benjamin 1968: 9-12). The situation had persisted through the colonial period but by the 1960s when he did his fieldwork attitudes of leaders and headmen appointed by the government had changed in the sense that enthusiastic and charismatic personalities have evolved as distinct political types. For *orang asli* groups in the south, political values had evolved earlier in close association with ideas held by Malays, since groups in this area were more involved with the latter. As an example, we can think of the Temuan, a society with leaders whose authority and responsibilities are clearly demar-cated in elaborate formal traditions and rituals (Baharon, op. cit., pp. 357-370).

With the increasing encroachments of the outsiders especially Malays into their lives over the centuries there is little escape for *orang asli* from being drawn into the wider political system. The process of politicisation began when they were caught in the ideological crossfire during the Emergency period of 1948-1960, or perhaps even before that period during the Japanese occupation. One outstanding event during the colonial period which left a particularly indelible mark in *orang asli* experience was the resettlement policy of the government. In a remarkable paper in which he reflected on the impact of this policy, Carey expressed how such a move "was a grave mistake" (Carey 1977:5). During the exercise the *orang asli* were put into "hastily established villages" which resembled "miniature concentration camps" (ibid: 6). The policy was disastrous and hundreds of *orang asli* perished from the severe mental and psychological trauma. The lessons they learnt from this experience were bitter. They showed how politically powerless, exploited and misunderstood they were in their unorganised 'apolitical' condition. Carey noted that the more intelligent of the *orang asli* escaped the resettlement camps and retreated to the deep jungle, to be away from the politically-smitten Malay world. In this respect it would hardly be surprising if, politically, *orang asli* perceive the Malay world to be an arena which is filled with political conflict. Being extremely sensitive people who are used to a more peaceful and relaxed existence in the forest there is little in the Malay world that particularly attracts them apart from its bright lights. Denten in his account of the Semai (1968) argues how their non-violent ideology pervades much of their activity and thought patterns, implying how alien systems, including that of the Malays, should learn from their ways. It must be admitted though that few societies today can remain as simple in organization and 'uncomplicated' in political structure as that of the Semai.

The change in economic values is closely related to *orang asli* ideas about the Malays. As was mentioned earlier it can he argued that the process of continuing exploitation has the net result of transforming a large number of *orang asli* into Malay-type peasants. Their plight is not far different from that of upland Malays as shown in many ethnographical reports in which the main form of activity engaged in by them is petty trading rather than larger business ventures. Among the Temiar of Kelantan, the Mah Meri of Selangor and the Semelai of Pahang, the transitional economies have placed more value on the acquisition of cash and "property". Cash has become an index of wealth more so than during pre-colonial and colonial times, such that the transition has been instrumental in unconsciously making successful *kampong* Malays as an important reference group to imitate. Styles of life have also changed towards imitating the relatively conspicuous consumption and patterns of spending of rural Malays. Indications of change can be seen in styles of dress, houses and acquisition of household furniture, including eletronic equipment. The paraphernalia of rural Malay life is obvious in many *orang asli* homes, especially among the 40 % are non-jungle dwellers.

The change in economic values and consequent transformation in life styles reflect a tendency towards integration with the wider social order generally. However, not to mention cases of rejection of such life-styles which also exist among some *orang asli* would misrepresent the real overall situation. Endicott is critical, for instance, of the "pattern settlement" strategy of the government to coerce some *orang asli* groups to adopt in certain parts of Kelantan (Endicott, op. cit., pp. 182-89) for the reasons that the village built for them is almost the exact opposite of what they look for in a living pláce. In many cases, they revert to their traditional style of life which they much prefer. Living in houses built in straight rows, for example, is unsuited to normal Negrito patterns of social life. This may perhaps be one aspect of Malay social value which *orang asli* do not wish to adopt. To *orang asli* the coolness of the forest is much preferable to the heat of the clearings where the Malays live.

With differences in social tastes it is reasonable to assume that not all *orang asli* would like to emulate the economic ways and social life-styles of the Malays. However, it may be predicted that with increasing monetization of the *orang asli* economy in general and the continuing shortage of land for them to utilize, there is the possibility that their life-styles would come to resemble those of the Malays in the near future.

Notes

1) Mention has been made frequently about the existence of the *orang asli* but scholars usually are not able to state what role they has played in the past. This has brought about a situation whereby much of the history of the country relates to the history of the coastal towns outlying villages and hardly anything at all about 'the peoples of the interior'. Perhaps archaeological research on an extensive and intensive scale may result in a 'rewriting' of some aspects of peninsula Malaysian history.
2) See *Batek Negrito Religion,* Clarendon Press, Oxford, which presents a balanced and sympathetic picture of Negrito cosmology and social life.
3) Endicott's detailed study of the Batek Negritos in the upper Lebir and Aring areas of Ulu Kelantan has produced remarkable insights into the nature of hunting and gathering peoples and certainly has done a service to *orang asli* ethnography by his meticulous and thorough methods of field research. There are few researches which have been conducted in the country which can match the study made by him, especially relating to the field of religion and beliefs.

References

Aboriginal Peoples Act
   1954 (Revised-1974) Laws of Malaysia, Act 134.

Baharon Azhar bin Raffie'i
   1967 *Marketing of Orang Asli produce.* Kuala Lumpur: Jabatan Hal Ehwal Orang Asli Malaysia.
   1966 *Masalah integrasi di kalangan Orang Asli.* Kuala Lumpur: Jabatan Hal Ehwal Orang Asli Malaysia.
   1967 *The New World of the Orang Asli.* Kuala Lumpur: Jabatan Hal Ehwal Orang Asli Malaysia.
   1973 "Parit Gong: An Orang Asli Community in Transition," Unpublished Ph. D. thesis, University of Cambridge.

Benjamin, Geoffrey
   1966 "Temiar Social Groupings," *Fed. Mus. J.*(N.S.), 11.
   1967 "Temiar Kinship," *Fed. Mus. J.*(N.S.), 12.
   1968 "Temiar Personal Names," *BTLV*, 124: 99-134.
   1968 "Headmenship and Leadership in Temiar Society," *Fed. Mus. J.* (N. S.), 13.

Bourien, P.
   1865 "On the Wild Tribes of the Interior of the Malay Peninsula," *Trasactions of the Ethnological Society of London* 3.

Carey, Iskander
   1976 *Orang Asli: The Aboriginal Tribes of Peninsular Malaysia.* Kuala Lumpur: Oxford University Press.

Dentan, R.K.
   1968 *The Semai: A Nonviolent People of Malaya.* New York: Holt, Rinehart and Winston.

Dunn, F.L.
   1971 "Rain-forest Collectors and Traders: A Study of Resource Utilization in Modern and Ancient Malaya," Ph. D. thesis, University of Malaya.

Endicott, K.
   1979 *Batek Negrito Religion.* Oxford: Clarendon Press.

Evans, I.H.N.
   1927 *Papers on the Ethnology and Archaeology of the Malay Peninsula.* Cambridge.
   1937 *The Negritos of Malaya.* Cambridge.

Favre, P.
   1865· *An Account of the Wild Tribes Inhabiting the Malayan Peninsula, Sumatra and a Few Neighbouring Islands.* Paris: The Imperial Printing

Office.

Gomes, Albert Gerard

1976   *The Social Demography of Jahai Negritos at Nural Post.* Kelantan, Latihan Ilmiah Jabatan Antropologi dan Sosiologi, Universiti Malaya.

Holman, Dennis

1958   *Noone of the Ulu.* London: Heinemann.

Jimin bin Idris

1972   *A Brief Note on the Orang Asli of Peninsular Malaysia and Their Administration.* Kuala Lumpur: Jabatan Hal Ehwal Orang Asli Malaysia.

1968   "Distribution of Orang Asli in West Malaysia," *Fed. Mus. J.* (N.S.), 13: 44-48.

Khadizan bin Abdullah and Abdul Razak Yaacob

1976   *Pasir Lenggi: A Batiq Negriot Resettlement Area in Ulu Kelantan.* Social Anthropology Section, School of Comparative Social Sciences, Unviersiti Sains Malaysia.

Mikluho-Maclay, N. von

1878   "Dialects of the Melanesian Tribes in the Malay Peninsula," *JSBRAS,* 1: 38-44.

Muhammad Razha Rashid, Syed Jamal Jaafar and Tan Chee Beng

1976   *Three Studies on the Orang Asli in Ulu Perak.* Social Sciences, Universiti Sains Malaysia.

Nagata, Suichi et al.

1973   "Peringkat-peringkat umur di kalangan orang-orang Kensiu di Kedah dan orang-orang Kintak dan Temiar di Ulu Perak-satu lapuran pendahuluan," *Manusia dan Masyarakat,* 2: 117-125.

Needham, Rodney

1956   "Ethnographic Notes on the Siwang of Central Malaya," *JMBRAS,* 29(1): 49-69.

Noone, Herbert Deane

1936   "Report on the Settlements and Welfare of the Pre-Temiar Senoi of the Perak-Kelantan Watershed," *JFMS Mus,* 19(1).

Polunin, Ivan

1953   "The Medical Natural History of the Malayan Aborigine," *Medical Journal of Malaya,* 8.

1968   "The Magical Medical System of the Jah Heut of Central West Malaysia," *International Congress on Anthropological & Ethnological Science,* 8th, 1:243-244.

Rajmah binti Abdul Samad

1971   "Komuniti Temuan di Kuala Kubu Bharu-suatu kajian mengenai Orang Asli di perkampungan semula, dengan menyentuh soal perubahan," M.A. thesis, Kuala Lumpur.

Safian bin Muhammad Nasir
    1976   *Kampung Temakah: A Temiar Community in Perak.* Social Anthropology Section, School of Comparative Social Sciences, Universiti Sains Malaysia.
Schebesta, Paul
    1973   "Among the Forest of Semangs and Sakais in Malaya," *Anthropologie,* 6.
Schmidt, P.D.
    1903   "The Sakai and Semang Languages in the Malay Peninsula and Their Relation to the Mon-Khmer Languages," *JSBRAS,* 39: 38-45.
Shahrum bin Yub
    1963   "The Museums Department Collections: Kuala Lumpur and Taiping. i. Mah-Meri Masks," *Fed. Mus. J.* (N.S.), 8: 18-23.
Shamsul Amri Baharuddin et al.
    1972   "Satu Kajian luar etnografi Orang Asli Senoi Semai, di Pos Telanok, Tanah Rata, Pahang," *Manusia dan Masyarakat,* 1:118-136.
Skeat, W.W. and Blagden, Charles Otto
    1966   *Pagan Races of the Malay Peninsula.* 2nd ed., London.
Statement of Policy Regarding the Administration of the Orang Asli of Peninsular Malaysia
    1961   Kuala Lumpur, Jabatan Hal Ehwal Orang Asli Malaysia.
Swettenham, F.A.
    1887   "On the Native Races of the Straits Settlements and Malay States," *JRAI,* 16: 221.
Wazir Jahan Begum Abdul Karim
    1974   "Participant Observation: Initial Problems of Acceptance and Adaptation amongst the Hma' Batisi of Pulau Carey, Selangor," *Manusia dan Masyarakat* 3: 82-90.
Werner, Roland
    1975   *Jah-het of Malaysia Art and Culture.* Kuala Lumpur: Penerbit Universiti Malaya.
    1973   *Mah-Meri Art and Culture.* Kuala Lumpur: Muzium Negara.
    1974   *Mah Meri of Malaysia Art and Culture.* Kuala Lumpur: Penerbit Universiti Malaya.
Wilkinson, R. J.
    1910   *Papers on Malay Subjects, Supplement: The Aboriginal Tribes.* Kuala Lumpur.
Williams-Hunt, P.D.R.
    1952   *An Introduction to the Malayan Aborigines.* Kuala Lumpur.

4   Anthropology and Sociology in Indonesia[1]

KOENTJARANINGRAT

Indonesian Anthropology and Sociology before World War II

Records on Indonesian Peoples and Cultures

The development of anthropology and sociology in Indonesia is based on a vast accumulation of records on Indonesian peoples and cultures left by foreign visitors who have come to the islands from time immemorial. Compared to the records left by the Chinese, Indian and Arab merchants, those left by Western European visitors are the most important. The earliest Western European records came from travellers and sailors, from missionaries, from translators of the Bible, from explorers, and from civil servants of the Dutch colonial administration.

On that vast amount of records there are more than 40 bibliographies, of which lists are included in *Gids van in Nederland Aanwezige Bronnen Betreffende de Geschiedenis van Nederlandsch-Indie/Indonesia 1816-1942*[2] compiled by F. G. D. Jaquet (1968) and in a textbook on social research methodology (Koentjaraningrat 1973: pp. 44-50). Therefore, no additional list of those 40 bibliographies is necessary to be included here. It should be taken into consideration, however, that the earlier part of those writings are of very dubious quality and not very useful for scientific studies. The Dutch scientific interest in Indonesia indeed began only during the second part of the 19th century. Since then the Dutch government required an extensive knowledge of the main languages and cultures of the peoples in Indonesia from civil servants and military officers who intended to make a career in the colonial service. This attention for Indonesian languages, peoples and cultures stimulated an intensive collection of data on those matters, and consequently the development of a complex of social sciences called *Indologie*. Although in a subsequent stage of her development the various specializations of *Indologie* could not be kept concentrated in one hand, the discipline was characterized by a minimum of differentiation. There were only three branches of specialization: studies with a dominantly literary-historical orientation, those with a dominantly socio-political orientation, and those with a dominantly socio-economic orientation.

Anthropology in the restircted sense did exist in the prewar period, and is usually considered to belong to the first group of studies. However, many which today can also be considered anthropology, such as the study of *adat* law, or the study of rural economics, was at that time considered to belong to the second and third categories of studies respectively. Sociology, on the other hand, belonged to the second branch of *Indologie*.

The Dutch specialists in *Indologie* have attempted to achieve an understanding of the peoples and cultures in Indonesia mainly through the normative approach, i.e. searching for basic principles and established norms of the cultural system, by using speculative and deductive comparative methods of investigation. Consequently they had to consider and take a look into the older phases of the culture, which results in their little interest in the problem of socio-cultural change.

The centers of Indonesian studies before World War II were mainly the universities and the scientific institutes and associations in Holland. Indonesian studies in Indonesia were also mainly in the hands of Dutch scholars as only few of the small number of Indonesians with a university degree has taken up an academic career. Instead, they usually went into the civil service. However, cases can be mentioned of the outstanding role of some three or four Indonesian academics in the development of Indonesian studies. A more detailed presentation of the development of *Indologie* and the relationship of anthropology and sociology within *Indologie* is unnecessary as a number of books and articles have been written on the development of various branches of Indonesian studies, such as on the development of *adat* law studies by C. van Vollenhoven (1928) and J. Prins (1962); on the development of Indonesian Anthropology by R. Kennedy (1949), G. J. Held (1953), A. G. Gerbrands (1959),

P. E. de Josselin de Jong (1960), and Koentjaraningrat (1975); on the development of sociology by H. J. Heeren (1953; 1956); and a review of government surveys on agrarian problems, household budget studies and population studies are included in E. A. van de Graaf's book on the development of statistics in Indonesia (1955).

Indonesian Anthropology and Sociology after World War II

Research Activities by Dutchmen

When after World War II Indonesia became independent, Dutch *Indologie* was never able to return to its previous glorious position. Before the war Dutch Indologists were placed as civil servants in even the smallest subdistricts throughout the country, and were thus in a position to have a close and continuous contact with the population as well as a full opportunity to observe and study them from nearby. Their high quality of academic training qualified them for adequate social research, an opportunity which disappeared when the independent Republic of Indonesia disposed of the Dutch civil servants.

A number of studies in *adat* law and anthropology published after the war by Dutch ex-civil servants can only be considered as continuations of studies already started before the war. Some examples of these are: G. J. Held's study on the social structure of the Waropen Papuans of the Nubuai on the eastern coast of the Cenderawasih (or Geelvink) Bay in West Irian (1947): H. Bouman's study on the development of Indonesian Nationalism in West Sumatra (1949); H. Th. Chabot's study on the kinship and social system of the Macassarese of the *adat* area of Borongloe in South Sulawesi (1950); and H. J. Burger's remarkable study on structural changes in Javanese society (1948-49).

After the war the chair in anthropology at the University of Indonesia was occupied by G. J. Held, and the chair in sociology by G. T. S. Mulia, a specialist in education and social-philosopher who among other things had done a library study on the concept of "primitive mentality" in the Lévy-Bruhlian sense. In 1951, however, Mulia became minister of education. Sociology was then taught by the Dutch trained Indonesian sociologist Ismael and subsequently by H. J. Heeren, a Dutchman who was trained in social geography.

During 1957-58 most of the Dutch scholars left Indonesia due to the tense relations between the two countries, which developed consequent to the West Irian issue. Indonesia became closed territory for Dutch scholars, and *Indologie* could only study her subject from a distance. Hence it only became part of *Niet-Westersche Sociologie* (Sociology of Non-Western Societies). The younger generations in Holland began to lose interest in Indonesia, and Indonesian studies was carried out only by a small group of an older generation of Indologist, most of who have had a civil service or academic career in the prewar colonial period.

Whereas Dutch interest in Indonesia diminished rapidly after 1958, interest in West Irian increased tremendously. Holland's interest in this part of her colonial empire was almost absent before the war, but after 1950 this situation changed. Many research activities, especially those in the field of anthropology were organized or sponsored by *Kantoor voor Bevol-kings-zaken* at Kotabaru (now called Jayapura). This research station was established by the first governor after the war, J. van Baal, who himself is a well-known anthropologist.

With the West-Irian issue solved and relations between Indonesia and Holland improved in 1963, the interest in Indoensia returned in the academic circles, although rather slowly. Until about 1960 it was still a continuation of older prewar interest. H. G. Schulte Nordholt, for example, submitted a dissertation to Vrije Universiteit te Amsterdam titled *Het Poli-tieke Systeem van de Atoni van Timor* (1966) which included data compiled during his period of service in the colonial administration in 1939-42 and 1945-47. Another example is H. J. Heeren, who submitted a dissertation to the University of Utrecht on *Transmigratie in Indonesia* (1967), the material of which he had started to collect during the period when he had lectured in sociology at the University of Indonesia between 1954-57. Currently, Dutch interest in Indonesia has returned, also among the younger generation of scholars.

Research Activities by Americans and Other Foreigners

After the war American anthropologists and sociologists became interested in Indonesia more than ever before. This was part of their general interest in postwar Southeast Asia, while at least three important centers in the United States were active in organizing anthropological and sociological research in Indonesia, i.e. Cornell University, Massachussetts Institute of Technology, and Yale University.[3]

Cornell University has a Southeast Asia Program as a division of the Department of Far Eastern Studies, which carried out research and trained also specialists through a Ph. D. program on that area. The graduate student has to be able to achieve a general comprehension of the total Southeast Asian region and can specialize in any one of the Southeast Asian countries based on a particular discipline, e.g. political science, economics, sociology, anthropology, history, or linguistics. Competence in any one of the principal Southeast Asian languages is also required. An important part of the program was te Modern Indonesia Project of which G. McT. Kahin was the director, a political scietist and author of a well-known book, *Nationalism and Revolution in Indonesia* (1952). Although political science and history seemed to have dominated the program, there was also sufficient input from the side of anthropologists and sociologists, e.g. the study done by R. Textor on community development (1954); D.E. Willmott's on the Chinese of Semarang (1956; 1957; 1960); whereas a number of Indonesian anthropologists and sociologists have studied under the program either for an M.A. or a Ph. D.

Another important center for Indonesian studies was the Center for International Studies of the Massachussetts Institute of Technology, which has as objective the study of postwar international problems, including the cultural, economic, and political aspects. Within this framework, three countries became the special focus of attention: Italy, India, and Indonesia. The coordinator of the program on Indonesia was the well-known economist B. Higgins. Although the main focus of attention of the Indonesian program was economic and political development, the trend of thinking which emerged in the late fifties concerning the noneconomic obstacles of economic developments, with B. Higgins himself as one of the early exponents, stimulated intensive study on the socio-cultural aspects of Indonesian society. The most important anthropological and sociological research project sponsored by M. I. T. in Indonesia was the Modjokuto study, carried out by a team of anthropologists and sociologists under leadership of a linguist, R. Handon, who studied a small town called Pare in East Java, which was given the assumed name Modjokuto. All the members of the team have subsequently written their Ph. D. theses on data obtained in

Modjokuto: C. Geertz on the religion in Modjokuto (1960); his wife, H. Geertz on the kinship system (1961); E. J. Ryan on the cultural value orientation of the Modjokuto Chinese (1961); A. C. Dewey on the small market economy (1963); and R. R. Jay on local small town politics (1963). Although most of them have also written a number of other articles in addition to their dissertations (Jay 1956; 1963; Dewey 1962; H. Geertz 1963), none of them has done better than C. Geertz, who has published a long series of books and articles on various aspects of his Modjokuto data, with special reference to the sociocultural and religious aspects of economic development (Geertz 1956; 1956-a; 1956-b; 1957; 1960; 1963; 1963-a; 1965) as well as on the results of his second Indonesian field work in Bali (1959; 1964; Geertz and Geertz 1964). Most of his works have been extensively discussed, not only in American, but also in Dutch and Indonesian social science journals, whereas a critical appraisal of the main theme of his work is included in H. J. Heeren's review article on Indonesian sociology, in Harsja Bachtiar's extensive review of *Religion in Java,* and in Koentjaraningrat's book on *Anthropology in Indonesia* (1975).

Yale's interest in Indonesia dated from the period before the war, when R. Kennedy who compiled *Bibliography of Indonesian Peoples and Cultures* (1948) was professor in anthropology at the Anthropology Department. Yale also had a Southeast Asia Program after the war, of which K. J. Pelzer, a geographer, became its director. Before the war this scholar had done work on resettlement programs in Indonesia and the Philippines, and has written a book on the subject, called *Pioneer Settlements in the Asiatic Tropics* (1949). After the war he has done another economic-geographic study in East Sumatra (Pelzer 1957), and his assistant, a Yale graduate student in anthropology, C. Cunningham, has during that trip studied the postwar migrations of Toba-Bataks to East Sumatra to occupy concession land of estates as squatters (Cunningham 1958). Another Yale student, L. Pospisil, did field work among the Kapauku Papuans of West Irian, and wrote an important dissertation on their *adat* law, to obtain an understanding of the five principles of law in non-literate societies (Pospisil 1956). P. R. Goethals did field work in West Sumba and wrote his dissertation and other articles on various aspects of West Sumba socio-political organization (1959; 1960; 1967). C. Cunningham returned several years later after his trip with Pelzer, to do field work among the Atoni of Timor, and also wrote his dissertation and a number of other articles on various aspects of Atoni culture (1964; 1964-a; 1965; 1967). E. M. Bruner, a member of the staff of the Anthropology Department made a study of Toba Batak urbanization in Medan (1959; 1961; 1963; 1972; 1972-a). F. L. Cooley did his field work for his dissertation in Ambon. A part of his dissertation and a number of articles on Ambon are published (1962; 1962-a; 1967).

The Human Relations Area Files of Yale University, which compiles systematically ethnographic data from all over the world, is naturally also interested in Southeast Asia and Indonesia. In a series of publications called Survey of World Cultures, there is a large volume on various aspects of contemporary Indonesia under the editorship of R. T. Mavey (1963). The anthropological chapter on peoples and cultures in Indonesia is written by H. Geertz. Two more strictly ethnographic volumes on Ethnic Groups of Insular Southeast Asia has been published, edited by F. Le Bar et al. The first volume on Madagascar and Indonesia has already appeared, whereas the one on the Philippines and Taiwan followed.

There are many other foreigners other than the Americans who are doing research in Indonesia. The number has increased especially since 1967. Table 1 presents a picture of the number of foreign anthropologists and sociologists according to their nationality, who started, or were doing research in Indonesia during 1971.

Research Activities by Indonesians

In 1953 the anthropologist G. J. Held wrote that: "... all scientific research in Indonesia is done by Europeans" (Thomas and Pickelis 1953). This was naturally due to the fact that at that time the teaching staff of the University of Indonesia was still predominantly Dutch. However, at the Gadjah Mada University in Yogyakarta, anthropology and sociology were taught by an Indonesian professor, M. M. Djojodigoeno, who unlike most of the first generation university professors in Indonesia whose previous prewar occupations were generally in the civil service, had compiled data on *adat* private law of Central Java, in cooperation with another *adat* law scholar, Tirtawinata.[4] He has therefore been able to stimulate an atmosphere of research among staff members and students of the Faculty of Law and the Faculty of Political Science of Gadjah Mada University.

A committee called Panitya Social Research, which was subsequently transferred into *Lembaga Sosiografi dan Hukum Adat* (Institute for

Table 1

Number of Foreign Scholars Who Conduct
Research in Indonesia in 1970-1972

Nationalities	Anthropology			Sociology			Other Social Sciences		
	1970	1971	1972	1970	1971	1972	1970	1971	1972
Americans	7	19	12	—	—	—	14	17	19
Australians	2	3	2	1	1	—	5	6	3
British	—	4	3	—	—	—	1	6	2
Dutchmen	1	2	1	—	—	—	2	6	3
Germans	1	1	—	—	—	1	1	3	1
French	—	3	2	—	—	—	—	1	—
Canadians	—	—	1	—	2	—	—	1	—
Singaporeans	—	—	—	—	—	—	—	2	—
New Zealanders	—	—	—	—	—	—	—	1	—
Italians	—	1	1	—	—	—	—	—	—
Ceylonese	—	1	—	—	—	—	1	—	—
Total	11	34	22	1	3	1	24	43	28

Source: Files of the Indonesian Institute for Sciences(LIPI)

Sociography and Adat Law) organized the research activities, of which the results were published as mimeographed papers, or included in the journal *Sosiografi Indonesia*. Of the 30 articles on research findings, the most important ones are those written by Soedjito Sosrodihardjo, who paid special attention to Javanese rural religion and leadership (1956; 1956-a; 1958), by Pandam Guritno, who studied social pathology and child health in rural Java (1958; 1959; 1960; 1963), and by Masri Singarimbun who did some research in the Karo Batak area of North Sumatra (1959). The first-mentioned staff member, Soedjito Sosrodihardjo, subsequently went to England to study at the University of London, where he worte an M. A. thesis on the sociology of religion: *A Sectarian Group in Java, With Reference to a Midland Village* (1959). Masri Singarimbun also had the opportunity to study abroad, where he was awarded a graduate fellowship from the Australian National University in 1962, and where he completed his dissertation on *Kinship and Affinal Relations among the Karo of North Sumatra* (1965).

At the University of Indonesia in Jakarta, anthropology and sociology were during the initial years after the independence taught by Dutchmen.

It was only in 1956 that two Indonesians who had received anthropological training abroad (one in Holland and the other in the United States) became available. They established a Department of Anthropology in 1957. A number of sociologists returned from overseas training at approximately the same time. However, only two of this first group remained in the academic position. In 1959 Harsja W. Bachtiar returned after submitting his M. A. thesis on *Twelve Sumatran Villages: An Exercise in the Study of Political Instiutions* (1956) to Cornell University, and in 1961 came Sulaiman Sumardi, after having submitted his M. A. thesis on *Regional Politicians and Administrators in West Java* (1961).

Sociologists of the University of Indonesia who succeeded in achieving a Ph. D. degree abroad are Selosoemardjan, who wrote a dissertation for Cornell University on *Social Changes in Jogyakarta* (1962); Tan Giok Lan,[5] who initially wrote an M. A. thesis for Cornell University on *The Chinese Community in a Sundanese Town* (1961) based on a previous community study which she had conducted in Sukabumi (West Java), and who later wrote a Ph. D. dissertation for the University of California at Berkeley on *The Chinese of San Francisco* (1968); Harsja W. Bachtiar, who received a Ph. D. from Harvard based on his dissertation *The Formation of the Indonesian Nation* (1972); Mochtar Naim, who had previously studied at McGill University, and who wrote a dissertation for the University of Singapore on *Merantau, Minangkabau Voluntary Migration* (1974).

Other Indonesian sociologists who have had a basic training in other disciplines are Harjono Sujono, who is basically a statistician, and who wrote a dissertation on *The Adaptation of Innovation in a Developing Country: The Case of Family Planning* (1974) for the University of Chicago; Herman Suwardi, an agronomist, who wrote a dissertation on *Respon Masyarakat Terhadap Modernisasi Produksi Pertanian* (1972) for the University of Padjadjaran at Bandung.

An important group of sociologists are connected with the Institute of Agriculture in Bogor. They studied agrarian problems and peasant economics, became interested in peasant communities in general and became rural sociologists. Among them are: Kampto Utomo from the Institute of Agriculture of Bogor, who has studied communities of Javanese "spontaneous resettlers" in the Way Sekampung area of Lampung in South Sumatra (Kampto Utomo 1957); Bachtiar Rifai from the same institute, who has studied comparatively forms of land property and sharecropping systems in two villages in the northern part of Central Java (Bachtiar Rifai

1958); Adiwilaga, an agronomist from the *Kantor Perantjang Tata Bumi* (Bureau for Land-Use Planning) in Bandung, now professor in agricultural sociology at Padjadjaran University of Bandung, has studied land-use and land-tenure in Sundanese villages of West Java in the early 1950's, and has paid special attention to the relationship between the wealthy and the poor farmers in his area of study (1954; 1954-a).

Kampto Utomo[6] was subsequently appointed professor in rural sociology at the Institute of Agriculture of Bogor, and has among his many graduate students who worked for their *Sarjana* degrees in agronomy, an annual average of 2.8% who chose a subject in socio-econmic problems in peasant communities for their *Sarjana* theses. To give an idea of the variety of problems in which Indonesian rural sociologists are interested, Table 2 presents a specification of 40 subjects of *Sarjana* theses written by graduate students in agronomy at the Institute of Agriculture of Bogor during 1958 and 1971. Today there is a *Pusat Penelitian Sosiologi Pedesaan* (Center for Rural Sociological Research) at the Institute for Agriculture of Bogor, with Sediono Tjondronegoro, a sociologist trained at the University of Amsterdam, as the director.

Involvement of Indonesian Universities in Large Scale Socio-Economic Surveys

Large scale extensive national or regional survey studies concerning agrarian or rural socio-economic problems are frequently carried out by government ministries or provincial governments, often in cooperation with research institutes of the universities or by political parties. Apparently, due to the low capacity for small-scale, more conceptual intensive social research, the large scale surveys dominated social research in Indonesia since the early 1950's until quite recently. Although some have produced important results, compared to the costs which had been put into those survey studies, the output is on the whole relatively meager. Those surveys generally involved rural sociologists, but only a few involved anthropologists.

An early example of a large scale extensive survey is one on rural demography, agrarian problems, and agricultural economics conducted by the *Lembaga Penyelidikan Ekonomi dan Masyarakat*, Institute for Economic and Social Research, the University of Indonesia, in cooperation with the Ministry of Interior, during 1954 and 1955. An extensive questionnaire and interview guide was meant to gather data on rural demography, sys-

Table 2

Subjects of Sarjana Theses on Socio-Economic Problems of
Peasant Communities, Written by Graduate Students of the
Institute of Agriculture of Bogor between 1957 and 1971.

Subject	Number of theses on various aspects of the subject
1. Problems of relationship between peasants and external institutions (Padi Sentra, sugar mills, forestry service etc.)	11
2. Categorizations of peasants in Indonesian village communities	6
3. Problems of local leadership in peasant communities	6
4. Problems of land tenure and land law	4
5. Problems of change in technology and methods of cultivation	4
6. Levels of living of peasant households	3
7. Estate workers	1
8. Opening up of new land	1
9. Marga Raja in North Tapanuli	1
10. Kinship system in Acehnese peasant communities	1
11. Rural social stratification	1
12. Tree crops and tree planting on mountain slopes	1
Total	40

tems of land tenure, land use and land ownership, subsistence agriculture,
peasant cash crops agriculture, cottage industries, rural cooperatives etc. in
23 villages scattered throughout Central and East Java. Although a substantial amount of data on those matters was collected, only a limited
number of reports have appeared. One general report was written by Emil
Salim (Salim et al. 1959), and there were three other small reports by
Ismail and Widjojo Nitisastro (Widjojo Nitisastro 1956; Ismail 1960).

Another, and apparently more successful survey was the Agro-Economic Survey which was initiated by the Ministry of Agriculture in early
1965, in close cooperation with research institutes of a number of important universities throughout the country, and with Financial assistance of
Ford Foundation. The management of the research was in the hands of an
appointed Work Committee under directorship of Sajogya, and the re-

search teams consisted of agronomists from the Ministry of Agriculture, but for a large part also from the Institute of Agriculture of Bogor, Gadjah Mada University of Jogya, and the Padjadjaran University in Bandung.

Fourteen teams of six to twelve investigators, the majority of which recruited from the above-mentioned universities, had concentrated on 14 problem areas relating to production, labor, marketing, agricultural services, cooperatives, and relating to crops in the subsistence cash crops as well as estate sector. At a later stage, when the surveys expanded to include areas outside Java, the teams also recruited staff members and students from the University of North Sumatra in Medan, the University of Andalas in Pdang, and Hasanuddin University in Ujung Pandang.

The subjects of the interviews and observation of the teams consisted of samples of 150 to 600 respondent farmers, estate workers, seasonal workers, traders, and other categories of people who played a role in the network of agricultural economics at the village, subdistrict, or district levels.

In between field work periods of one month or more, the various teams often convened for inter-team workshops to exchange findings, discuss common methodological problems, and stimulate further investigation. Officials from the Ministry of Agriculture and other policy-makers were often invited to join the workshops. This close cooperation between the university research teams and the policy-makers seemed to have caused a remarkable impact which, according to a foreign observer, E. de Vries (1969) the agro-economic survey seemed to have on the agricultural policy of the Indonesian government. Apart from that impact, the eight-volume report of the 14 surveys seemed to be a sufficiently successful result of this large scale survey.[7]

Anthropology and Sociology in National Development

Relationship between Anthropology and Sociology in Indonesia

The opinion on anthropology and sociology held by Indonesian academics during the period immediately after 1950 was divided: one group was in favor of sociology as compared to anthropology, which they considered inappropriate for a growing country as it has to look into the future rather than pay attention to its backward, primitive, and static aspects; another group, however, recognized the importance of anthropology as a means of acquiring knowledge of and insight into an area with a large diversity of ethnic groups, while they also recognized the advantages of the anthropological method of qualitative inquiry and observation in socio-cultural research in a country with a large portion of illiterates and peasants among its population. T. S. G. Moelia, the first postwar professor in sociology at the University of Indonesia has expressed his view in an article (Moelia 1951), in which he regarded anthropology suspiciously as based on colonial interest.

Differences concerning the history of the two sciences indeed exist. Anthropology emerged inductively, when several scholars, lawyers, psychologists, archeologists or geographers started to integrate a vast compilation of descriptive data on a great variety of peoples and cultures all over this globe during the second half of the previous century, into macro-histories of social evolution or diffusion. Sociology, especially in the Netherlands, started in a similar way as did social geography, although it was also partly diverted deductively from social philosophy.

Concerning their subject matter and field of study, anthropology as well as sociolgy in Indonesia study both urban and rural problems, although it has been suggested that anthropology in Indonesia was to concentrate mainly on socio-cultural problems at a regional level, and sociology on socio-cultural problems on a national level. This division of labor, however, proved to be hard to maintain. Some Indonesian anthropologists still insist that anthropology is more holistic in its approach, whereas sociologists tend to look at particular social phenomena and problems. However, if we look at some of the research projects which a number of Indonesian anthropologists are carrying out today, e.g. cultural aspects of fertility, the economic cost of children in peasant communities, variations in value orientation of students with Chinese school and national school backgrounds, comparative study of divorce in peasant and urban communities etc., the above-mentioned distinction becomes irrelevant.

It might make sense to make some distinction based on the fact that anthropologists indeed have more experience and more adequate concepts to deal with the phenomena of ethnic diversity, but it is my opinion that this is only a matter of training and that it is not difficult to provide students in sociology of Indonesia with concepts and facts that will enable them to cope with similar problems of ethnic diversity in their country.

If the difference between the two disciplines is difficult to formulate in terms of subject matter and field of study, there seems to be some difference of emphasis in terms of the methodology. Anthropologists claim to have developed more accurate qualitative methods, of intensive interview, observation, content analysis, the case study approach etc., whereas sociologists are proud of their skill in utilizing quantitative methods, accurate probability sampling, and statistical techniques. However, as some Indonesian anthropologists are also getting interested in and have actually started to use quantitative methods in their studies, this difference will also disappear rapidly.

Despite the large similarity between the two disciplines, the structure of the current Indonesian universities is actually not very conducive for frequent contact between anthropology and sociology. Anthropology departments are part of the Faculty of Letters, whereas sociology departments belong to the Faculties of Social and Political Science. This organization goes back to the Dutch period, when anthropology was considered to be part of Indonesian studies, which is closely related to the study of Indonesian languages, literature, and cultural history. Although Dutch universities have changed this structure and moved anthropology to the Faculties of Social Sciences (*Faculteit der Sociale Wetenschappen*), in Indonesia this development has not yet taken place. Sociology, one the other hand, has according to the tradition of Dutch universities always been associated with the study of law, and has after the separation of the Faculty of the Social Sciences from the Law School become part of this new faculty. The idea of moving the Department of Anthropology to the Faculty of Social Sciences has been advanced, but at Indonesian universities where faculties have existed as virtually autonomous institutions, each with its own teaching staff, and administratively separated from the other faculties, with separate libraries etc., such a reorganization proved to be a complicated and costly endeavor.

Anthropologists and sociologists are difficult to distinguish in Indonesia, except by their difference in educational background. In their profession they practically share the same knowledge, theories and concepts; are interested in similar national as well as regional problems, in urban as well as rural areas, and both utilize similar qualitative and quantitative methods.

However, I consider it necessary to maintain the distinction even if it is only to be in accordance with the situation in the international scientific community, where anthropology and socioloy are still considered as two separate disciplines. Anthropology and sociology in Indonesia, however, should be in one department, share the same curriculum at the under-graduate level, and only separate at the graduate level when teaching starts to put emphasis on theories and concepts.

Problems of National Development

Before the war anthropology in the broader sense includes not only ethnography and ethnology but also the study of *adat* law and of agricultural and peasant economics. It has therefore developed knowledge to administer the country. In the postwar period anthropology has, in close cooperation with sociology, studied problems of nation building. This study of national problems is considered "urgent anthropology". The meaning of this concept therefore differs significantly from the way in which it is perceived in developed countries, where it is considered to be the study of vanishing cultures, before all traces have disappeared. Especially after 1965, when Indonesia became fully committed to national development, anthropological and sociological research activities also became oriented towards a number of important national problems in the area of: (1) national integration, (2) population increase, (3) socio-cultural change, (4) education, (5) community development, (6) reorganization of administration (see Table 3), are relevant for anthropological as well as sociological research projects, and can best be analyzed with anthropological or sociological concepts and methods.

In the framework of national integration, inter-ethnic relations, inter-racial relations, and relations between religious collectivities, there are problems of great interest to anthropolgists as well as sociologists, and can be studied in rural as well as urban situations with qualitative as well as quantitative methods. In this respect, anthropologists can also be of par-ticular importance in promoting a better understanding between the ethnic groups in Indonesia, by writing recent, up-to-date, and modern ethnog-raphies. These can become source books for popular literature, novels, children books etc., where themes on ethnic customs and beliefs may promote a better understanding among peoples from different ethnic groups in Indonesia. There is of course a vast ethnographic literature on many of the ethnic groups in Indonesia. However, most of that literature has now become obsolete, whereas consequent to the fact that it is for the

Table 3
Problems of Nation Building in Indonesia

Main problem areas	Actual problems
1. National integration	Inter-ethnic relations; inter-racial relations; promotion of the national language; relations between religious collectivities; relations between the national center and the regional communities etc.
2. Population increase	Resettlement programs; control of urbanization; unemployment and disguised unemployment; planned parenthood programs; ecological consequences of high population densities etc.
3. Socio-cultural change	Changes in fundamental cultural value orientation; changes in traditional social systems; changes in adat law systems; changes in traditional social stratifications; changes in patterns of leadership; changes in the meaning and content of socio-cultural systems and artistic expression due to the impact of tourism etc.
4. Education	Discrepancy between the national ideal and actual practice of education in different local situations and cultures; national aspirations for the educational system; the people's perception of the educational system at the local level; socio-political function of the school as a non-traditional institution in the local community; political, economic, social and ideological impediments to equality of educational access; teaching and learning processes in both formal and informal educational systems; the nature of the interpersonal relationship between teacher and student, teacher and parents, teacher and government administrators etc.
5. Community development	The impact of illiteracy campaigns; the constraints and impact of the green revolution; changes in household budgets and cost of living; the constraints in the development of rural cooperatives; sociocultural aspects of infant and child mortality and morbidity etc.
6. Reorganization of administration	The value systems behind administrative structures; principles, perceptions and conceptions about cooperation and competition in bureaucratic systems; perceptions and conceptions about leadership; corruption etc.
7. Problems of Environment	Erosion as a consequence of population growth; tropical forest conservation and slashing cultivation; health and environment; changing food habits; tourism and environment; etc.

greatest part written in Dutch, it has became virtually useless to most Indonesian intellectuals under 40 years of age. Besides, several areas of Indonesia have never been adequately described. There are still many gaps in the ethnographic literature of Indonesia, e.g. on West Java, Madura, the islands of Lombok, Sumba, Flores, and those between Flores and Timor, Halmahera, a large part of South Maluku, most of North Sulawesi, Central and East Kalimantan, the Gayo area of North Sumatra, the Lampung area of South Sumatra, and most of Malay East Sumatra.

Studies to compile ethnographic data can best be carried out within the framework of Ph. D. study programs. The dissertation serves as a goal and stimulator to motivate graduate students to spend the traditional one-year anthropological field work period to observe intensively and to study qualitatively one particular ethnic culture. Two anthropologists from the University of Indonesia, i.e. Junus Melalatoa and J. Danandjaja have conducted such kinds of field work; the first has written his dissertation on the Gayo of North Sumatra, and the latter on the non-Hindu Balinese of Trunyan. One anthropologist from Satyawatjana Christian University, N. L. Kana, has written a structural ehnography of the people of Sawu.

Inter-ethnic relations can best be studied in urban environments where people of different ethnic backgrounds meet and compete for limited economic, educational and political opportunities, or where processes of cultural adjustment, accomodation, or assimilation, occurs. Such studies have been carried out by a team of anthropologists in the city of Bandung, directed by E. M. Bruner, who has worked on similar problems in Medan (North Sumatra). A number of interesting reports have come out from the study (Bruner 1971; Parsudi Suparlan 1971; Hirokoshi 1971; Djuwariah Utja 1971).

The study of relations between religious categories and groups have not yet been done on the basis of sociological approaches. After Geertz's book *The Religion of Java* (1959), no major study on the sociology of religion has been carried out in Indonesia. A number of specific studies for doctoral dissertations in theology have been carried out, e.g. on Javanese religious movements (Hadiwijono 1967; Jong 1973), on missionary activities among the Batak (Schreiner 1972), or among the Ngaj of Central Kalimantan (Ukur 1971), or some data collection on facts about Christianity (Cooley 1968; Widyapranata 1973). This material may be a good start for more intensive anthropological or sociological studies on the interaction between religious groups in Indonesia.

In the framework of population increase problems in relation to re-settlment programs, control of urbanization, unemployment and disguised unemployment, there are areas where only anthropological and sociological research can contribute to the understanding. Also in family planning, however, especially in regard to the problem of the sociocultural aspects of fertility anthropologists can be of primary importance, whereas studies on the impact and follow-up of family planning programs will be a specific task of sociologists.

Numerous studies which evaluate the effectiveness of various contraceptive devices and studies on the knowledge, attitudes and practice (KAP studies) of family planning among the population have been carried out mainly on Java by public health officers and sociologists. A complete annotated list of the studies, of which the Jakarta KAP studies are the most adequate ones, are included in a volume: *Kumpulan Ichtisar Hasil-Hasil Penelitian Keluarga Berencana 1961-1972* (BKKBN, LP3ES 1972). Anthropologists have done studies on indigenous midwives, on the condition of women or on family structures and household compositions at various places in Java (BKKBN, LP3ES 1972: pp. 69-71, 79-80, 82-85). Excellent studies on the role of indigenous midwives (*dukun bayi*) and curers (*dukun*) or the socio-cultural aspects of fertility have been conducted by anthropologists and sociologists who participated in the Serpong project. This joint project between the University of Indonesia and Leiden University to study and evaluate traditional as well as modern contraceptive methods, the significance of the rural public health clinics for the follow-up care of acceptors, and the total complex of socio-cultural factors that interfere with or stimulate family planning, the role of the indigenous midwives and curers in that respect,[8] has published a series of over the 20 reports, of which the most outstanding are those on the role of the traditional midwives in rural Jakarta society (Lubis, Borkent-Niehof, Pudjiastuti 1973). One remarkable study that focuses on the role of women in family planning in Indonesia is carried out in seven areas in Sumatra, Java and Bali by a team of women anthropologists and sociologists (Ihromi *et al.* 1973).

All the actual problems in the framework of socio-cultural change are typical problems for anthropological and sociological research. Studies on changes in fundamental cultural value orientation (Koentjaraningrat 1969-a; 1974), in traditional social system and in *adat* law systems, are especially for the anthropologists. Sociologists may have more experience in studies on changes of social stratification, whereas studies on changes in patterns of leadership in various parts of Indonesia should be carried out in interdisciplinary cooperation between anthropologists and sociologists.

In the framework of education the actual problems are also specific problems to which anthropological and sociological research have a great deal to contribute, although often in cooperation with psychologists.

Problems that related to community development are basically anthropological or sociological ones. Although on the surface they concern illiteracy campaigns, the introduction of new techniques of agricultural production, improved public administration, public health, ecology, and better technology, the core of the problems concern the change of traditional value orientations. Many routine surveys on illiteracy, illiteracy campaigns, and the results and consequences of such activities have been carried out by the Ministry of Education of the Republic of Indonesia. Numerous studies relating to problems of the introduction of new techniques of agricultural production have been carried out by the rural sociologists of the earlier mentioned Agro Economic Survey, or the Center of Research in Rural Sociology of the Institute of Agriculture in Dogor. Routine surveys on special studies on village administration and public administration at the village level have been done by the Ministry of Interior, by the National Institute for Administration, or by students of faculties of Political Science and Public Administration (*Fakultas Sosial Politik*) of various universities who work for their *Sarjana* theses.

Some studies in the field of public health need special mention. They are the studies on nutrition and food habits. Numerous studies on food and nutrition have been done in Indonesia, but a realization of the importance of anthropological and sociological concepts for the understanding of nutritional problems only started in the early 1950's when the WHO assigned a British anthropologist, M. Freedman, to study the socio-cultural aspects of nutrition in Indonesia (Freedman 1954). A study on the nutritional status at two economic levels in two Sundanese villages is done by nutritionists Lauw Tjin Giok, I. Tarwotjo, Djokosaptono, and R. Rasidi (1962); a socio-economic study on nutrition in another group of Sundanese villages is done by sociologist H. Suwardi and nutritionist M. Enoch (1960), whereas a study to evaluate the attempts to improve the nutritional content of the daily food in Indonesian households is done by a team of rural sociologists, agronomists and nutritionists (Sajogya *et al.* 1974). A study on the social and cultural aspects of food patterns and food habits among the social categories of households in West Javanese Central Javanese, East Javanese, Balinese, and South Sumatran villages is done by a team of social scientists and nutritionists (Tan *et al.* 1973).

Problems relating to the reorganization of administration need anthropological and sociological research, especially where it concern the human element, the value sytems behind the administrative structures, principles, perceptions and conceptions about cooperation, competition and leadership, corruption etc. However, despite the numerous studies that have been made in the field of public administration, many of which are doctoral dissertations for the University of Indiana, few have studied the human element in public administration from a particularly anthropological or sociological point of view. Only H.A. Abdul-Rachman's dissertation, *Suatu Pendekatan K'earah Pembinaan Kepemimpinan Kerja di Indonesia* (1963) submitted to Padjadjaran University, has utilized some sociological concepts on leadership and management, whereas S. P. Siagian's dissertation, *The Development and Problems of Indigenous Bureaucratic Leadership* (1964) focuses on the same problem.

National and regional planners in Indonesia indeed make frequent use of anthropologists as well as sociologists as consultants; the latters are also often invited as consultants by special committees of government departments or special committees of the army and navy staffs. A special committee of the Ministry of Internal Affairs, for example, as the assignment to draw up a new law on village communities, and an anthropologist was invited to be consulted on the problem of diversity and typology of Indonesian villages.

Development planners in Indonesia are now beginning to feel deeply concerned about problems of ecology in Indonesia due to the heavy pressure of population growth, especially about problems of human ecology. In the overcrowded volcanic island of Java the almost complete disappearance of the forests on the mountain slopes have frequently caused extensive floods; on the arid East Indonesian islands the chronic shortage of water forms an important obstacle to socio-cultural and economic development; the inadequate garbage disposal methods and shortage of running water have caused serious health problems in the overcrowded towns and cities, whereas chemical waste of industrial plants has begun to cause serious problems of heavy pollution to human habitat in the areas surrounding the industrial centers. The Indonesian government does not conceptualize those problems as technological ones, but rather for a large part also as problems of human mentality. A special minister for ecological problems has therefore been appointed, and one of his numerous activities is supporting and financing the development of centers for Ecological Studies at various state universities in Indonesia.

At the University of Indonesia (located in Jakarta) the Ministry of Ecological Problems is supporting the study of human ecology and subsidizing the Center for Environmental Studies and Human Resources. The "Human Resources" component of that center is now what used to be the Institute of Anthropology of the University of Indonesia, which merged with the Center for Ecological Studies of the same university in 1980.

Teaching of Anthropology and Sociology in Indonesian Universities

The Nature of Anthropology Courses at Indonesian Universities

There are two kinds of training in anthropology at Indonesian universities: one which consits of only a 60-hour, one-year introductory course in the anthropology of Indonesia at Law Faculties, at all the Departments of the Faculties of Social Science (Department of Political Science, Department of Administration, Department of Publicistic, Department of Social Works, Department of Sociology), at most of the departments of the Faculty of Letters (Departments of Indonesian Studies, Linguistics, History, and the Area Studies Departments), at the Faculties of Psychology, Faculties of Public Health, and at the IKIPs. The other kind of training in anthropology provides full training in the discipline at the Department of Anthropology, which is part of the Faculty of Letters.

The 60-hour, one-year introductory course is meant to provide students of various branches of study with a preliminary insight and understanding of the socio-cultural variety in Indonesia, and of some of the main principles which underlie the differences. The course is often also meant as a subsidiary subject which will help law students to understand the ways of thinking which form the basis of many norms in Indonesian *adat* law in the rural areas.

The way this one-year introductory course in the anthropology of Indonesia is taught at the 40 state universities and over 200 private universities all over the country, naturally varies widely. However, there is a striking similarity in the way the course is outlined. I have made a survey as part of the LIPI project and have glanced through a number of lecture notes of students from a number of departments of various universities throughout Indonesia, and one kind of syllabus can be distinguished easily in lectures of introductory anthropology of Indonesia at Faculties of Law in most of Central and East Java and the universities of East Indonesia. According to this syllabus, this course usually starts with an explanation of the meaning and objectives of anthropology, i.e. the study of man, especially of man from non-literate "primitive" cultures. Later a great deal of time is spent to explain the concept of "primitive" in the Lévy-Bruhlian sense. Then follows an illustrative description of an Indonesian primitive culture (about 20% of the notes included a description of the Mentawai cultures), followed by notes on kinship systems, where great attention is often paid on the interaction between unilineal kingroups, in relation to systems of asymmetrical cross-cousin connubium. Then there were notes on elements of primitive religion (animism, magic etc.), and subsequently followed by partial description of cultural elements from three of four different ethnic groups in Indonesia; finally a brief explanation of a number of schools in anthropological theory such as evolutionism, the culture historical school, functionalism, etc.

This similarity in the syllabus and main theme of the courses at law schools can be traced back to the teaching material of one of the first lecturers in anthropology at the law school in Jakarta of the 1930's, J. P. Duyvendak. An introductory textbook on Indonesian Anthropology, called *Inleiding tot de Ethnologie van de Indische Archipel* (1937), previously meant as a textbok for high schools, remained the only main textbook in Indonesian anthropology until long after the war (i.e. until about 1958), whereas another small one written by an anthropologist from the University of Utrecht, J. Th. Rischer, *Inleiding tot de Culturele Anthropologie van Nederlandsch-Indie* (1935) which was actually meant as a popular exposition of the diversity of Indonesian cultures for the general public, was translated into the Indonesian language and used as an additional source book on variations in Indonesian cultures.

Duyvendak's lecture notes were apparently handed down through several generations of lecturers, especially those outside the University of Indonesia, in upgrading courses for teachers. After the war, the professor of anthropology at the University of Indonesia, G. J. Held, basically shared

Duyvendak's viewpoint concerning the concept of ancient social structures in Indonesia, both being J. P. B. de Josselin de Jong's former students. However, Held has had more contact with American anthropology, and his lecture notes included the subject of genetics, principles of physical anthropology and the issue of race, problems of culture change, a great deal on kinship systems and Lévi-Strauss, but nothing on the concept "primitive" and the Mentawai islanders. Held's list of readings included M. Mauss' *Essays sur le Don,* C. Lévi-Strauss' *Structure Elementaire de la Parente,* R. Firth's *Human Types,* and a number of American textbooks, such as for instance A. L. Kroeber's *Anthropology Today.* Lectures based on Held's syllabus were given by anthropology teachers at law schools in Jakarta and West Java, but not at the law school of the University of Indonesia.

Also the university departments such as those for political science etc. which were usually younger departments and which only started to include anthropology in their curriculum since 1958, usually followed neither the Duyvendak nor the Held syllabus. Those who lectured at these younger departments were usually former students of the two first Indonesian anthropology lecturers; one started teaching in 1957 at the newly established Padjadjaran University at Bandung. Although he has also been a student of Held's, he has developed his own view of Indonesian anthropology. The other Indonesian anthropologist, also a former student of Held's but who has had an additional American training, started teaching at the University of Indonesia in 1957. These two Indonesian anthropologists have published a number of anthropological textbooks in the Indonesian language, which are now being used for the teaching of anthropology at Indonesian universities.

There are five Indonesian universities that offer full professional training in anthropology at the respective anthropology departments, which are part of the respective Faculties of Letters, but only one has the actual qualification to have a doctorate program in social anthropology. The other four (of which one is a joint sociology-anthropology department) are only capable of offering undergraduate training which lead to *Sarjana Muda* degrees.

The *Sarjana Muda* or undergraduate study at the Department of Anthropology of the University of Indonesia requires four years of class work, while graduate study leading to a *Sarjana* degree requires a minimum of one year of class work or a maximum of two, and the submittal o´

Table 4
List of Institutions Which Offer Training in Anthropology and Sociology (1972)

City	Institution	Type of training
Jakarta	*University of Indonesia*(U.I.)	
	Faculty of Social Sciences, Department of Sociology	Undergraduate and graduate training and doctoral program in Sociology
	Faculty of Letters, Department of Anthropology	Undergraduate and graduate training and doctoral program in social anthropology
Bogor	*Institute of Agriculture*(IPB)	
	Department of Rural Sociology	Graduate training and doctoral program in rural sociology
Bandung	*University of Padjadjaran* (UNPAD)	
	Faculty of Letters, Department of Anthropology	Undergraduate and graduate training in social anthropology
	Faculty of Agriculture, Department of Rural Sociology	Graduate training in rural sociology
	Parahiangan Catholic University	
	Department of Anthropology and Sociology	Undergraduate and graduate training in anthropology and sociology
Jogyakarta	*Gadjah Mada University*(UGM)	
	Faculty of Social and Political Science, Department of Sociology	Undergraduate and graduate training in social sociology
	Faculty of Letters, Department of Anthropology	Undergraduate training in social anthropology
Manado	*Sam Ratulangi University* (UNSRAT)	Undergraduate training in social anthropology

a small *Sarjana* thesis based on field work. The courses at the department are classified into four categories:

(1) *Courses in main subjects,* which include: introductory anthropology, kinship systems, social organization, peasant communities, religious systems, ethnography of Indonesia and Irian, ethno-linguistics, introductory sociology, prehistory of Indonesia, introductory physical anthropology, research methodology, and basic statistics. The stu-

dent must take a total of 40 semesters of these courses during his four years of undergraduate study.

The main subjects at the graduate level include: theoretical anthropology, ethnography of Southeast Asia, anthropology and development (applied) anthropology, and sociology of Indonesia; all of which have to be completed during seven semesters of class work.

(2) *Courses in subsidiary subjects,* which include: the ethnographies of other parts of the world, like Africa, Oceania, America; folklore of Indonesia; Islam in Indonesia; and ten semesters of these are required in the undergraduate or graduate level.

(3) *Introductory courses in related subjects,* which includes: introduction to economics, law, psychology, demography, political science, archeology, linguistics, etc., of which ten semesters are required during the undergraduate four years of class work.

(4) *Courses in other subjects,* which can be anything that is offered at other faculties or schools, and range from arts, literature, geography, political science, to languages. The student may select a total of ten semesters on these subjects, of which six are to be in languages. This may be an Indonesian ethnic language other than one's own or any other Asian or European language, except English.[9]

If we consider the main features of the curriculum explained above, we notice the main focus on social anthropology of the geographic area of Indonesia (although another focus on the whole of S. E. Asia, and another one on East Asia, will develop in the near future), detailed factual knowledge of the most important ethnic cultures, qualitative as well as quantitative research methodology, introductory knowledge of related disciplines, some knowledge of other disciplines, introductory knowledge of other cultures, of the principal area of the globe. Other Indonesian or foreign languages, especially Asian languages, and anthropological theory and concepts, are taught at the graduate level.

Anthropologists with a *Sarjana Muda* degree are therefore only able to teach at high schools, or become assistants in research. The type of research they can do is data collecting without a complex theoretical or conceptual framework. The graduate *Sarjana* degree, however, enables them to carry out more sophisticated research.

The curriculum discussed above is currently only followed by the Departments of Anthropology of the University of Indonesia as the department of the other four universities are unable to follow this curriculum. As is illustrated in Table 4, those departments have a dominantly regional character. They train people who will become experts in the regional ethnic culture and society, its features and problems, and have little capacity to study even other Indonesian cultures.[10] Because of their weakness in anthropological theory and concepts they are also only capable of doing data collecting.

The Nature of Sociology Courses at Indonesian Universities

Similar to anthropology there are also two kinds of training in sociology at Indonesian universities. One kind offers only a 60-hour, one-year introduction in all the faculties and departments where anthropology is also taught, but also at the College of Technology, the Institute for Management, the School for Banking, the Training School for the Immigration Service etc. The other system of teaching sociology provides full professional training in the discipline at Departments of Sociology, which form part of the Faculties of Social Sciences or the Institute of Agricultures.

The 60-hour, one-year introductory course is meant to provide students of various branches of study with some insight into the main components, aspects, and principles of human society. At least this seems to have been the objective when the course was first taught at the Batavia Law School in 1924 by B. J. O. Schrieke, a philologist-turned-sociologist, and subsequently by F. D. Holleman, a lawyer, from 1930 to 1934. After the war the course at the University of Indonesia, and the Law School, which became part of the University of Indonesia, was taught by T. S. G. Moelia who had no training in sociology, and subsequently by Ismael and H. J. Heeren, both social geographers.

Beginning with H. J. Heeren, who returned to Holland and was succeeded by P. A. Postma and Harsja W. Bachtiar in 1958, the course became more empirical in orientation, and more related to Indonesian sociological problems. This trend in the teaching of sociology improved, especially when lecturers like Harsja W. Bachtiar acquired additional training, and when other sociologists like Selosoemardjan and Mely G. Tan returned from their training abroad. Yet, the other type of courses with the social-philosophical orientation still prevailed, mainly at universities in the regions which, to a large extent corresponded to areas where in the field of anthropology the "Duyvendak lecture notes" were taught. Indonesian sociologists of today call it the "Bouman sociology" as the students were usually assigned P. J. Bouman's textbook *Sosiologi: Knosep2 dan Masalah2* (a very inadequate Indonesian translation of the Dutch original called *Sociologie: Begrippen en Problemen*) by lecturers who taught sociology.

Sociology departments which offer full training in sociology exist at five Indonesian universities, and are part of the respective Faculties of Social Science of those universities (cf. Table 4). Undergraduate study at these departments require three years of class work, whereas graduate studies need an additional two years. The study is designed to train Indonesian sociologists who have the ability to understand: "the social structure and social processes including the social changes which spread about, develop and become functional in the Indonesian society ... and to integrate their ability in sociology with other disciplines in the social sciences in an interdisciplinary way, while it is also expected that they comprehend one area of specialization in the field of sociology, and on the other hand are able to apply theory in research, policy and application ..." (Buku Pedoman 1969: p. 36).

The study, which makes it possible to achieve this objective, requires three years of undergraduate and two years of graduate class work, of which the courses are distributed as follows:

(1) At the *Persiapan* (equivalent to "freshman") and *Sarjana Muda I* level (sophomore), the students receives a general education in the social sciences, which include introductory courses in sociology, anthropology, law, economics, psychology, political science etc.

(2) At the *Sarjana Muda II* level (junior) the student starts to focus on various specialized branches of sociology, and can take courses in economic sociology, political sociology, urban sociology, rural sociology, sociology of the family, industrial sociology, sociology of development, whereas courses in research methodology are obligatory.

(3) At the *Sarjana* or graduate level, theoretical sociology and sociological problems which the student can select in relation to the specialization he has chosen, are required. These problems are, for instance, feudal society, conflict, poverty, political movements and revolutions, alienation, corruption *etc.*

The curriculum of the Department of Rural Sociology of the Institute of Agriculture of Bogor is different in that it is a graduate specialization after a four-year undergraduate study in agricultural engineering and agronomy. During their undergraduate study, however, the students in agronomy are required to take eight courses in agricultural economics and six courses in rural sociology. After the *Sarjana Muda* the student in agronomy may choose a specialization and work for a degree in rural sociology at the Department of Rural Sociology by taking a total of six courses in sociology including theoretical sociology and after submitting a *Sarjana* thesis in rural sociology or agricultural economics to the Department.[11]

Teaching Staff in Sociology and Anthropology

As has been mentioned earlier, the majority of lecturers who teach the one-year introductory courses in anthropology and sociology at law schools, the departments of political sciences etc., are usually students of the various schools or departments who has received good grades for the compulsory courses in introductory anthropology and introductory sociology and who, therefore, after they had received their degrees in another discipline, were appointed as assistants to help the lecturers when the latter retired or left the academic profession. This explains the striking uniformity in lecture notes throughout the country, as those lectures have mainly been a continuous repetition of the same lecture notes.

Naturally, many of those assistants and lecturers have improved their knowledge in anthropology or sociology, through their own efforts and occasional reading, but of course their general knowledge of the discipline remains weak. Some of them have had the opportunity to improve their knowledge of anthropology or sociology abroad, while other lecturers have had their training at any one of the five above-mentioned anthropology or sociology departments. Table 5 presents the number of lecturers in anthropology and sociology available in Indonesia in 1972. The category "other" under national training refers to those afore-mentioned lecturers who did not have a full training in anthropology or sociology, but who had taken a course in introductory anthropology and sociology. Under the category "exclusively trained abroad" is classified a Dutch anthropologist who has become an Indonesian citizen. Generally this category is meant for those who have started their training abroad in the discipline concerned, all the way from the freshman level.

Table 5
Number of Anthropologists and Sociologists in Indonesia(1980)

Training	Degree	Anthropologists	Sociologists
Domestic:	Sarjana	128*	60
	Doktor	8	2
	Other	82	86
Partly overseas:	Master of Arts	8	10
	Doctor/Ph.D	5	5
Exclusively	Master of Arts	—	2
overseas:	Doctorandus	—	—
	Doctor/Ph.D.	1	2

Note: Some of the anthropologists and sociologists classified under "Partly overseas" may have a domestic *Sarjana* degree.

* About 30 Sarjana in Anthropology have graduated in 1973, 1974 and 1975 from the Department of Anthropology of Padjadjaran University (in Bandung).

Anthropological and Sociological Textbooks and Libraries

Textbooks and reading material are another principal weakness in Indonesian academic training in general, and in anthropology and sociology in particular. Jakarta is the only place where for reasons of library facilities a doctorate program can be set up by an anthropology or sociology department, although a graduate or Ph. D. student of the Anthropology or Sociology Department of the University of Indonesia cannot exclusively rely on his university library. The library of the Faculty of Letters, of which the Department of Anthropology only forms a part, only has over the 5,000 titles of older books in the field of anthropology and sociology, and only 39 journals (Dutch, American, British, Australian, German, Austrian, Indonesian, Russian, and some scattered issues of Swedish, Rumanian, Indian and Japanese). This library has not caught up very well after 1960 due to monetary problems suffered by the country during the period of "running inflation", which made it impossible for the library to purchase foreign books and to subscribe to foreign journals. Until now the library has not yet recovered from this situation. Fortunately, however, the limited number of graduate students in anthropology have easy access to other libraries in the city. The library of the National Central Museum has the best prewar collection on Indonesian cultures, societies and languages. They can also use the library of the Law School, which has over 3,000 titles in anthropology and sociology and a number of journals. The students usually also make extensive use of their professors' private libraries.

Another school with reasonably adequate facilities in sociology is the Department of Rural Sociology at the Institute of Technology in Bogor. Over the 5,000 more recent titles and more than 60 journals in sociology and anthropology are listed in the catalogue of the centralized library of the Institute.

The other departments of anthropology and sociology own libraries that are still far below any minimal standard, although the Department of Anthropology of Gadjah Mada University in Jogyakarta can make use of the good prewar collection of *Perpustakaan Islam,* which is located in the city, and also if necessary the rapidly developing library of the Institute for Social Science Research of Satya Watjana Christian University at Salatiga, a town only 90 kilometers (about two hours by car) from Jogyakarta.

Student Enrollment in Anthropology and Sociology

The general public in Indonesia is still not aware of the function of anthropology and sociology, and their importance to the understanding of social problems. A large part of the students who choose to study social sciences at the Law School are, probably stimulated by the image that to become a civil servant will be the kind of career which gives the greatest security and prestige. Another large number of students go to the Faculty of Economics as they may be stimulated by the fact that many economists seem to obtain high positions since the 1970's in Indonesia. Students with less ambitions choose the Teachers' College. However, only very few enroll at the Department of Sociology, whereas those who failed to be accepted at any other school or department were usually glad to get a place at the Department of Anthropology to try an academic education. Anthropology departments, especially in Jakarta, therefore get very poor attendance as those who enroll are usually not the best students. In cities outside Jakarta anthropology departments are greater attendance, due probably to the fact that the people in the provinces are less materialistically inclined than those from Jakarta. Another reason may be because the youth in the provinces have some interest in their own ethnic culture. Table 6 shows the enrollments of four anthropology departments in the freshmen year during 1960 to 1970.

Until recently almost all the *Sarjana's* graduated from the Department of Anthropology of the University of Indonesia and the Department of Anthropology of Padjajaran University, were absorbed in the teaching occupation except for three who taught at high schools. Most of them, however, are employed by their own department, although others teach at faculties of other universities or run the embryonic anthropology departments in Jogyakarta and Manado (North Sulawesi). One anthropologist works as consultant at the staff headquarters of the Indonesian Navy, whereas another at the provincial government administration of East Sumatra.

Table 6
Number of Students at Anthropology and Sociology
Departments, and the Output of Sarjana's from 1960 to 1970

	1960	1961	1962	1963	1964	1965	1966*	1967	1968	1969	1970
Dept. Anthr. UI											
enrollment	16	15	12	11	15	13	—	12	7	8	2
output	—	—	1	3	3	4	5	1	2	3	1
Dept. Soc. UI											
enrollment	—	—	—	—	—	5	—	5	6	4	3
output	—	—	—	—	—	—	—	—	—	—	—
Dept. Anthr. NPAD											
enrollment	19	29	38	49	28	19	—	35	21	13	5
output	—	—	—	—	—	—	22	21	3	1	3
Dept. Anthr. UGM											
enrollment	—	—	42	38	25	29	—	31	21	15	12
output	—	—	—	—	—	—	—	—	—	—	—
Dept. Soc. UGM											
enrollment	.... no information available									30	24
output										—	—
Dept. Anthr. NSRAT											
enrollment	—	—	—	7	6	7	—	5	7	8	11
output	—	—	—	—	—	—	—	—	—	1	1

* Due to student activities in the year of the political change in Indonesia there is on 1966 enrollment.

Recommendations for the Future Development of Anthropology and Sociology in Indonesia

Considering the trends in the development of anthropology and sociology, during the pre-as well as post-war periods and the need for anthropological and sociological research for national development, the following points may be summarized:

(1) Anthropology and sociology, although originating from different backgrounds, are very hard to distinguish in Indonesia in terms of objectives, subject matter, fields and areas of studies, as well as in terms of approaches and methodology. However, for purposes of maintaining contact with the international scientific world in which the two disciplines are still separated, it is advisable to maintain the separation, also in Indonesia.

(2) On the university structure, however, there should be one department of sociology and anthropology; or at least both disciplines should be in the same faculty. In planning new departments this structure should be planned from the start.

(3) The Sociology Department of the University of Indonesia (with a staff of 17 sociologists in 1972, four of whom hold a Ph. D, and the Institute of Rural Sociology of the Institute of Agriculture of Bogor (with a staff in 1972 of eight sociologists, among whom one is a Ph. D.), should be responsible for the deveopment of sociology in Indonesia and supply the need for lecturers in other institutions of higher learning and the country's need for sociologist research workers. It is also due to the favorable location of both institutions to be in and near Jakarta, the only city in Indonesia where archives and sufficient library facilities make a Ph. D. training program possible.

(4) Similarly, the Anthropology Department of the University of Indonesia (with a staff of eight anthropologists, of whom two hold Ph. D.'s), is responsible for the development of anthropology in Indonesia. We can call the three latter departments the "feeder" departments, compared to the other "developing" departments.

(5) The deveopment of at least five other joint sociology-anthropology departments should be carefully planned from now on. Potentially favorable sites are the Badjadiaran University, the Gadjah Mada

University, Satya Watjana Christian University in Salatiga, Hassanu-
din University in Ujung Pandang (Macassar), and Sam Ratulangi
University of Manado. Another one should be deliberately developed for Sumatra, e.g. at the IKIP of Medan, whereas at
Udayana University in Denpassar, Bali, and at Cenderawasih University in West Irian, the Anthropology Departments should be developed.

(6) Considering the urgent need for research in the so-called "national
problems" listed in Table 3, and assuming that theoretically each
problem needs to be tackled by at least one anthropologist or
sociologist, the country must have about 40, and attempts are to be
made as far as possible to combine the research projects with the
Ph. D. program.

(7) Facilities for interdisciplinary research should be created by the research training field stations which today are established at Syah
Kuala University in Banda Aceh and at Hasanuddin University.
There, a number of social scientists, including anthropologists and
sociologists, annually recruited from different universities in Indonesia, can devote full attention to research work and acquire experience in interdisciplinary cooperation for a period of one year, which
are made possible with research grants.

Notes

1) This paper has been published in Koenjaraningrat (ed.), *The Social Sciences in
Indonesia*, Jakarta, Indonesian Institute of Sciences (LIPI), 1975, pp. 167-201.
2) "Guide to the Sources in the Netherlands Concerning the History of the Netherlands
Indies/Indonesia, 1816-1942".
3) A survey of the first period of development of Indonesian studies in America is
included in four articles written by A. Van Marle for the journal *Indonesië*
(1956-57). See also G. Mct. Kahin (1952) and B. S. Dohrenwend (1957).
4) They published the voluminous book *Het Adat Privaat Recht van West Java* (1940).
5) After 1966 Tan Giok Lan's works are listed under her name Mely G. Tan.
6) He changed his name into Sajogya, and his subsequent works are therefore listed
under his new name.
7) For a fuller description of the Indonesian agro-economic survey, see the
above-mentioned article of E. de Vries (1969) and another one by the director of
the survey, Professor Sajogya (1969; 1973).
8) For further information on the Serpong project, cf. Plan of Operation n.d.; Lubis,
Borkent-Niehof, Hdiati Amal 1974.
9) Only a limited number of foreign languages are offered at the University of Indone-

sia in 1970: Chinese, Japanese, Arabic, Russian, Dutch, German, and French. According to plan Tagalog will be taught, as well as Thai.

10) Only occasionally, when they happen to have students from other regions, who are native speakers and participants of the languages and cultures of the regions concerned, can they assign papers or theses on those other regions to the students concerned.

11) To get a picture of the kinds of socio-economic problems which the Bogor Agronomists are interested in, see Table 2, which lists the subjects often tackled by them for their *Sarjana* theses.

References

Abdurachman, H. A.
  1963 "Suatu Pendekatan Kearah Pembinaan Kepemimpinan Kerdja di In-
         donesia," Bandung (Doctoral thesis, Padjadjaran University).
Bachtiar, H. W.
  1972 "The Formation of the Indonesian Nation," Cambridge, Mass. (Unpub-
         lished Ph.D. Dissertation, Harvard University).
Bachtiar Rifai
  1958 "Bentuk Milik Tanah dan Tingkat Kemakmuran; Penjelidikan Pedesaan
         Didaerah Pati, Djawa Tengah," Bogor: University of Indonesia
         (mimeographed doctoral dissertation, University of Indonesia).
BKKBN, LP3ES
  1972 *Kumpulan Ichtisar Hesil-Hasil Penelitian Keluarga Berentjana
         1961-1972.* Jakarta: BKKBN, LP3ES.
Boeke, H. J.
  1938 "Keuze en Opleiding van den Candidaat-Indische Bestuursambtenaar,"
         Verslag van de Algemene Vergadering V. V. A. B.-B. N. I. *Koloniaal Ti-
         jdschrift,* XXVII: pp. 219-261.
Bouman, H.
  1949 "Enige Bewchouwingen over de Ontwikkeling van het Indonesisch
         Nationalisme op Sumatra's Westkust," Groningen, Batavia: J. B. Wol-
         ters (Doctoral dissertation, University of Utrecht).
Buku Pedoman
  1969 *Fakultas Ilmu Pengetahuan Kemasjarakatan.* Djakarta: Universitas In-
         donesia
Bruner, E. M.
  1959 *Kinship Organization of the Urban Batak of Sumatra.* New York: Trans-
         actions of the New York Academy of Science, 22, Series II.
  1961 "Urbanization and Ethnic Identity in North Sumatra," *American
         Anthropologist,* LXIII.
  1963 "Medan, The Role of Kinship in an. Indonesian City," *Pacific Port
         Towns and Cities: A Symposium.* A. Spohr, editor, Honolulu: Bishop
         Museum Press, pp. 1-12.
  1971 "The Expression of Ethnicity in Indonesia," Champaign: University of
         Illinois (mimeographed manuscript).
  1972 "Kin and Non-Kin," *Urban Anthropology,* A. Southall, editor, London:
         Oxford University Press.
  1972-a "Batak Ethnic Association in Three Indonesian Cities," *Southwestern
           Journal of Anthropology,* XXVIII: pp. 207-229.

Burger, D. H.
1948-49 "Structuurveranderingen in de Javaanse Samenleving," *Indonesia*, II:
pp. 381-98, 521-37; III: pp. 1-18, 101-23, .225-50, 381-89, 512.
Chabot, H. Th.
1950 "Verwantschap, Stand en Sexe in Zuid Celebes," Djakarta: J. B. Wol-
ters (Doctoral dissertation, University of Indonesia).
Cooley, F. L.
1962 *Ambonese Adat: A General Desciption*. New Haven: Yale University
Southeast Asia Studies.
1962-a "Ambonese Kin Groups," *Ethnology*, I.
1967 "Allang: A Village on Ambon Islad," *Villages in Indonesia*, Koentjaraningrat, editor, Ithaca, N.Y.: Cornell University Press, pp. 129-156.
1968 *Indonesia: Church & Society*. New York: Friendship Press.
Cunningham, C. E.
1958 *The Postwar Migrations of the Toba-Batak to East Sumatra*. New
Haven: Yale University Southeast Asia Studies, Cultural Report Seires
No. 5.
1946 "Orser in the Atoni House," *Bijdragen tot de Taal-, Land- en Volkenkunde*, CXX: pp. 34-69.
1964-a "Atoni, Borrowing of Children: An Aspect of Meditation," Proceedings
of the Annual Meeting of the American Ethnological Society, Seattle.
1965 "Order and Change in an Atoni Diarchy," *Southwestern Journal of
Anthropology*, XXI: pp. 359-383.
1967 "Soba: An Atoni Village of West Timor," *Villages in Indonesia*, Koentjaraningrat, editor, Ithaca, N. Y., Cornell University Press, pp. 63-89.
De Hollander, J. J.
1861-64 *Handleiding bij de Beoefening der Land- en Volken- kunde van
Nederlandsch-Indie*.
Dewey, A. C.
1962 "Trade and Social Control in Java," *Journal of the Royal Anthropological Institute*, CXII: pp. 177-190.
Djojodigoeno, M. M., R. Tirtawinata
1940 "Sundanese Organization in Pasundan," Bandung (mimeographed
manuscript).
Dohrenwend, B. S.
1957 *Courses Related to Southeast Asia in American Colleges and Universities, 1955-1956*. Ithaca.
Echols, J. M.
1966 "In Memoriam G. F. O. Ochekoen, 1904-1966," *Indonesia*, II: pp.
157-159.

Freedman, M.
  1954   *A Report on Some Aspects of Food, Health and Society in Indonesia.*
         Geneva: W. H. O.
Geertz, C.
  1956   "The Social Context of Economic Change, An Indonesian Case
         Study," Cambridge, Mass.: M. I. T. (mimeographed manuscript).
  1956-a *The Development of Javanese Economy, A Socio-Cultural Approach.*
         Cambridge: M. I. T.
  1956-b "Religious Beliefs and Economic Behavior in a Central Javanese Town,
         Some Preliminary Considerations," *Economic Development and Cul-
         tural Change,* IV: pp. 134-58.
  1957   "Ethos, World View and the Analysis of Sacred Symbols," *Antioch
         Review,* XVII.
  1957-a "Ritual and Social Change: A Javanese Example," *American Anthro-
         pologist,* LIX: pp. 32-54.
  1959   "Form and Variation in Balinese Village Structure," *American Anthro-
         pologist,* LXI: pp. 991-1012.
  1960   *The Religion of Java.* Glencoe, Ill.: The Free Press.
  1960-a "The Javanese Kijai: The Changing Role of a Culture Broker," *Com-
         parative Studies in Society and History,* II: pp. 228-249.
  1961   "Boekbespreking: Bali, Studies of Life, Thought and Ritual: Selected
         Studies on Indonesia, 5," *Bijdragen tot de Taal-, Land- en Volkenk-
         unde,* CXVIII: pp. 498-502.
  1963   *Agricultural Involution, The Process of Ecological Change in Indonesia.*
         Berkeley.
  1963-a *Peddlers and Princes, Social Change and Economic Modernization in
         Two Indonesian Towns.* Chicago: University of Chicago Press.
  1971   "A Program for the Stimulation of the Social Sciences in Indonesia," A
         Report to the Ford Foundation, Princeton (mimeographed manuscript).
Geertz, H.
  1961   *The Javanese Family: A Study of Kinship and Socialization.* Glencoe:
         The Free Press.
Goetals, P. R.
  1959   *Aspects of Local Government in a Sumbawan Village, Eastern Indone-
         sia.* Ithace, N.Y.: Monograph Series Modern Indonesia Project, South-
         east Asian Program, Cornell University.
  1960   "Task Groups and Marriage in Western Sumbawa," *Intermediate
         Societies, Social Mobility and Communication,* V. Ray, editor, Seattle:
         University of Washington Press.
  1967   "Rarak: A Swidden Village of West Sumbawa," *Villages in Indonesia,*

Koentjaraningrat, editor, Ithaca, N. Y.: Cornell University Press, pp. 30-62.

Graaf, E. A. van de
1955 *De Statistiek in Indonesie.* Gravenhage, Bandung: W. van Hoeve.

Hadiwijono, H.
1967 "Man in the Present Javanese Mysticism," Baarn, Bosch & Keuning N. V. (Doctoral dissertation in theology, Vrije Universiteit Amsterdam).

Harjono Sujono
1974 "The Adaptation of Innovation in a Developing Country: The Case of Family Planning" (Unpublished dissertation, University of Chicago).

Heeren, H. J.
1965 "Recente Sociolgische Literatuur over Indonesie," *Sociologische Gids,* III: pp. 179-186.
1967 "Transmigratie in Indonesie, Interne Migratie en de Verhouding van Immigranten/Autochtonen, Speciaal met Betrekking tot Zuid- en Midden-Sumatra," Meppel, J. A. Boom en Zoon (Doctoral dissertation, University of Utrecht).

Held, G. J.
1947 *De Papoea's van Waropen.* Leiden: E.J. Brill.
1953 "Applied Anthropology in Government: The Netherlands," *Anthropology Today,* A. L. Kroeber, editor, Chicago: University of Chicago Press, pp. 866-879.

Hermana
1971 *An Annotated Bibliography of Food and Nutrition Research in Indonesia.* Bogor: Nutrition Research Institute.

Hoevell, W. R. Baron van
1849 "De Uitbreiding van het Hooger Onderwijs in de Oostersche Talen an de Nederlandsche Akademien," *Tijdschrift voor Nederlandsch-Indie,* XI, 2: pp. 68-78.

Horikoshi, H.
1971 "The Changing Ethnic Attitude in an Indonesian City: Bandung," Champaign: University of Illinois (Mimeographed manuscript).

Ihromi *et al.*
1973 *The Status of Women and Family Planning in Indonesia.* Jakarta: Indonesian Planned Parenthood Association.

Ismail, J. C.
1960 *Keadaan Penduduk di 23 Desa di Djawa.* Djakarta: Lembaga Penjelidikan Ekonomi dan Masjarakat Fakultas Ekonomi, Universitas Indonesia.

Jay, R. R.
1956 "Local Government in Rural Central Java," *Far Eastern Quarterly,* XV: pp. 215-227.

1963   *Javanese Villages: Society and Politics in Rural Modjokerto.* Glencoe, Ill.: The Free Press.

1963-a   *Religion and Politics in Rural Central Java.* New Haven: Cultural Report Series No. 12, Southeast Asia Studies, Yale University.

Jong, S. de

1973   "End Javaansche Levenshouding," Wageningen, H. Veerman & Zonen B. V. (Doctoral dissertation in Theology, Vrije Universiteit Amsterdam).

Kahin, G. Mct.

1952   *Nationalism and Revolution in Indonesia.* Ithaca, N. Y.: Cornell University Press.

1952-a   *Teaching and Research Relating to Southeast Asia in American Colleges and Universities.* Ithaca.

Kampto Utomo

1959   "Masjarakat Transmigran Spontan di Daerah W. Sekampung," Djakarta: Penerbitan Universitas (Doctoral dissertation, University of Indonesia).

Kinderen, T. H. der

1892   "Levensbericht van Dr. G. A. Wilken," *Bijdragen tot de Taal-, Land- en Volkenkunde,* XLI: pp. 139-156.

Koentjaraningrat

1958   "Beberapa Metode Anthropologi Dalam Penjelidikan2 Masjarakat dan Kebudajaan di Indoensia (Sebuah Ichtisar)," Djakarta: Penerbitan Universitas (Doctoral dissertation, University of Indonesia).

1962   *Some Social-Anthropological Observations of Gotong-Rojong Practices in Two Villages of South Central Java.* Ithaca: Modern Indonesia Project, Cornell University.

1966   "Bride-Price and Adoption in the Kinship Relations of the Bgu of West Irian," *Ethnology,* V: pp. 233-244.

1969   *Masjarakat dan Kopra Rakjat di Pantai Utara Irian Barat.* Djakarta: Bhratara, Terbitan Takberkala Lembaga Ekonomi & Kemasjarakatan Nasional, LIPI.

1969-a   *Rintangan2 Mental Dalam Pembangunan Ekonomi di Indonesia.* Djakarta: Bhratara, Terbitan Takberkala LIPI No. I/2.

1973   *Methodologi Penelitian Masjarakat.* Jakarta: Lembaga Ilmu Pengetahuan Indonesia.

1974   *Kebudayaan, Mentalitet dan Pembanguman.* Jakarta: P. T. Gramedia.

1975   *Anthropology in Indonesia, A Bibliographical Review.* Leiden: Koninklijk Instituut voor de Taal-, Land- en Volkenkunde.

Koentjaraningrat, H. W. Bachtiar (eds.)

1963   *Penduduk Irian Barat.* Djakarta: Penerbitan Universitas.

Lauw Tjin Giok, I. Tarwotjo, Djokosptono, R. Rasidi

1963 *A Study of the Nutritional Status at Two Economic Levels in Tjiwalan and Amensari: Villages of West Java.* Bogor: Academy of Nutrition.

Lindgren, E. J.
1948 "Obituary, Bertram Johammens Otto Schrieke: 1890-1945," *Man.*

Lubis, F., A. Borkent-Niehof, Pudjiastuti
1973 *Laporan Survey Dukun Bayi di Kecamatan Serpong.* Jakarta: Universitas Indonesia.

Lubis, F., A. Borkent-Niehof, S. Hidayati Amal
1974 "Proyek Kerjasama Penelitian dan Latihan dalam Bidang Keluarga Berencana Antara Universitas Indonesia dengan Rijksuniversiteit Leiden di Serpong," *Berita Antropologi,* VI: pp. 25-30.

Marle, A. von.
1956-57 "Mededeling Betreffende Indonesie op Amerikaanse Unversiteiten," *Indonesie,* IX-X, 1956: pp. 418-20, 524-26; 1957: pp. 172-73, 433-35.

McVey, R. (ed.)
1963 *Indonesia.* New Haven: HRAF Press.

Moore, F. W. (ed.)
1961 *Readings in Cross-Cultural Methodology.* New Haven: HRAF Press.

Moelia, T. S. G.
1951 "Indonesische Sociologie," *Cutureel Nieuws,* XI: pp. 28-32.

Naim, M.
1974 "Merantau, Minangkabau Vountary Migration," (Unpublished dissertation, University of Singapore).

Nieuwenhuis, A. W.
1900 *In Central Borneo.* Leiden: E. J. Brill (Vols. I-II).
1904-07 *Quer Dutch Borneo.* Leiden: E. J. Brill (Vols. I-II).

Pelzer, Kl
1957 "The Agrarian Conflict in East Sumatra," *Pacific Affairs,* XXX: pp. 151-159.

Parsudi Suparlan
1971 "The Javanese in Bandung," Champaign: University of Illinois (mimeographed manuscript).

Pijnappel, Gz. L.
1859 *De Koninklijke Akademie to Delft, als Inrigting tot Opleiding voor Indische Ambtenaren.* Amsterdam: F. Muller.
1863 *Drie Stellingen over de Opleiding der Indische Ambtenaren.* The Hague: M. Nijhoff.
1868 *De Rijksinstelling van Onderwijs in Indische Taal-, Land- en Volkenkunde te Leiden en de Hoogeschool.* The Hague: M. Nijhoff.

Plan of Operation
n.d. "Family Planning Project Serpong, Indonesia," Leiden: Universitas In-

doneiea-Leiuen State Unviersity, Serpong Paper No. 1.

Pospisil, L.

1956 *The Kapauku Papuans and Their Law*. New Haven: Yale University Publications in Anthropology, No. 54.

Ressers, W. H.

1921 *De Pandji Roman*. Antwerpen: D. de Vos-van Kleef.

Ryan, E. J.

1961 "The Value Systems of a Chinese Community in Java," Cambridge, Mass.: Harvard University (Unpublished Ph. D. dissertation).

Salim, E. *et al.*

1959 *Kehidupan Desa di Indonesia, Suatu Case Study Daripada 23 Desa di Djawa*. Djakarta: Lembaga Penjelidikan Ekonomi dan Masjarakat, Fakultas Ekonomi, Universitas Indonesia.

Sajogya

1969 *Summary of Agro-Economic Survey Activities from September 1963 to October 1969*. New York: The Agricultural Development Council.

1973 "Penelitian Ilmu-Ilmu Sosial dan Aplikasiny," *Methologi Penelitian Masjarakat*, Koentjaraningrat, editor, Jakarta: LIPI, pp. 423-453.

Schreiner, L.

1972 *Adat und Evanglium: Zur Bedeutung der Altvolkischen Lebensordnungen fur Kirche und Mission unter der Batak in Nordsumatra*. Gerd Mohn: Gutersloher Verlegshaus.

Schulte Nordholt, A. G.

1966 "Het Politieke Systeem van de Atoni van Timor," Driebergen: Van Manen & Co. (Doctoral dissertation, Vrije Universiteit Amsterdam).

Selosoemardjan

1962 *Pembangunan Masjarakat di Desa*. Djakarta: Lembaga Penjelidikan Ekonomi dan Masjarakat, Universitas Indonesia.

1962-a *Social Changes in Jogjakarta*. Ithaca, N. Y.: Cornell University Press.

1963 *The Dynamics of Community Development in Rural Central and West Java: A Comparative Report*. Ithaca, N. Y.: Modern Indonesia Project, Cornell University.

Shadily, H. M.

1955 "A Preliminary Study of the Impact of Islam on a Community and Its Culture in Indonesia," Ithaca, N. Y. (Unpublished M. A. thesis, Cornell University).

Siagian, S. P.

1964 "The Development and Problems of Indigenous Bureaucratic Leadership" (Unpublished Ph. D. dissertation, Indiana University).

Singarimbun, M.

1965 "Kinship and Affinal Relations among the Karo of North Sumatra,"

Canberra: Australian National University (Unpublished Doctoral dissertation, Australian National University).

Slamet, I. E.
1963 *Pokok2 Pembangunan Masjarakat Desa, Sebuah Pandangan Antropologi Budaja.* Djakarta: Bhratara.

Snouck Hurgronje, C.
1893-94 *De Atjehers.* Batavia: Landsdrukkerij (Translated into English in 1906: *The Achehnese.* Leiden: E. J. Brill (Vols. I-II)).
1924 "De Opleiding van Ambtenaren voor de Administratieven Dienst in Nederlandsch-Indie," Bonn, Leipzig, K. Schroeder, *Verspreide Gesohriften,* IV(2): pp. 51-76.

Sudjito Sos. odihardjo
1959 "Kedudukan Pemimpin Dalam Masjarakat Desa," Jogyakarta: Lembaga Sosiografi dan Hukum Adat (Mimeographed manuscript).

Sulaiman Sumardi
1961 "Regional Politicians in West Java: Social Background and Career Patterns," Ithaca, N. Y. (Unpublished M. A. thesis, Cornell University).

Suwardi, H.
"Respon Masyarakat Terhadap Modernisasi Produksi Pertanian" (Dissertation, Padjadjaran University).

Suwardi, H., M. Enoch
1960 *Pendahuluan Penjelidikan Sosial Ekonomi dan Gizi Didesa Tjiwalan, Patjet dan Desa Amansari Rangkasdengklok.* Bogor: Akademi Pendidikan Nutrisionis dan Ahli, Gizi.

Tan Giok Lan
1961 "The Chinese Community in a Sundanese Towm," Ithaca, N. Y.: Cornell University (Unpublished M. A. thesis).

Tan, M. G.
1974 "Aspek Sosial-Budaya dari Polandan Kebiasan Makanan pada Lima Daerah Pedesaan Indonesia," *Berita Antropologi,* VI: pp. 45-56.

Tan, M. G. *et al.*
1973 *Social and Cultural Aspects of Food Patterns and Food Habits in Five Rural Areas in Indonesia.* Jakarta: LEKNAS and Directorate of Nutrition.

Textor, R. B.
1954 *Notes on Indonesian Villagers' Participation in Programs to Modernize Rural Life.* Ithaca, N. Y.

Thomas, W. J., Jr., A. M. Pikelis
1953 *International Directory of Anthropological Institutions.* New York: Wenner Grenn Foundation for Anthropological Research, Inc.

Tobing, Ph. O. L.
1956 "The Structure of the Toba-Batak Belief in the High God," Amsterdam: Jacob van Kampen (Doctoral dissertation, University of Utrecht).

Ukur, F.

    1971　"Tentang-Djawab Suku Dajak, Suatu Penjelidikan Tentang Unsr2 Jang Menjekitari Penolakan dan Penerimaan Indjil Dikalangan Suku-Dajak Dalam Rangka Sedjarah Geredja di Kalimantan (1835-1945)," Djakarta: B. P. K. Gunung Mulia (Dissertation, Sekolah Tinggi Theologia, Jakarta).

Umar Khayam

    1966　"Aspects of Interdepartmental Coordination in Indonesian Community Development," Ithaca, N. Y. (Unpublished doctoral dissertation, Cornell University).

Van Doorn, J. A. A.

    1956　"The Development of Sociology and Social Research in the Netherlands," *Mensch en Maatschappij,* XXXI: pp. 189-264.

Van Leur, J. C.

    1932　"De Opleiding der Indische Bestuursambtenaren," *Koloniaal Tijdschrift,* XXI: pp. 577-585.

Veth, P. J.

    1854　*Borneo's Wester-Afdeeling, Geographisch, Statistisch, Historisch,* Zaltbommel, Joh. Noman en Zoon. (Vols. I-II).

    1875-82　*Java: Geographisch, Etonologisch, Historisch.* Haarlem: Erven F. Bohn. (Vols. I-II).

    1881-92　*Midden-Sumatra, Reizen en Onderzoekingen der Soematra-Expedities, Uitgerust door her Koninklijk Nederlandsch Aardrijkskundig genootschap, 1877-1879, Beschreven door de Leden der Expeditie Onder Toozicht van P. J. Veth.* Leiden: E. J. Brill (Vols. I-IV)

Vries, E. de

    1969　"The Agro-Economic Survey of Indonesia," *Bulletin of Indonesian Economic Studies,* V: pp. 73-77.

Widjojo Nitisastro

    1956　*Some Data on the Population of Djabres, A Village in Central Java.* Djakarta: Lembaga Pendidikan Ekonomi dan Masjarakat, Fakultas Ekonomi Universitas Indonesia.

Widyapranawa, S. H.

    1973　*Benih Yang Tumbuh, Suatu Survey Mengenai Gereja2 Kristen Indonesia, Jawa Tengah.* Jogyakarta: Lembaga Studi dan Penelitian D. G. I.

Willmott, D. E.

    1956　*The National Status of the Chinese in Indonesia.* Ithaca, N. Y.: Interim Report Series No. 1, Modern Indonesia Project, Cornell University.

    1959　"The Chinese Family System in Central Java," Ithaca, N. Y. (Unpublished Ph. D. dissertation, Cornell University).

    1960　*The Chinese of Semarang: A Changing Minority Community in Indonesia.* Ithaca, N. Y.: Cornell University Press.

5 Anthropological Studies in the Republic of China during the Last Three Decades

CHI-LU CHEN

Taiwan, an Island for Anthropological Researches

For its complexity and heterogeneity in racial-cultural stucture rarely seen in other parts of the world, Taiwan constitutes an excellent field for anthropological researches. The two racial-cultural strata of Taiwan are the aboriginal and the Chinese. However, each of these two strata again is subdivided into layers which are quite distinct from each other.

The Taiwan aborigines are Austronesian-speaking people. They may be culturally grouped, not to include those formerly occupied the western plains and are now already completely sinicized, under at least ten tribal names: Atayal, Saisiat, Thao, Bunun, Tsou, Rukai, Paiwan, Puyuma, Ami, and Yami.

Anthropologists are still divided in opinion as to when the first settlers arrived in Taiwan. Most anthropologists believe that the first Austronesian migration into Taiwan took place in the third millenium B.C. However, recent archaeological discoveries, by the result of carbon 14, gave a much older date of more than ten thousand years than formerly thought to be.[1] Thus the relation of this date with the aboriginal population became a new and important issue to be solved.

The ancestors of most of the Taiwan aborigines were immigrants from Southeast Asian Archipelago. They are believed to have come from different localities of that vast region and in many migration waves. Therefore they brought to the island a good many varieties of Southeast Asian cultural traits.[2] To enumerate them here surely will bore you. I wish only to mention that Professor A. L. Kroeber who studied Southeast Asian culture, discovered there are at least twenty-six cultural traits "common respectively to several peoples of the Philippines, of the remainder of the East Indies, and of Assam or other parts of the Indo-Chinese mainland."[3] What is worth mentioning is that most of the twenty-six cultural traits are also found in aboriginal Taiwan. Professor Shun-Sheng Ling has added another twenty-four to them after his careful studies of Southeast Asian culture. Professor Ling pointed out most of these fifty cultural traits were also found in ancient China south of the Yangtze River. He is of the opinion that the Old Southeast Asian Culture was originated in the Liang-hu or Two-lakes Region of the Yangtze Valley.[4] Professor Ling's theory has gradually gained support from both Chinese and foreign scholars. At least, this new theory can serve as the basis for explaining the direct migratory movement of the Taiwan aborigines from China-mainland to the Island of Taiwan.

The aboriginal Taiwan is regarded as the northeastern limit of Austronesia. That means beyond the north of Taiwan, we found no Austronesian culture. Because of its historico-geographical factor, Taiwan had been isolated for several millenia prior to the coming of the Chinese in the seventeenth century. While other parts of the Austronesia had been influenced by the Indian and the Islamic cultures, Taiwan remained unaffected. In Taiwan even Chinese contact occurred rather late. So the culture of the Taiwan aborigines may be said to be relatively "pure" as compared with other parts of the Southeast Asia. The Taiwan aboriginal culture with old traits thus preserved represent an older stratum or the archaic form of the Austronesian culture. In this sense, Taiwan could be regarded as the cultural depository of Southeast Asian region, and the study of the Taiwan aborigines has an important place in the study of the whole Austronesian area.

The Chinese, the upper racial-cultural stratum, is also a complex one. There are recent immigrants, the so-called "mainlanders" who came after the restoration of the island to China. The mainlanders though mainly the Han Chinese, also include the Mongols, the Tibetans, the Manchus, the Uigurs, the Kazaks, and many minority nationalities of Southwestern China, such as Paiyi(Thai), Miao, Yao, Tung, Chungchia, and others. Almost all important components of the Chinese nationality are present in the so-called mainlanders in Taiwan.

The Taiwan Chinese or "Taiwanese" are descendants of the early

Chinese immigrants who migrated into the island mainly during seventeenth, eighteenth, and nineteenth centuries. The Taiwanese, like the mainlanders, are not a special ethnic entity. They are grouped under one name simply because of historical reasons. A great majority of the Taiwanese were from Southeast China, mainly Amoy dialect and Hakka dialect speaking people. Generally speaking, immigrants first settle in the more convenient and fertile localities, and then gradually extend to the less fertile and mountainous areas. The Amoy people including those hailing from Chuan-chou and Chang-chou, moved in earlier to Taiwan, therefore they settled mostly in the western plains. Among them, those hailing from Chuan-chou came still earlier, therefore they settled mostly along the coastal areas and ports, and were shop or factory owners or workers; those hailing from Chang-chou came a little later, therefore, they settled mostly in the inland plains areas and devoted themselves to agriculture. Even today, there are more Chuan-chou people following commercial and industrial activities, and more Chang-chou people, as compared to Chuan-chou people, engaging in agriculture. The Hakka people moved in later than the Amoy people. In the time when they came to Taiwan, the western plains had already been densely inhabited, so they had to concentrate and till land on the Yaoyuan-Miaoli Tableland and in the Taichung and Kaohsiung-Pingtung Foothill Region. The Fuchou and Hsinghua people move in still later than the Hakka. When they came, even the tableland and foothill regions were occupied. Therefore they had to place themselves in cities and towns and followed different occupations.

Chinese culture has a long history. It started in Chung-yuan (中原), the down-stream regions of the Yellow River; it gradually expanded its sphere to cover the whole area of China, and absorbed many other cultures within the boundary of today's China. Taiwan as the most recent area to be cultivated by the Chinese people, gave us a clearest picture of how Chinese culture has developed. Therefore, the study of the Chinese development in Taiwan can help us to understand the whole Chinese cultural history. In this paper, I will not describe its development because I have discussed it elsewhere. I only wish to point out that, like Austronesian culture, Taiwan is also a depository of Chinese culture. It is really a grievous thing to say that under political suppression, Chinese traditional culture is now in peril in China mainland. So, it is our responsibility to preserve our cultural heritage in Taiwan.

Anthropological Studies in China before 1945

Whether there is such a discipline in a country can always be judged by whether there is an academic organization of that discipline or by whether there is a department of that discipline in a university. The existence of an academic organization means there are at least a dozen or more such scholars in that country. Probably France is the first country to have anthropological societies ——the Société des observateurs de l'homme, established in 1800; the Société ethnologique de Paris, in 1839; and the Société d'Anthropologie de Paris by Pierre Paul Broca, in 1859——therefore, we may say France is the vanguard of anthropology. As compared to France, England and the United States of America came a little behind. The American Ethnological Society of New York was organized in 1842, and the Ethnological Society of London in 1843. Then, Germany followed suit. But it was not until 1869 when the Deutsche Gesellschaft für Anthropologie, Ethnologie, und Urgeschichte was founded by R.L.K. Virchow and P.W.A. Bastian. In 1871, the Ethnological Society of London was reorganized and renamed as Royal Anthropological Institute of Great Britain and Ireland, and had been the center of anthropological studies of the world until World War II.

In Asia, Japan is the forerunner. The Tokyo-Jinrui-Gakukai(東京人類學會 the Tokyo Anthropological Society) was established in the campus of Tokyo Imperial University in 1884. It had been quite active until the Second World War when its leading position was replaced by the Nippon-Minzoku-Gakukai (日本民族學會 the Japan Ethnological Society) which was organized in 1934.

Probably, it was only a coincidence that the Chung-kuo-min-tsu-hsueh-hue (中國民族學會 the Chinese Ethnological Society) was also founded in Nanking in the same year 1934. The society had only less than fifty charter members in its inauguration; however, it is indicative that anthropology as a scientific discipline had already been established in China at that time.

In 1937, three years after the founding of the Chinese Ethnological Society, saw the outbreak of Sino-Japanese War. Following the government's removal to inland China, the Chinese anthropologists quickly set themselves to work on the task of field studies and opened up the anthropological treasury of the Southwest. From 1937 to 1945, many field investigations were undertaken as follows: Cheng-Tsu Shang (商承祖) : investigation of the Yao of Kwanghsi resulting in the publication of Kwanghsi-ling-yun-yao-jen-tiao-ch'a-pao-kao (*Report of Investigatio among the Yao People of Kwanghsi);* Shun-Sheng Ling (凌純聲) and Yih-Fu Ruey (芮逸夫) : investigation of the Miao people of Western Hunan resulting in the publication of Hsiang-hsi-miao-tsu-tiao-ch'a-pao-kao (*Investigation Report of the Miao Tribe of Western Hunan);* Cheng-Chih Yang (楊成志) : investigations of the Lolo tribe of Szechuan and Yunnan, and the Yao tribe of Peichiang of Kwangtung resulting in the publications of Hsi-nan-min-tsu-tiao-ch'a-pao-kao (*Investigation Report of the Southwestern Minority Groups),* Yun-nan-lo-lo-tsu-ti-wu-szu-chi-ch'i-ching-tian(*The Shaman and the Scripts of the Lolo Tribe of Yunnan*), Kwangtung-pei-chiang-yao-jen-ti-wen-hua-hsien-hsiang-yü-t'i-chih-hsin (*The Cultural Phenomena and Physical Types of the Yao Tribe of Peichiang of Kwangtung);* Ting-Liang Wu (吳定良) : investigation of the Miao tribe of Kweichour resulting in the publication of Shui-mian-miao-tiao-ch'a-chi-yiao (*Investigation Report of the Shui-mian Miao);* Yiao-Hua Lin (林耀華) : investigation of the Lolo people resulting in the publication of Liang-shan-yi-chia (*The Lolo of Liang-shan)* and others, to enumerate only a few.[5] To sum up, during the eight years of Anti-Japanese War, the Chinese anthropological studies forged ahead into a new period.

However, following the victory over Japan in 1945, there was a short period of stagnancy because most of the academic institutions and their staff were busy with moving back from the inland to reestablish themselves in the recovered area. Anthropological field studies in the Southwest were inevitably affected and discontinued. Soon afterwards in 1949, because of the Communist usurpation of Mainland China, most of the anthropologists evacuated with the Government to Taiwan, and the center of Chinese anthropological researches has since removed to Taiwan.

Anthropological Studies in Taiwan before 1945

An account of anthropological studies in Taiwan is not complete without mentioning the previous researches undertaken by Japanese scholars.

Anthropological studies in Taiwan began with the studies of the Taiwan aborigines. Although the Dutch missionary in the seventeenth century and the Chinese scholars in the Ch'ing dynasty (17th to 19th century) left to us many valuable documents on the aborigines, scientific studies did not begin until Japanese occupation period. Ryuzo Torii (鳥居龍藏) and Yoshinori Ino (伊能嘉矩) were among the earlier anthropologists who investigated the Taiwan aborigines. Torii was the first to undertake anthropological studies and to classify the Taiwan aborigines. However, Ino's reports on the Plains tribes are of no less importance because they are the only scientific records of these extinct tribes.

More important works on the aborigines were those undertaken by the Rinji-Taiwan-kyukan-chosakai (臨時台灣舊慣調查會) or the Special Commission for Inquiry on the Olden Customs of Taiwan. This commission was planned by the Taiwan Colonial Government in 1899 and was actually set up in 1901. The director was Dr. Santaro Okamatsu (岡松參太郎) who had been a student of Professor Josef Kohler, one of the leading scholars in the German school of comparative jurisprudence. The primary aim of the commission was to survey the customary law of the Taiwan Chinese and the Plains tribes (the Pingpu) and to compile the reports thereof in view of meeting the administrative requirements. After having published scores of volumes, for example, the 13 volumes Taiwan-Shiho (台灣私法 *Taiwan Private Law*) which were the excellent reports on the family, kinship, property, etc. of the Taiwan Chinese, the commission began to concentrate the effort mainly upon the similar works concerning the aborigines since 1909. The effort resulted in the 27 volumes of report on the Taiwan aboriginal culture.

As far as compilation work covering various aspects of customary law in colonial land is concerned, the parallel of these would be the 44 volumes of *Adatrechtbundel* issued by the "Commissie voor het Adatrecht" which was organized at Leiden since 1911. This series of publications contain valuable informations not only about Indonesian peoples but also about Chinese and Arabs in the East Indies. And shortly after the "Commissie" set out the work, the Dutch Ministry of Foreign Affairs sent letters of inquiry as to whether there were similar projects, respectively to those countries such as Britain, France, Belgium, U.S.A., and Germany. The reply was generally negative, except that Germany had a systematic plan of surveying customary law in her colonial land under the leadership of Professor Kohler (cf. *Adatrechtbundel,* deelen I,V,VI, and VII). It would deserve notice that Japan had already laid a plan for such a compilation work at the end of the nineteenth century. However, the commission was dissolved in 1918 because of the apathetic attitude of the governor toward this undertaking.

The period of the commission was followed by a stagnation for a considerable duration of time, except some of rather sporadical researches by a few persons such as Magane Koizumi (小泉鐵) and Ki-ichiro Ando (安藤喜一郎)

However, the establishment of the Taihoku Imperial University (now National Taiwan University after the retrocession of Taiwan to China) in 1928 brought our anthropological study of the Taiwan aborigines to a new period. In this period, the study of the Taiwan aborigines was mainly undertaken by the Institute of Ethnology, under the leadership of Professor Nenozo Utsurikawa (移川子之藏), a student of Professor Roland B. Dixon of Harvard University. At the outset, the members of the institute, including Nobuto Miyamoto (宮本延人), and afterwards Toichi Mabuchi (馬淵東一), had engaged in an extensive survey in reference to a work of historical reconstruction. The result was the two volumes of *The Formosan Natives: A Genealogical and Classificatory Study* published in 1935 by the University, which is considered one of the most important contributions of the Japanese scholars in anthropology.

Professor Mabuchi, a student and an associate of Utsurikawa, said that Utsurikawa was not a narrow-minded person, and he also accepted functionalism. He admired Raymond Firth, and read his *Primitive Economics of the New Zealand Maori* with great interest. Therefore his work on the Taiwan aborigines may be said to be both extensive and intensive.

At that time, functionalism was in vogue at least among a number of younger anthropologists and sociologists in Japan. Yuzuru Okada (岡田謙), then lecturer of Sociology with Taihoku Imperial University, was one of them. He engaged himself in both rural sociology on the Taiwan Chinese and social anthropology on the aborigines, and concentrated his effort especially in the study of family life of the latter. Though his trip covered only a short duration of time respectively on several tribes, the procedure of his research would deserve a notice as one characterized by a combination or mixture of social anthropology and rural sociology.

On the other hand, Kiyoto Furuno (古野清人), one of the prominent Dukheimians in Japan and also a functionalist (on the side of Radcliffe-Brown) who was then with the Imperial Academy of Tokyo, visited the aboriginal area several times. As a specialist of sociology of religion, he was naturally concerned with the survey on the ritural life of the aborigines. But he was prudent, his reports were descriptive rather than theoretical, as far as the study on the Taiwan aborigines was concerned.

Now I wish to say a few words on the studies of material culture. Studies of material culture of the Taiwan aborigines is closely related with the development of anthropological museums. In Taiwan, more important anthropological museums are the Taiwan Museum and the Anthropolgical Museum of the National Taiwan University. Both of them made collections from the beginning of this century and each owns about 10,000 pieces of aboriginal specimens, not counting archaeological artifacts. My book *Material Culture of the Formosan Aborigines*[6] is a study based on these collections.

The Japanese scholars who have contributed more on studies of Taiwan aboriginal material culture are Tadao Kano (鹿野忠雄), Kokichi Segawa (瀬川孝吉), Suketaro Chichiiwa (千千岩助太郎), and Bun-ichi Sato (佐藤文一). Dr. Kano deserves special mention. As a biologist, Kano extended and revised the northern portion of the Wallace Line and pointed out the difference of the fauna and flora between the main island of Taiwan and Botel Tobago, which also helps us to explain the cultural relations of their inhabitants. Kano's fieldwork in Taiwan covered almost all aboriginal villages, and he published many articles on ethnology, especially on material culture of the Taiwan aborigines. In these articles he tried to link the Taiwan aboriginal culture with cultures in Southeast Asia and establish a chronology for the Taiwan aborigines.

Even more important contribution of Dr. Kano is his excellent work collaborated with Mr. Segawa in the fine volume in English entitled *Illustrated Ethnography of the Formosan Aborigines: The Yami Tribe*[7] published first in 1945 and later reprinted in 1956, which is a 400-page book of 12 by 6 inches format with full illustration. I share with the authors that material culture studies cannot be made without illustration. Dr. Kano's original plan was probably to write 10 volumes of such book, each for a separate tribe of Taiwan. Unfortunately, his dream did not actualized because of his own disappearance in Borneo in the end of the Second World War.

Anthropological Studies in the Republic of China During the Last Three Decades

When the Central Government of the Republic of China removed to

Taipei in 1949, many members of the Chinese Ethnological Society were among the large population who followed the Government to Taiwan. As mentioned before, Taiwan is an excellent field for anthropological studies rarely seen in the world, the newly coming anthropologists soon joined their local colleagues to set out their researches, actively in this field in many parts of the island. Of the numerous field studies carried out concerning the Taiwan aborigines, the notable one was the Expedition to Pinsebukan, believed to be the ancestral land of the Atayal. Members of the expedition included late Professors Chi Li (李濟), Tso-Pin T'ung (董作賓), and Shao-Hsing Ch'en (陳紹馨). The report of this investigation, though preliminary, was soon published. This expedition has opened up the research work of the Chinese anthropologists in Taiwan. Soon afterwards in 1954, the Chinese Ethnological Society reactivated in Taipei with a even larger membership of 66, and anthropological studies in Taiwan became even more active.

However, the real great stride forward of the anthropological development in this period was the establishment of the Department of Archaeology and Anthropology at the National Taiwan University in 1949. In China, though anthropology was taught at several universities —— such as Peking, Chungshan, Ch'inghua, Yenching, Fujin, Chungyang, Chingling, Tahsia, Huahsi, and others, it was included in the curricula of the department of history or the department of sociology —— it was not until 1953 when the first class students graduated from the Department of Archaeology and Anthropology of the National Taiwan University that we have anthropologists produced by our own school system, and that we have scholars classified as anthropologist.. This is why it was mentioned earlier that a department of a discipline in a university may serve as an indication of the establishment of that discipline in a country.

Anthropology, though possessing utilitarian value, is mainly an academic discipline. Therefore, members of the Department of Archaeology and Anthropology regard their research as the important part of their work and have achieved fruitful result. Besides the semi-annual *Bulletin of the Department of Archaeology and Anthropology*[8] for carrying short articles, field reports, and miscellanea, there are occasional monographs published by the Department. My own *Ethnological Researches among the Thao of Sun-Moon Lake, Formosa*[9] and *Woodcarving of the Paiwan Group of Taiwan*[10] were published in this series.

Somewhat similar to the extension courses of Western universities, the

Department of Archaeology and Anthropology also conducted seminars on Taiwan for those who were interested in local studies. In these seminars, papers on folk beliefs, folk literature, folk arts, social structure, cultural change, etc. were read and discussed. The proceedings of these seminars were also published as two numbers of this series which entitled: *Proceedings of the Seminars on Taiwan Studies,* [11] and *Supplementary Proceedings of the Seminars on Taiwan Studies.*[12]

However, the most important event following the establishment of the Department of Archaeology and Anthropology at the National Taiwan University obviously was the founding of the Institute of Ethnology in Academia Sinica. Academia Sinica is the highest academic institution of the country. Originally, anthropology was installed as a section in 1928 under the Institute of Social Sciences, and afterwards, when the institute was suspended in 1934, it was then transferred to the Institute of History and Philology. However, because of the growing importance of anthropology as an academic discipline, now we saw the need to establish a new separate and independent insitution, and the Institute of Ethnology was created. It is noteworthy that this new institute is the only institute of sociological and behavioral sciences, besides the rather specialized Economics Institute, in this highest learning institution.

Ever since its establishment,. the Institute has been conducting research in the areas of: (1) cultural and ethno-history of China, (2) culture of Taiwan aborigines, (3) Chinese society and folklore in Taiwan, (4) overseas Chinese in Southeast Asia, and (5) social and cultural changes in Taiwan and its adaptation. In the Institute there are now 24 full-time research staff members. Being an academic institution, the main responsibility of its staff members is to carry out researches. The Institute has several series of publications: (1) *Bulletin* —— the first issue, March 1956: the latest issue No. 48, Autumn 1979[13]; (2) *Monographs* —— totally 25 numbers were published since 1962[14]; (3) *Monograph Series B* —— totally 8 numbers were published since 1970.[15] The fruitful achievement of the Institute deserve admiration.

This paper purports only to give a descriptive account of the anthropological research status of my country. Evaluation of each contribution made by my colleagues is beyond the capacity of the paper and the author. Therefore, I wish to conclude my paper by only mentioning a few trends of anthropological development in my country.

From Study of Taiwan Aborigines to Study of Chinese Society

Taiwan is an excellent field for anthropological research. The rich aboriginal cultures, especially, have attracted many anthropologists, both local and abroad, to come and study them. This was also one of the principal reasons of the establishment of the Department of Archaeology and Anthropology at National Taiwan University and the Institute of Ethnology in Academia Sinica. The early publications of these two institutions show that most of the researches undertaken by their members were aboriginal studies. However, in recent years, the trend has changed. The collective projects conducted by the Institute of Ethnology in the last decade were largely studies of Chinese society.[16] This trend of shifting from the studies of primitive people to the studies of one's own culture and society, needless to say, is universal. However, the rapid cultural and social changes which had taken place among our aborigines and which transformed their societies from "closed" to "open" status, and made them less "exotic" and less "interesting", may also be the reasons for anthropologists to shift their interest to their own.

From the Pole of the Humanities to the Pole of Social Science

Whether anthropology be considered a discipline among the humanities or a social science, scholars are still divided in opinions. Before the establishment of the Department of Archaeology and Anthropology of National Taiwan University, anthropology courses were taught at the Department of History. Therefore, the Anthropology Department may be regarded as an offshoot of the History Department. Again, the Anthropology Department is put under the College of Liberal Arts of National Taiwan University. We may thus say, anthropology in the Republic of China is genealogically and substantially regarded as a discipline of the humanities. However, in recent years, it has gradually slided from the pole of the humanities to the pole of social science. In this trend, though coordinated with some objective conditions, there were also subjective factors. Professor Yih-Yuan Li (李亦園) has purposefully set the direction when he was the director of the Institute of Ethnology. In his article "Institute of Ethnology 1955-1971: Retrospect and Prospect," he says: "In the last couple of years, the Institute of Ethnology has stressed two principles, these are: (1) direction toward behavioral science interdisciplinary cooperation and synthetic research; and (2) emphasis on analytical studies of current social problems".[17] Therefore this trend was also shown in their recent publications. Many of them are community studies, social-economic change studies, or social structure studies.

A New Type of Area Studies

However, cultural-historical studies of anthropology are still persisting. The Seminar on Taiwan Studies started by the Department of Archaeology and Anthropology of National Taiwan University is still continued and sponsored by the Lin-pen-yuan Cultural Fund (林本源中華文化基金會), a private foundation founded for the promotion of local studies of Taiwan. The participants of the seminar, therefore, besides anthropologists, consist mostly of local historians or local gazetteers. Local gazette is a special form of Chinese history writing. Most Chinese provinces, counties, prefectures, even towns or villages, had their own gazettes compiled by local scholars. Local gazettes in modified form, such as the Tai-wan-sheng-t'ung-chih (台灣省通志 *The Taiwan Gazette),* the Tai-pei-shih-chih(台北市志 The Taipei City Gazette), and others, were still compiled lately. The getting together of anthropologists and local gazetteers has introduced anthropological methodology into local gazette compilation, and resulted in the formation of a new type of "area studies".

Contribution of Anthropological Studies to National Construction

During the last three decades, the entire nation of the Republic of China successfully pursued their task of economic and social construction with determination and dedication, such as the enforcement of land reform program, the six four-year economic construction plans, the agricultural development plans, the extension of compulsory education to nine-years, and the recent Ten Major Construction Projects. The people of the Republic of China are now able to enjoy higher living standard comparable to the developed nations. It is now the appropriate time to start our undertaking of cultural construction. The government thus promoted a Chinese Cultural Renaissance Movement in 1966, including the Cultural Center Construction Plan (which cover the construction of a library, a music hall, and a museum in each prefecture) as one of the Twelve New Construction Projects proclaimed 1976, and promulgated the Cultural and Recreation Activity Plan in 1979. These three undertakings consist of many items, such as preservation and enhancement of cultural properties, training of cultural personnel, establishment of museums and other cultural institutions, etc., which are closely related to anthropology, because anthropology itself is to study culture. Anthropology though an academic discipline, needless to say, possesses also utility values. I think we should sometimes come out from our ivory towers to help our society and to serve our nation. Then I think they will in turn help us. I hope this will be one of the new trends of anthropological studies in my country.

Notes

1) Wen-Hsun Sung, "Changpinian, A Newly Discovered Preceramic Culture from the Agglomerate Caves on the East Coast of Taiwan" (Preliminary Report), *Newsletter of Chinese Ethnology,* No. 9, 1969, pp. 1-28 (in Chinese).
2) Such as clan system (patrilineal clan among the Saisiat, the Thao, the Bunun, and the Tsou, matrilineal clan among the Ami and the Puyuma), feudalistic class system (the Rukai, the Paiwan, and the Puyuma), moiety (the Ami, the Puyuma, and the Rukai), parent-child linkage naming system (most groups), teknonymy (the Yami), house-name system (the Paiwan and the Rukai), age-set (mainly matrilineal groups), semi-subterranean dwelling (typically the Atayal and the Bunun), pile-building (most groups), betel-nut chewing (mainly southern groups), horizontal back-strap loom (all groups), shellbeads (the Atayal, the Ami, and the Bunun), multicolor-glass-beads (the Paiwan, the Rukai, and the Puyuma), bead-work (southern groups), embroidery and appliqué (the Paiwan and the Rukai), basketry (all groups), rafts (the Ami and the Puyuma), dugout canoes (the Thao), plank-boats (the Yami), mortar and pestle (all groups), harpoon type throwing spears (most groups), bow-and-arrows (except the Yami), cross-bows (the Saisiat and the Tsou), long shields (most groups), animistic belief (all groups), indoor burial (most groups), platform burial (the Yami), head-hunting (except the Yami), various kinds of taboo observation, dream omens (most groups), ornithomancy (most groups), bamboo divination (the Ami and the Puyuma), hair pulling, tooth knocking, ear-lobe piercing (most groups), body tattooing (the Paiwan and the Rukai), face tattooing (the Atayal and the Saisiat)......

3) A. L. Kroeber, *People of the Philippines*, 1943, New York, pp. 227-228.

4) Shun-Sheng Ling, "An Introduction to the Study of Ancient Southeast Asian Culture", Chu-*i-yu-kyo-ts'e*, No. 44, pp. 1-5 (in chinese).

5) For more detail, please see Chi-Lu Chen, "Ethnological Studies in China, Retrospect and Prospect," *Chinese Cultural Renaissance Monthly*, Vol. 13, No. 4, 1978, pp. 5-10 (in Chinese).

6) Chi-Lu Chen, *Material Culture of the Formosan Aborigines*, 422 pp., 20 color plates, 1968, The Taiwan Museum, Taipei (in English).

7) Tadao Kano and Kokichi Segawa, *An Illustrated Ethnography of Formosan Aborigines*, Vol. 1, *The Yami*, 456 pp., 1956, Maruzen, Tokyo (in English).

8) Up to date, 41 numbers were published.

9) Chi-Lu Chen, et al., *Ethnological Researches among the Thao of Sun-Moon Lake, Formosa*, 166 pp., 1958, National Taiwan University, Taipei (in Chinese with English summary).

10) Chi-Lu Chen, *Woodcarving of the Paiwan Group of Taiwan*, 198 pp., 86 plates, 1961, National Taiwan University, Taipei (in Chinese).

11) Chi-Lu Chen(ed.), *Proceedings of the Seminar on Taiwan Studies*, 102 pp., 1967, National Taiwan University, Taipei (in Chinese).

12) Chi-Lu Chen(ed.), *Supplementary Proceedings of the Seminar on Taiwan Studies*, 60 pp., 5 plates, National Taiwan University, Taipei (in Chinese).

13) Up to date, 48 numbers were published.

14) The authors, titles, and publishing date of the 25 numbers are:

No. 1, Hwei-Lin Wei and Pin-Hsiung Liu, *Social Structure of the Yami, Botel Tobago*, 1962.

No. 2, Yih-Yuan Li et al., *Material Culture of the Vataan Ami*, 1962.

No. 3, Shun-Sheng Ling, *Bark-cloth, Impressed Pottery, and the Invention of Paper and Printing*, 1963.

No. 4, Pen-Li Chuang, *Panpipes of Ancient China*, 1963.

No. 5, Yih-Yuan Li et al., *The Atayal of Nan-ao*, Vol. 1, 1963.

No. 6, Yih-Yuan Li et al., *The Atayal of Nan-ao*, Vol. 2, 1964.

No. 7, Chi-Chien Chiu, *Social Organization of the Take-Bakha Bunun*, 1966.

No. 8, Pin-Hsiung Liu et al., *Social Structure of the Siu-ku-luan Ami*, 1965.

No. 9, Lin-Ts'an Li, *A Study of the Nan-chao and Ta-li Kingdoms in the Light of Art Materials Found in Various Museums*, 1967.

No. 10, Shun-Sheng Ling, *The Dolmen Culture of Taiwan, East Asia and the Southwestern Pacific*, 1967.

No. 11, Jen-Ying Wang, *Population Change of Formosan Aborigines*, 1967.

No. 12, Chung-I Wen, *Aspects of the Culture of Ch'u*, 1967.

No. 13, Sung-Hsing Wang, *Kwei-shan Tao, A Study of a Chinese Fishing Community in Formosa*, 1967.

No. 14, Chi-Wan Liu, *Great Propitiatory Rites of Petition for Beneficence at Sungshan, Taipei, Taiwan*, 1967.

No. 15, Shun-Sheng Ling, *The Mound Cultures of East China and Southeastern North America*, 1968.

No. 16, Shun-Sheng Ling, *A Study of the Raft, Outrigger, Double, and Deck Canoes of Ancient China, the Pacific, and the Indian Oceans*, 1970.

No. 17, Raleigh Ferrell, *Taiwan Aboriginal Groups: Problems in Cultural and Linguistic Classification*, 1969.

Nos. 18-19, Chang-Rue Yuan, *The Makutaai Ami of Eastern Taiwan, an Ethnog-*

raphic Report, 1969.

No. 20, Shun-Sheng Ling, *Turtle Sacrifice in China and Oceania,* 1972.

No. 21, Lei Shih, *Su-Paiwan, An Anthropological Investigation of a Paiwan Village,* 1971.

No. 22, Chi-Wan Liu, *Essays on Chinese Folk Belief and Folk Cults, 1974.*

No. 23, Lei Shih, *Cognatic Kinship Systems among Formosan Aborigines, A Comparative Study of Rukai, Paiwan, and Puyuma,* 1976.

No. 24, *Proceedings of the Seminar on Juvenile Problems in Changing Society,* 1978.

No. 25, Jih-Chang Chester Hsieh, *Structure and History of a Chinese Community in Taiwan,* 1979.

(In Chinese, except No. 17 in English)

15) The authors, titles, and publishing date of the 8 numbers are:

No. 1, Yih-Yuan Li, *An Immigrant Town, Life in Overseas Chinese Community in Southern Malaya,* 1970.

No. 2, Pin-Hsiung Liu, *Murngin, A Mathematical Solution,* 1970.

No. 3, Chien Chiao, *Continuation of Tradition in Navajo Society,* 1971.

No. 4, *Symposium on the Character of the Chinese,* 1972.

No. 5, Sung-Hsing Wang and Raymond Apthorpe, *Rice Farming in Taiwan, Three Village Studies,* 1974.

No. 6, Chung-I Wen et al., *Social Change in a Suburban Village of Taipei,* 1975.

No. 7, Chung-Min Chen, *Upper Camp, A Study of a Chinese Mixed*-cropping *Village* in Taiwan, 1977.

No. 8, Ying-Chang Chuang, *Lin Yi Pu, The Social and Economic History of a Chinese Township in Taiwan,* 1977.

(Nos. 1,4,6,8 in Chinese; Nos. 2,3,5,7 in English)

16) For example: The socio-cultural change and adaptation in Northern Taiwan. Anthropological and environmental investigation of the Cho-shui and Tatu River Valleys in Central Taiwan. Studies of social development in rural Taiwan. Population studies in Taiwan, and Overseas Chinese stuides.

17) Yih-Yuan Li, "Institute of Ethnology 1955-1971, Retrospect and Prospect," *Bulletin of the Institute of Ethnology, Academia Sinica,* No. 31, 1971, p. 2.

6 Sinology and Sino-Anthropology: Family Study as an Example

SUNG-HSING WANG

Sinology or Anthropology?

Han Chinese society which is a highly complicated society with historically long civilisation, is very different in nature from those primitive-small scale societies with no historical record which are the object of study for previous anthropologists. Due to perpetual historical development, the Chinese society has attained highly complicated political and economic systems, with specific way of thought and world view. If anthropologists still persist on using theories such as those applied to African kinship system as studying means, they surely would face the limitation in understanding problems. Some anthropologists doing research on Han Chinese society have borrowed Redfield's conceptual frame of great tradition and little tradition as the studying focus, viz., the literary-historically recorded complicated cultural institutions are belonging to the great tradition level of the Chinese culture, and thus should under the jurisdiction of sinology. For anthropology, the jurisdiction should be retreated to study the little tradition of peasant and village communities.

Such an arrangement, in a quick glance, seemed to provide a foothold for anthropological study of China. However, in reality, anthropologists are always shifting between past and present, great tradition and little tradition when they are handling data derived from their long-term participant observative study of village communities. They even have a series of explanations on why they cannot completely surrender the great tradition.

In B. E. Ward's proposed three consicous models from Chinese culture, it has significantly reflected such a dilemma of anthropologists. Even though anthropologists have made use of field investigation to study native's culture of 'immediate model', on the other hand, they ought to have explained Chinese culture's integrity and perpetuality, which surpasses regions, classes and historical periods. For such, they proposed a 'believed--in traditional model' to conclude.

The conceptual framework of 'conscious model' can, in contrast to the strict dialectical approach of great tradition and little tradition, better explain the internal dynamic of Chinese socio-culture. Due to affection of specific social and ecological condition, the cultures of different Chinese regions and social classes have developed into different 'immediate models'. However, they persistently adhere to an unique 'believed-in traditional model', thus, making possible Chinese culture to maintain her integrity and perpetuality. The cultural contents 'believed-in traditional model' emphasizes, such as clanship and ethical relations, are relatively uniform to that of the 'immediate models' among various regions or classes. Other than that stressed by the 'belived-in traditional model', the various 'immediate models are left to develop freely. Thus, wide differences are expected among various regions levels upon areas like role specification between male and female, village organization and religious belief of the popular masses (Ward 1965).

Disregard great and little traditions, or conceptual frame of 'conscious models', they all are, in reality, built on the same postulation. That is, the cultures of the scholar-gentry and the popular masses separately represented the two-level of Chinese culture. Sinologists and anthropologists can make use of their specific means of study to carry out, without any inter-intrusion, individual field of study. Sinologists can make use of their intelligence on classical Chinese literature to elaborate the namely Confucian-based great tradition, a 'believed-in traditional model' cultural pattern, whereas anthropologists can go through field investigation to carry out study of the culture of 'immediate models'.

However, anthropologists are growing dissatisfied with such a division of work and they are crying for the study of Chinese socio-culture as an entity (Freedman 1974). They believe that the great tradition of the scholar-gentry or that revealed by literary classics is in fact rested upon a common base as the popular masses' little tradition, representing two versions of the same entity.

On the other hand, sinologists commonly deny the existence of the differentiated scholar-gentry culture and the popular masses culture. Taking the recently deceased Kojiro Yoshikawa as an example, he postulates that, in contrast to other ethnics, Chinese cares seriously the classics which are regarded as the norms of life. From this, it gives birth to certain characteristics of the Chinese, viz.: (1) The classics for norms of life, the 'five classics' are selective and specifically assigned. (2) The 'five classics' are to be looked upon as an eternal truth. (3) The unanimity of practical life and the classics are reforced (Yoshikawa 1964:1-8). Yoshikawa carries on to say that:

"Those who have got the opportunity to read the 'five classics', i. e. the so-called 'literati', are limited. There are multiples of non-literati, the so-called 'popular masses.' However, even for the popular masses, their sentimental life is basically indifferent to that of the literati. Their standard is no further than respecting precedence, following the 'five classics' as an ideal and....at least, the popular masses having got not any concept of life to confront that of the literati's" (1964: 28-29).

Undeniably, anthropologists studying China must be familiar with Chinese classics and traditional sinological works, and Chinese anthropology should also be collaborated with Chinese history and sinology which study great tradition. Tambiah has pointed out that anthropologists for long go into the field to study live action and take the derived pattern as their theoretical basis. Because when an anthropologist "is already committed to an anthropological level of reality and social facts,....(he) who works in complex 'historical' societies is likely to view the literary culture of that society as constituting another 'level' or order equivalent to the level of 'live action' he has managed to record. Moreover, this static view of the literature and recorded history may be an inevitable result of the fact that an anthropologist is not primarily interested in them; they are the province of the Orientalist or the Indologist and the historian" (Tambiah 1970: 371). "In short, what needs to be emphasized is that anthropologists dealing with complex literate societies should pay greater attention to the role of literacy and the traditional networks of learning and transmission of knowledge" (ibid.:373). Even though Tambiah divides Thai religion into the jurisdiction of historical and present he never regards them as two mutually rejecting levels. What he wants to inquire about is the continuities and transformations of the two (ibid.: 4).

On the same time, M. Freedman, an anthropologist studying Chinese society, corresponds with such a viewpoint by taking the study on Chinese religion as an evidence. He believes that the elite and the peasant religion rest upon a common base, representing two versions of one religion. Freedman has quoted two prominent scholars working on Chinese religion as exmaples to support that the two versions are the same religion bearing two external appearances due to difference in living conditions only. De Groot's Chinese religious study begins with fieldwork and is from the peasant to the elite; whereas Granet is just a reverse, he starts from Chinese classical texts and, from the elite to the peasant. Though standing from opposite polars, both eventually come to the same religion. On the other words, no matter started from where, the concluded answer is that there is only a single religion in China (Freedman 1974).

It becomes rather significant that anthropology concerning Chinese socio-culture must take into greater concern the attainment of sinological study. Such a touch can also be seen from the Han civilization embracing Japanese community of anthropology. Chie Nakane believes that social anthropologists doing research on this civilization realm must bear satisfactory literary knowledge as well as be concern to the works of the neighbouring disciplines. Among them, the most important is history. It is because East Asia is a region possessing the wealthiest historical literature. Such a fact, however, may also be chains constituting to the development of social anthropology in the region. If conciliatory relationship can be established, then the growth of social anthropology in the East Asia region is just a matter of time (Nakane 1975).

Undeniably, a series of publications on Chinese society published by Stanford University Press is inclined to such an approach. The authors of these series are mainly historians and anthropologists. The outcome of the dialogue of the two disciplines proves that such is necessary and important. The first publication of the series is: *Family and Kinship in Chinese Society* edited by the anthropologist Freedman. The following is based on Chinese family study to discuss the possibility and necessity of collaboration of sinology and anthropology.

History, Fieldwork, and Family System

Coincidentally, many anthropologists like to refer to the process of the collapse or transformation of family system after carrying out their fieldwork on the Chinese family system. They have a common postulation that traditional or ideal type of Chinese families should be large families with five generations together. Thus, when they come across a live peasant's family pattern contrary to it, they responsively cry for the drastic collapsing of Chinese family system.

The renowned Chinese legal historian Noboru Niida is especially resent to such a viewpoint. In his criticism to an aticle, 'Fen-chia-dispersing process of Chinese big family system', he is especially dissatisfied with the unthoughtful conclusion drawn by the anthropologists. His criticism may represent sinologists' opinion to a certain research outcome of anthropology. Below is a brief introduction of Niida's criticism:

The author starts by raising the number of heads in the peasant families of Shansi, Shantung and Hopei as evidence and continues to say, "I had expected to see a great number of big families existing in the villages of North China, but such an expectation is completely in vain because the overall majority households are with average of around six heads". If a typical modern family pattern is composed of a couple and their unmarried son(s) and/or daughter(s); and that a family, then, modern family pattern in villages of North China may be said as with absolute majority: According to Yao-Yu Wang's article, the transformation of households and cultivated lands in the fifty villages of I-tu Hsien, more than forty villages doubled their households in the recent twenty years. He believes that 'fen-chia' (division of family) is the main reason accountable." "Furthermore, according to field investigations of the villages, it proves that 'fen-chia' is largely carried out in the recent decade, especially caused by the Sino-Japanese War". ... "Not to separate when the parents are still alive is the ethic of past family system. By then, a family with three generations amounting to more than ten heads together should have been very obvious. However, now situation changes. Fen-chia while parents are still alive is with an increasing tendency". Eventually, the author draws to a conclusion that "such a change of idea unevitably is a collapse of past family system". On the other words, it also is a shattering of old ethics (quoted from Niida 1952: 96-97).

Such a proposition can easily be detected from works of the anthropologists. When facing a family pattern in contrast to that of a big family with five generations together, despite it being in favour of nuclear family, 'rotating, stem families'[1] or federal family[2], anthropologists will unhesitatedly regard it being a process of transformation of family systems, and a product of economic change or social modernization.

Niida does not agree to such a proposition. He thinks that the questions lie on: (1) To what degree was the norm of past family ethics on the live society in traditional times? With special reference to peasant societies, it is worth questioning. (2) What is the transformation or qualitative change of the ethics that practically tie up the olden society in the recent years? (3) Is it real that past family pattern is mainly with three generations and more than ten heads? (Niida 1975: 97-98)

Pinning on the third question, Niida says, "the ancient peasant families, which Mencius based on to advocate his 'ch'ing-tien' or well-field system[3], were not exceeding ten heads each. The late Ming scholar Yen-Wu Ku had also pointed out that it was obvious that brothers fen-chia before the death of their parents in the Six Dynasties period. Such has been agreed by historians too. The trend could also be seen after T'ang. In the T'and Code, division of family property or separation of 'chia' by brothers before death of parents were not strictly forbidden. The law codes after T'ang were even more lenient to these. If just taking the inclination of family dispersion ro family heads or family composition for inference, then, shattering or collapsing of family system is not a matter of recent years but somewhat as early as 2000 years ago or even earlier (ibid.: 99).

The route of Niida on studying Chinese family system is the same as Granet mentioned previously. He initiated from classic literary. His well-known works, like *Gleanings on Tang Code* (1934), *Status-Legal History of China* (1942), are outstanding in the field of sinology. Even so, he does not neglect the study of live social life of the popular masses. From 1940 to 1942, he participated in the survey of rural customs in North China.[4]. His book *The Family in Rural China,* is namely based on data derived from that investigation. In ther preface, he repeatedly stressed the importance of taking into concern both classical history studies and live field investigation. He says:

"This field survey is very meaningful in reflecting the history of Chinese society, and, this is not only so to others but me too, for I hence, in the earlier publication of 1942, awared of the need for such a revision. Of course, in the *Status-Legal History of China,* I first opined that looking back at past Chinese society is helpful in understanding the linkage between present and past society....The present cannot be distinctly separated from the past or the future. They are from the very beginning within the pulse of historical development. Furthermore, history should always be reviewed, reconstructed, and repeatedly supported by the contemporary viewpoint. The contents of field investigation, except giving subject review to historical study, cannot completely get rid of the bound of historical conditions...." (ibid.:5-6).

Niida's viewpoint, in fact, is relevant to what has been repeatedly emphasized by a group of anthropologist, like L. Dumont and D. Pocock, studying India in the series *Contribution to Indian Sociology* (Tambiah 1970: 369-372).

However, Niida's study on live society is not so deep as that groups of anthropologists on India. He was just a guest investigator in the North China Rural Customs Investigation team. He can only proceed to the extent as detected in his book (1942), and use the conceptual framework to reorganize and analyse the materials got from the North China Rural Customs Investigation. The theme reflected to historical study by that field investigation has, according to Niida, substantially enlightened his two new viewpoints: The first is that the well-known Chinese family property equal-divisionism produces equilibrium among the dispersed families. Therefore, it cannot establish, like that of Japanese society, a super-inferior relationship between the original and the separated families. Such equal-divisionism is structurally linked with patriarchal authority and the law of family labor. Another discovery is the problem of matriarchate (house-wife-in-charge), which has for long been neglected by those studying history of Chinese family system, and is also a theme not touched by Niida in his publication of 1942 (ibid.: preface 5).

Undeniably, the North China Rural Customs Investigation is rather striking to those scholars engaging in the study of Chinese family history or literature. Shuzo Shiga, a younger legal institutionist to Niida, is a typical example to it.

In 1950, Shiga published *On Chinese Family Law*. Same as Niida's 1942 book, it is a historical work based on literary classics. Even though Shiga had not directly participated in the North China Rural Customs Investigation, he had totally absorbed all the data from the Investigation, made full active use of them to rewrite the original book and renamed it as *Principle of Chinese Family Law* (1967). Shiga take a metaphor that the original book —— i.e. historical study of literary clasiscs —— is the *seed*, and the rewritten book —— i.e. with injection of data from lively practical social survey —— is the *body* after complete germmation and growth (cf. 1967, preface).

What worth mentioning is that of the methodology used by Shiga to deal with Chinese family law, in which lies the problem why data of literary classics and popular customs can indifferently be quoted. He believes that state law and common law are not confronting each other, but is homogeneously related. As somewhat minor may have change of time or difference in region, but they are fundamentally with unchangeable principles. From the characteristics of traditional Chinese society, it is made understandable why the postulation can be established. It is because traditional Chinese society has never developed a seclusive inheritance or feudal social class. Between the scholar-gentry class, the 'Shih' or the 'literati', and the productive toiling popular masses, following the transferrence of generations, there is constant interflow of upraising and down-grading. People's concept of life or value system is one: those who can adequately experiment and experience it is called sholar-gentry. Others who, upon restrictions, cannot wholly put it into practice is belonging to the popular masses (1967:15-16). On the other words, Shiga believes that the principle of family law of scholar-gentiv and the popular masses is the same in reality.

In this case, what is meant by '*chia*' as referred by Shiga, after having made detailed comparison and analysis with Japanese '*ie*', opined that the basic elements of Chinese 'chia' are that of the component members and property, and it can be illustrated by the relationship of 'same household with common property' (同居共財) (ibid: 68). However, the phrase 'same household common property' does not especially mean living under the same roof. The Explanatory notes on T'ang Code (唐律疏議) says, "Even though living together, it still is under different household"(雖復同住 亦爲異居). It clearly indicated that the reality of living together does not necessarily attribute to the relationship of under the same household. Contrariwise, the biography on Shih-Chih Chang in Shih Chih has recorded that Chang had been a official in the Capital for ten years, but was as one household as his brother living in the home country. Definitely, whether living together or separately is not with absolute tie to the relativeship of under the same household or not. The data from North China Rural Customs Investigation has also had the idea of 'in the same household but under neighbouring roof' (同居隔宅居住). Therefore, the relationship of 'same household with common property' should include the following three contents:

(1) The toiling production of each individual member should include into the common economy of the 'chia'.

(2) The necessitated daily expenses of all in the household should be born

by the chia's common economy.

(3) The surplus of the chia's common economy is accumulated as the common property or 'chia-ch'an' (家產).

In other words, the 'chia' basing on the 'same household with common property' is founded on economic function. 'Fen-chia', division of family property, is the stoppage of the 'same household with common property' relationship between brothers (ibid.:69-85).

On the whole, the analysis and viewpoint of Shiga on Chinese family is acceptable. However, he mixed up 'chia-ch'an or family property with common family economy, believing that if family property is commonly possessed by the brothers, then there must also be a common economy too. Thus forming his so-called 'under the same household with common property'. Whether it is the fact or not is rather hard to agree unanimously on the standpoint of anthropologists' study of Chinese 'chia'.

Anthropologists are comparatively inclined to the dynamic study of the development of family. Supposing that a couple gets married and gives birth to offsprings, before the marriage of the latter, of course it is a 'chia' of 'same household with common property'. But when all of them have got married, daughters moving out and daughter-in-law moving in, a family may thus include more than two 'fang' (房) formed by individual brothers. If they still live together and share the same stove and eat rice from the same cooker, then the feature of 'same household with common property' complies with Shiga's three contents.

But, if each 'fang' lives separately, then such a 'family' includes more than two 'household'. In this case, whether family property has been scattered or family economy being communal or not is worth considering.

M. Cohen (1970) believes that Chinese 'chia' has got three component elements: chia estate, chia group, and chia economy. Each component can have two possible alternative characteristics: the chia estate is either concentrated or dispersed; the chia group may be either concentrated or dispersed; the chia economy may be inclusive or non-inclusive. Cohen further suggests that Chinese family has always been described as estate concentrated, group concentrated and economy inclusive.

However, according to the explanation of Shiga, this suggestion is not quite the fact. Shiga's family of 'same household with common property' is in reality including the two possibilities of family estate and group, except that family economy must be inclusive. In respect to the two possibilities of family estate, even though has not paid special attention on, he has specifically evidenced on the two possible arrangements of family members.

As what is said, living together or separately does not affect the integrity of a 'chia' and Shiga's three contents on the relationship of 'same household with common property' are all aiming at the inclusive nature of chia economy. As to whether non-inclusive chia economy can be called a 'chia' or not is a question worth arguing.

Fen-chia or the division of family property is a split and dissolution of a family. In other words, common possession of family property is an essential criteria for formation of a family. It means that a family is established on the basis of common family property. But, whether the division of family property is once and for all is rather doubtful.

When the sons get married, the aged father always shares part of the family property to let them manage individually. Depending on a share from their father, the sons will become independent and not to mix up their family economies. In the villages, the habit of 'retirement field' (養老田) can also be seen: the aged father initially divides up the major portion of his estate among his sons and retains a small portion calling 'retirement field', waiting to be settled by the sons only after the death of himself. All such arrangements reveal that the division of family property may be processed by several stages. By then, the married sons with patrimony are with independent family economies but, the parental centred family has not been completely dissolved. We may see from that of the rural religious activities that the mutually independent 'fangs' of the brothers are still all included into the family headed by the aged father, instead of listing their names individually. That means under the condition of non-inclusive family economy, it is still possible to maintain a single unit family. Ying-Chang Chuang names such as a federal famly, a family with dispersed estate, dispersed group and non-inclusive economy (Chuang 1976).

From the discussion of this section, what the author wants to stress is that the literary-diachronic sinologists' study and the live field-investigated anthropologists' study should be correlated. Taking family study as an example, the defect anthropologists easily commit is hasty reckoning: presenting a pattern of traditional family, disregard it being an extend family or a family of estate concentrated, group concentrated and economy inclusive, and then basing on their data about family got from field investigation to reckon whether the observed family is a pattern undergoing the process of metamorphosis. Such scamping and insecure thesis has been explicitly discussed in this passage. However, live field study is definitely of enlightening and introspective value to literary-history. Except the previously mentioned 'house-wife-in-charge' interested to Niida, the proposed non-inclusive family economy should be historically existed, only that it is not explicitly exploited by sinologists and thus, anthropologists' analytical concept of Chinese family study has been neglected.

Notes

1) In Taiwan and other part of China, especially in rural areas, there is a modified form of the stem family which is commonly called by the term of 'rotating stem family'. The so-called rotating stem family exsists when more than two sons are married and family division has already taken place. To accommodate the parents, the sons adopt a system in which the parents live with them on a rotating basis. An example would be an old couple with three married sons among whom an agreement is reached to take turns caring for their parents. The parents live with the family of the eldest son for a period of ten days, or whatever length of time has been agreed upon, and then, in a rotating fashion, stay with the second and third sons for the same period of time. When the cycle is finished, it recommences with the parents living with the eldest son (Chen 1977: 116-119).
2) Mr. Ying-Chang Chuang has coined a new term, federal family, which he defines as "a family unit in which the members do not share the same residence but maintain close social contacts, do not share common property but maintain a high degree of economic cooperation." He went further to point out that this new family system is a product of modernization (Chuang·1972).
3) The arable field, *t'ien* was assigned in sections to eight peasant families each. Every section was plotted in a form resembling Chinese character for well, *Ching*, the eight outer plots being cultivated in common by the eight families and central plot being reserved for residences and the raising of the produce which went to the lord.
4) Field reports were published by Iwanami-shoten under the title *"Chukoku-noson-- kanko-chosa"*, six volumes, 1952-58.

References

Chen, Chung-Min
  1977   *Upper Camp, A Study of a Chinese Mixed-Cropping Village in Taiwan.*
         Taipei: Institute of Ethnology, Academia Sinica, Monograph Series B
         No. 7.
Chuang, Ying-Chang
  1972   "T'ai-wan Nung-ts'un Chia-tsu tui Hsien-tai-hua te shih-ying" (The
         Adaptation of Family to Modernization in Rural Taiwan), *Bulletin of the
         Institute of Ethnology, Academia Sinica,* 34:85-98.
Cohen, Myron L.
  1970   "Development Process in the Chinese Domestic Group," in Maurice
         Freedman, ed., *Family and Kinship in Chinese Society,* Stanford Uni-
         versty Press, pp. 21-36.
Freedman, Maurice
  1974   "On the Sociological Study of Chinese Religion," in Arthur Wolf, ed.,
         Religion and Ritual in Chinese Society, Stanford University Press, pp.
         19-41.
Nakane, Chie
  1975   "Shakai Jinruigaku to Higashi Ajia" (Social Anthropology and East
         Asia), *Journal of Japanese Ethnological Society,* 39:344-349.
Niida, Noboru
  1952   *Chugoku no Noson Kazoku (Family in Rural China),* The Institute of
         Oriental Culture, The University of Tokyo.
Shiga, Shuzo
  1967   *Chugoku Kazokuho no Genri (Principle of Family Law in China),*
         Sobunsha.
Ward, Barbara
  1965   "Varieties of the Conscious Model: The Fishermen of South China," in
         Michael Banton, ed., *The Relevance of Models for Social Anthropology,*
         Tavistock, pp. 113-37.
Yoshikawa, Kojiro
  1964   *Sinajin no Koten to Sono Seikatsu (Chinese Classics and Life),* Iwana-
         mishoten.

7   Anthropological Studies in Korea

KWANG-KYU LEE

Introduction

Anthropological studies about Korean people and Korean culture can be referred to go back to the 18th century when a group of scholars who belong to the school of Silhak (or Practical Learning) published various kinds of books on rural life, folk customs, and agricultural technology. But in this paper only the review or evaluation of achievements on anthropological researches made since 1920's will be dealt with, because it was not until 1920's that we found, so called, results of anthropological research with its contents and style comparable to those of recent scientific researches.

We will exclude from this thesis all the comments on other branches of anthropology, such as archaeology, linguistic and physical anthropology. For each of these branches has established different schools respectively and our concerns lie mainly in the area of the cultural and social anthropology.

The history of anthropological studies in Korea can be divided into four periods; that is, dawning, beginning, folkloristic, and systematic research period.

The first period is applicable to the 15 years from 1920 to 1935. At these times Mr. Nam-Sun Choi and Mr. Nung-Hwa Yi were remarkable scholars. Mr. Choi is known to be a historian but he published several important books and articles which deal with the mythology and shamanism. Basing his works on the bibliographical research he compared the myth of earlier kingdom with those of the neighboring countries. His study on shamanism is marked with wider comparison of the Siberian Shamanism. We owe to his extensive learning our acknowledgement of many

curious folk customs of rural life. Mr. Neung-Hwa Yi has the same characteristics as Mr. Choi in the point of his interests and research methods in
his book. He also published several books on Korean shamanism, Buddhism, Confucianism, Taoism, ancestor worship and women's customs. His
researches are also based on the bibliographical study as Mr. Choi did so.
But Mr. Yi's works are noticeable for the accuracy of the historical
approach rather than for comparative study. Therefore anthropological
study of the dawning period in Korea is characterised by the bibliographical study with the historical approach, and two pioneer scholars, Mr. Choi
and Mr. Yi, indicate the main direction of the research in the future.

The second period begins from 1932 when the Korean Folklorist
Society was established, and Mr. Chin-Tae Son, Sok-Hwa Song and
In-Sup Chung are counted on as prominent scholars. Even though the
Society disappeared in a few years, the members of the Society and other
young scholars published important works related to anthropology. Especially Chin-Tae Son is more remarkable for his methodology of field research than any other scholars. His interest in the Korean culture was
connected with the earliest days of Koreans, and concentrated mainly on
making clear folk belief, shamanism, oral traiditon and mythology. He
continued to extend his concerns even into the research of megalithic
culture, marriage customs and material culture. His books on Korean history, *A General History of Korean Nation,* has been estimated as the best
qualified work even in general history. He based his research methodology
of Korean culture on the comparative study and ethnohistorical method
which are similar to those of the diffusionists. The works of Mr. Sok-Hwa
Song are greatly different from those of Mr. Son's. His interests lie principally in the area of folklore, such as folk dance, folk mass play, and mask
dances, etc. He made field research throughout all the area of Korean
peninsula but left us only ethnographical materials. Judging from his works
we can consider him as folklorist. Most of scholars in this period were
concerned with collecting ethnographical materials as Mr. Song did. Holding their special areas of study respectively, they extended their interest
into the whole range of folklore, such as folk song, folk tale, folk drama
and even traditional clothing, etc. With these native folklorists, we should
count on the achievements of Japanese scholars in this period. They published some important works related to the field of anthropological study,
and their scholastic activities were directed toward more systematic research and broader questionaire survey using administrative network than

those of native scholars. We also should not lose sight of the fact that there were considerable cooperations between Korean and Japanese scholars in the course of field research, and that jointly they arranged and published some interesting field data. Holding wider concerns for Korean culture, these Japanese scholar touched all the field which can be now called as the area of anthropological study.

The third period, so-called, folkloristic period extends from 1945 into 1970. Most of the researchers of this period are interested in folk customs and folk religions, annual customs, rites of passage, to celebrate these rites and quarreled against one another. One household god worship, village god worship, shamanism, folk beliefs, folk songs, mask dances, mythology, proverbs, cooking, house building, traditional clothings, etc. These kinds of research areas turn out to be the very places in which anthropological works are made in Korea. Researches are mainly practiced through individual efforts, and the collection of ethnographical materials forms the main stream of the anthropological studies in this period. But since 1970 the research team for synthetic survey of Korean folklore has been organized to collect ethnographical materials all over the country and has published 10 voluminous books titled as *The Report of the Synthetic Research of Korean Folklore,* covering such areas as kinship, community, religion, material culture, folk custom, production process, oral tradition, etc. This joint research team enabled the anthropological studies to face a new period. Before this new period, there were already some comparative studies. But after this joint research the comparison between or among different districts came to be actively made throughout the nation and opened a new tendency of joint work in the research activity.

Especially in this period we should notice that some universities established the department of anthropology: Seoul National University founded Dept. of Achaeology and Anthropology in 1961 but this Dept. was devided into two different Dept.'s, Archaeology and Anthropology respectively in 1975. Yeong-Nam University also established its Dept. of Cultural Anthropology in 1972. Recently Ann-Dong University founded Dept. of Folklore in 1979 and Gyeong-Bug University Dept. of Archaeology and Anthropology in 1980.

Korean Society for Cultural Anthropology was organized in 1958 and has published annual magazine, total 11 volumes. The branch of folklore was separated from this society in 1968 and also has published its annual magazine.

In this paper the achievements of these two periods, that is, the folkloristic period and systematic research period, will be dealt with as main contents. The works and research materials which will be discussed here are limited to those of Korean anthropologists and folklorists and foreign scholars which treat with Korean culture and society. We will classify all the materials into 5 parts according to each subject, such as, first, social anthropology in narrow sense including family, kinship, village and social activities; second, folk customs including rites of passage, annual customs, folk mass dance, mask dance, etc.; third, material culture including cooking, clothing, housing, farming tools, etc.; fourth, oral tradition including folk song, proverbs, folk tales, etc.; fifth, religion including folk belief, household god worship, village god worship, shamanism, and new religion.

Social Anthropology

The meaning of social anthropology in this paper is used in a narrow sense, including family, marriage and kinship, lineage, village community, social behavior, social grouping and social organization. Besides in this area of social anthropology there are some articles and books dealing with the same contents studied from other disciplines such as sociology, law and history. Naturally all of these achievements from these sister sciences have not been made from the stand point of anthropology. But there are some articles worth while to be considered as anthropological achievements.

Social anthropology is the most important area in Korean anthropology as in the other countries. The achievement of studies in this area could be summarized quantitatively as the following table 1.

As a single item, family is the most popular area of study in Korea as the statistics show. When the lineage and kinship are considered on together, the number of articles comes to surpass that of family. As to the publication of the books, village community is regarded as the most important study area. Anthropological research of family structure is examined in the different region, and so it divided into rural family, urban family, and middle size town family. However, it is noticed that the dominant interest in the study of family system lies in the rural family. According to the statistics collected, more than 80 percent of studies of family is connected with rural family. In the light of the contents of the subject, we are able to make clear that most of the articles are treating with various problems,

Table 1
Studies in social anthropology

Subject area	Artcles	Books
Family	64	6
Marriage	21	2
Woman	46	5
Kinship	50	3
Lineage	32	1
Village	33	12
Social grouping	21	1
Peasant	20	
Urban life	32	
Shifting cultivation	4	1

such as the family size, power structure in family, division of the role among the family members or under the name of family structure or family form.

There are two kinds of methods in the study of the family system; one is statistical method, and the other is comparative method. Especially with the comparative method, two different classes within the same area, or two different regions, that is, as in farming and fishing communities are chosen to make comparison according to researcher's interests. However, almost all the scholars participating in the family study are largely concerned about the traditional type of Korean family. In the results of these studies, we are able to find that the senior male, usually the head of the family, holds strong power and so that Korean type of family is defined as patriarchal family. And also it is noticed in the general agreements that the typical Korean family is not extended family but stem family and that the father's authority is conferred to as institutionalized one rather than as social one. Another area of the family study lies in the changing aspect of family concerning family size, attitude toward family authority, family function, division of role, psychological problem in changing family. Scholars concernd about this study area try to find proper answer for the question of how such changing aspects are generated. They seem to understand clearly that changing agents always derived from social change and that the change of family system is only a part of the social change.

One of the interesting areas of family study lies in, as we already noticed it, the traditional family system. Family cycle within the time dimension is an important aspect to understand Korean family type, along with the rule of family division, kinship system and the problem of inheritance and succession. Retirement system of the head of the family and housewife is an interesting issue in the study of Korean family. Mother-in-law complex is the another finding of family problem in traditional family. One important area of study is the family system in Che-ju Island. Che-ju Island is the largest one in Korea, located in the southern part of Korean peninsula. Che-ju Island is so widely noted not only for the peculiar family system but also for all aspects of culture that it is regarded as the ideal place for anthropological research in Korea.

There are a few articles and one book which compare the Korean family with that of China and Japan. As patrilineal and partriarchal family, the families of three nations share common characteristics but there are also many differences in basic pattern among them which may neglect the different characteristics of three cultures in East Asia.

The study of marriage has been examined in the various directions as in family study. The popular and principal subject of the study on marriage lies in the history of marriage system, especially the formation of rule of exogamy in the past. Another topic in the historical perspective is on the marriage as an indicator of social change in recent period. One of the interesting topics in marriage is the ghost marriage which is being performed even today.

Woman is the important subject of study for feminists in recent times. The achievements in this area are divided into 4 areas; woman herself, woman in family system, woman in social acitivity and woman in special occupation like the diver in Che-ju Island. Woman holds the psychological problems about another woman within the family, as we notice it in the woman's characters which are reflected on the novel, religious activities and criminal records, etc. Woman in family system should keep her moral role as housewife in her house-keeping activities and in polygyny system in the past. More than half of the achievements on the study of woman deal with these topics. Woman's activities in society have been done always in unequal condition compared to male's ones. The most interesting topic in the study of woman is that of diver in Che-ju Island, which deal with diver's practice, social life, annual customs of diver and psychological problem of the woman diver in Che-ju Island.

Kinship including lineage is the most popular area for anthropological study in Korea as the statistics show. The study of kinship is divided into 5 areas; that is, kinship system in general, kinship terminology, inheritance, adoption and kinship organization, the lineage. Kinship system in general deals with historical development of kinship or Chinese influences on Korean kinship system in the past. In the study of kinship terminology are dealt with such detailed subjects as structure of terminology, terms of reference in the past and semantic analysis of terminology.

There are about 15 articles which deal with inheritance and succession. This topic is also connected with the study of patrilineality or matrilineality in the past. Recent achievement in this area is the different type of inheritance which is connected with the ancestor worship, namely the division of ancestor worship among the offsprings which is found in remote area and in the past. There are some articles which deal with adoption.

Lineage organization plays important role to organize social group in modern times, and the scholastic interest in the study of lineage is also high. There are about 9 articles which deal with general character and system of lineage in Korea. In these articles various sub-topics such as division of lineage, formation and differences of lineage along the social classes and localities are treated with. There are also several achievements which deal with function, conflict of lineage and historical development of lineage organization in the past. The main interest, however, is in the lineage organization under the connection with ancestor worship and its historical development. There are also a few articles which compare the lineage organization of Korea with that of China and Japan especially on Ryukyu Islands.

Village community is also regarded as an important area of study by anthropologists in Korea. From the interest of scholars in the occupation of Korean people, the researches are concentrated on the farming, fishing, and mountain village. From the sociological viewpoint there has been some researches on religious villages, but greater interest of anthropologists tends to be in lineage village, which are occupied by famous lineages. Most of the village researches are ethnographical explanations. However, in each recent study there are among researchers new tendencies to search for interesting viewpoints; for example, one is interested in village's dynamics concerning to conflict and harmony and the other deals with ecological approach to consider the problem of productions and the third pays attention to socio-economic stratification of the village. Though social grouping is interesting topic for the study of village life, it is dealt here separately because it is also connected with urban life. Social grouping in this case are concerned with financial associations or labor exchanges. From earlier time there were many financial associations in rural villages and also informal organization of labor exchanges in village communities. Most of the researchers engaging in the study of social grouping are interested in collecting ethnographic data on financial associations. In the results of their efforts, we find some achievements in the area of study of the functions of labor exchanges, attitude toward financial associations, economic value of such social grouping, and labor mobility among social groupings.

The study of the peasant and their societies in Korean anthropology belongs to another separate area: it deals with social character and social activities of the peasant, and further, information networks among them, and various problems of tenant farmer. Recent studies on the peasant are concerned with the change of their attitude and value, due to the social change.

With the studies of the peasant, interests in the urban area has been greatly increased in the recent anthropological study in Korea. Researcher's concerns turn continuously towards family and kinship structure in residential area, populace distribution and life mode of the middle class. Researches on slum area, urbanization, laborer's life on street corner and market belong to entirely new areas in the anthropological study. There are also a few researches on small towns.

One interesting area of the study in social anthropology was on the shifting cultivation in Korea. Most of the researches in this area are ethnographical descriptions of shifting cultivators in mountainous area, but there are some interesting suggestions worth noticing for the future research of shifting cultivation in East Asia.

Folk Customs

Folk customs in this paper deals with rites of passage, annual customs, folk play and game, folk dance and folk drama. As social behavior and social activities are so, the folk customs are included in ethnographical records of village communities. But here we will discuss only the articles and books which mention the folk customs. The results of the study practiced on this subject for the last 35 years are showed in the following tabel 2.

Table 2

Studies on the subject of the folk customs

Subject area	Articles	Books
Rites of passage	48	2
Annual customs	14	7
Folk game and play	20	4
Dance and drama	28	19

According to this table, rites of passage appear as the most popular topic in the research area of folk customs. In fact, at any places, it has been regarded as important area of anthropological studies but there are some special reasons for having dominant interests in this area in Korea. In the past, Yi dynasty (1392-1910) adopted Confucianism as the state religion and put special emphasis on observing the four decorum or rites as the state law. If one did not observe the regulation of four rites, he was punished by criminal law of Yi dynasty. Not only from the stand point of the state law but also from the historical event the four rites were important issues in the past. There were the big disputes about four rites throughout the Yi dynasty, especially about mourning period of the queen. Because of the disputes of rites, every famous scholars in the past wrote books about these rites.

The four rites in the Yi dynasty is slightly different from the rites of passage in anthropological sense. Rites of passage which the anthropologists have studied include rite of birth, initiation, marriage and funeral. But the four rites in the Yi dynasty include rites on the occasion of initiation, marriage, funeral and ancestor worship. This paper will comment on all the materials which deal with rites of passage in anthropological as well as traditional standpoint.

Most of the researches in this area are included in the ethnographical works dealing with local customs or interesting customs connected with child birth and marriage. There are very few works dealing with initiation ceremony because today this custom disappeared. Most of the researches on child birth are connected with the folk beliefs such as mountain-god worship or rock worship for pregnancy. Antenatal training is also an interesting topic of the research.

While the studies of the rites of child birth and marriage were carried out in the process of ethnographical data collection, those of the rites of funeral and ancestor worship tended toward historical studies. The basic issues of the disputes about the four rites in the past are analyzed from the standpoint of the social development. There were also several articles comparing the four rites of Korea with original ones of China. And a great number of scholars from different schools insisted on the proper process of interesting topics in this area which is found in the multiple burial custom which is still carried out on remote small islands off the south and southwestern coasts of Korean peninsula. Multiple burial custom is also known as bone washing burial and considered as common aspects of the special culture of Pacific islands or circum-Pacific culture stream. Since Korean peninsula has four distinct seasons and her basic economy has been based on agriculture, naturally annual customs have been well developed as in the other agricultural societies. The achievement of research in this area can be divided into two dimensions as in the other area; ethnographical research and historical study. Ethnographical researches dealt with local customs or general information of one special holiday, such as New Year's Day, May 5th, July 7th, August 15th, September 9th by lunar calendar.

Most of the books which deal with annual customs are characterized by the historical study through the reference of books written about anuual customs in the past. Among 7 books of this topic, 5 books belong to the latter category. There are few articles which investigate the relations of the annual customs with the religious rites or folk belief.

The area of folk game and play includes mass games in the past such as wrestling, swing, tug of war etc.

Most of the researches on this topic consist of presentations of ethnographical data in rural areas. A few achievements has been made on the study of the traditional gamblings and child games, but few deal with the folk game in the past such as ball-kicking and ball-striking, and no one deals with the folk games involved in rice cultivation. The area of folk dance and drama covers the different kinds of folk theater and mask dance. Besides these kinds of folk dance, folk theater, there are different kinds of religious dances and court dances with court music. These religious dance and court music are performed still now during the Confucian rituals and are being taught in high schools for traditional music. But these classical music and dance are excluded here because they are not carried out by common people in the past as well as at the present.

Folk dances are conducted in the process of performing folk theater or mask dances. The well-known folk theaters are the puppet theater and folk theater troops, called "Namsadang". We can find a few researches made on these puppet theater and folk theater troops, but most of them are included in ethnographical reports. The most important and well developed area is the mask dance drama. More than two-thirds of researches in this mask dance drama are also investigated in the ethnographical reports of mask dances in different regions. However, there are several articles which are explaining mask dance drama in relation to literature, religions. Surely the field of origin of dance, structure of mask dances, functions of dances force us to pay our attention to them, increasing our interests in comic conflict in the mask dance drama or an element of Oedipus complex in mask dance. There were once hard debates on the origin of mask dance drama in Korea. Even though the debate was over, the interest of historical aproach is main area of research in this study.

Material Culture

Material culture includes clothing, dietary life, architecture, traditional arts and crafts, and folk paintings. Some works from sister sciences such as architecture, dietetics or home economics are included in this area side by side with those of anthropologists. The following table 3 is quantitative tabulation of works on material culture.

Table 3
Studies on material culture

Subject area	Articles	Books
Clothing	24	9
Dietary life	15	5
Architecture	31	5
Arts and crafts	6	11
Folk painting	2	5

Even though clothing, dietary life and housing are important area in daily life, the material culture is one of the less studied areas of anthropological study. In the subject of clothing, there are only a few folklorists who can not be called as specialists.

Researches on the subject of clothing could be divided into two areas;

one is related to the historical works and the other present habits. More than two thirds of researches are connected with historical study. Especially in this area there are strong tendency of historical approaches. Some scholars concern the clothings in 3 kingdom's period; those of Shilla, those of people and aristocracy in Koryo period, the clothings of earlier, middle and later period of Yi dynasty. There are some interesting topics such as the study of prehistorical clothing as indicators of cultural influences of Korea upon Japan, and the study of different style and colors of clothings as symbols of class difference in Yi dynasty. A study on different hats in the past began with collecting them.

Researches on habits of clothings deal with several topics such as woman's dresses in rural area, changing types of upper garment, ceremonial dresses in marriage and funeral, needleworks for Korean clothing and personal ornaments. Most of researches in this area are included in ethnographical reports.

Compared to that of clothing, the study of dietary life obtains poorer results. There are two books which deal with history of Korean dishes and dietary life. Another works through historical approaches are on the diffusions of potatoes in Korea, method of making Korean soy sauce, and tea ceremony in the past.

The other direction of the study on the dietary life deals with food habits or food customs in rural areas, showing in the main dishes and side dishes of the seasons, and special dishes in ceremonial table such as marriage, funeral rites and ritual service for ancestor worship.

Another area of research is connected with dietetics. There are researches on protein of Korean foods, vitamin C in bean sprouts and nutritional content of traditional pickled young radishes.

Most articles of material culture concentrate on the architecture. Architects and anthropologists have cooperated well in this area because the architects also desired to find out the basic type or original form of Korean architecture. There are about 8 works dealing with the history of architecture or house style. A few works concern the house types in prehistorical period. There are a few articles which deal with the origin of "Ondol", under-floor heating system of room.

Most of works in architecture are ethnographical reports of large house of higher officials in different regions and communal houses of common people in different areas. For example, there are reports of characteristic house type in mountainous areas or fishing villages, different roof styles according to the local differences. Very few articles deal with the using of spaces in architectural design.

From earlier times the traditional art and craft has been well known to foreign people. Researches in this area are still at the ethnographical level as in the other areas of material culture. Several special technologies, such as making Korean hat, brassware, pipe, chest, furniture, fan, embroidery, etc., have been reported. As a part of national policy of preserving traditional art and craft, the holders of technology have been designated as national treasure, and most of the existing studies are concerned about the works of such people. One important area in material culture is farming tools which are reported as a part of village life.

Folk painting has become popular topic of amateur folklorists these days and there are some publications on this topic. I hope that it will be dealt by scholars in near future.

Oral Tradition

Many anthropologists have majored in Korean language and literature in their training, producing already many works on this oral tradition. Oral tradition in Korean case includes mythology, folktales, riddle and proverb, folk song and folk music. Table 4 is result of studies in this area.

Table 4
Studies on oral tradition

Subject area	Articles	Books
Mythology	14	3
Folktale	57	45
Riddle and proverb	5	14
Folk song	44	20
Folk music	21	13

The studies of mythology deal with the myths of founding fathers of ancient dynasties such as Old Cho-Sun or Shilla. Most of the studies are ethnographical reports and interpretations related to cultural origin. However, there are a few studies which deal with the Korean mythology in comparison with Japanese or concern migrations of between the two countries and the interrelations between those cultures in earlier period.

The richest production in oral tradition has been achieved in folk tales. There are 45 books on this area besides many articles. The achievement in this area could be divided into also three dimensions like the other areas of oral tradition, ethnographical, historical, and theoretical ones. More than three fourths of existing works are ethnographical data collections, which can be divided into two branches, regional collections and subjective ones. Most of the studied regions were administrative or political centers of earlier period such as the capital of Shilla kingdom, that of Baek-je. Province and sub-provinces are also the boundary of folk tale collections. Items, such as dragon, bird, swan, white horse, culture hero, etc., were topics of tales. Some interesting topics such as rebirth motive, dream, humour, spirit, house god are important subjects of studies. In this case, there are some interpretations of the origin and diffusion of stories.

There are a few historical studies of folk tales which deal with the historical records as data for research. Such studies on folk tales are concerned with the relationship of folk tales to novels or the other genres of literature. Some studies compare the Korean folk tales with Chinese and Japanese ones. Theoretical studies of folk tales are concerned with the structure of tales especially from the standpoint of culture pattern.

The studies of riddle and proverb have been published mainly in books as a dictionary form and most of them are ethnographical collections without regional considerations. A few collections are dealing with the special topics such as proverbs on taboo, special behavior, etc. Even though there are many publications on folk songs, most of them are ethnographical data collections of folk songs in different regions, for example, folk songs of Che-ju Island and those of northern province and southern part of the Korean peninsula, or mountainous areas. Topical collections are concerned with such subjects as lady's song, song for family life, song on the mother, marriage and stone, and one sung in field.

One of the interesting topics for historical studies is the famous folk song "Arirang". Some articles deal with the origin and diffusion and different types of Arirang song. Theoretical studies deal the songs in connection with folk tales and musical instruments, as reflections of the national character or values of folk people, or workers.

In folk music there are three areas for research: Korean minstrel epic, shaman song, and farmer's band music. Earlier studies of folk music were collections of texts of songs but recent studies translated the rhythm of different songs into musical note.

Religions

Religion has been one of the important areas for anthropological study. Especially Korean and foreign scholars have paid attention to Korean shamanism. In the study of Korean religion, the studies of Buddhism, Confucianism and Christianity should be included and there are many valuable articles and books on these areas, but this paper excludes Buddhism, Confucianism and Christianity because there are no appreciable works from the anthropological point of view. Here then folk beliefs, village god worship, shamanism and newly-rising religions are included. Table 5 is statistics of achievements in this area.

Table 5
Studies on religions

Subject area	Articles	Books
Folk beliefs	37	3
Village god	38	2
Shamanism	85	16
Newly-rising religion	14	3

Folk beliefs include worship of natural gods such as wind god, water god and house god. The works on this subject could be divided into three kinds; historical, ethnographical, and theoretical ones.

The historical studies of folk beliefs deal with the origin and diffusions of special topics such as totemism, cereal god worship, prayer for rain, white-horse worship, worship of well and spring, etc. There are also a few works which concern the history of religions in Korea.

Most of the works on folk beliefs are ethnographical data. The popular topics in this area are child-birth god, farming god, house god, rock worship, prayer for rain, stories about ghost, phalicism, etc. Fortunetelling and geomancy are also important topics of folk beliefs.

Theoretical studies of folk beliefs deal with the belief behavior or objects of belief in consideration of philosophy, mythology, psychology, psychiatry and morality of people.

Village-god worship was a regular annual events of villages in the past. Each village has village-god, pole-god or other gods. In some villages the ritual service was carried out by ceremony masters who had been selected by villagers or shaman. After the ritual service there were festivals accompanied by farmer's band music.

Most of the researches in village-god worships are ethnographical reports on villages. Some deal with that of fishing villages in islands and some that of mountainous areas. There are also some articles which deal with pole god and bamboo pole god which are considered as symbol of village god in southern part of the Korean peninsula.

The ritual service for village god by shaman is considered as an old style of village-god worship. There are some reports and discussions on old type of village-god worship for community life of village community.

As table 5 shows, shamanism is the most popular topics in anthropological studies in Korea. Though established religions such as Buddhism, Confucianism and Christianity influenced on religious life and belief system of Korean people, they are of foreign origin and thus had some limits in religious influences. However, shamanism is considered the oldest religion and indigenous belief of Korean people. The shaman's songs which are continuously recited a few days without break include myths and legends of people, happy and sorrowful stories of humble people. Not only the shaman's songs but shaman's rituals of dancing are important in studying folk dance and folk belief.

Studies of shamanism could be divided into 6 areas. There are few works of shamanism from the historical point of view. Today shaman belongs to the lower class in social strata, but in earlier times, the shaman was honored and even the sister of king was shaman. The crown of Shilla king is considered the imitation of shaman's head decoration. Some studies bear on shamansitic ritual performance in royal court.

One area of shamanism is about shaman shrines and shaman god or deities. About 12 articles deal with this subject. Shaman shrines have different types in accordance with the local difference. Usually there are 12 deities of shamanism, but more than 200 deities have been discovered in Korea as the result of an analysis into shaman's songs. The classification of shaman gods is main topic in this area.

Less than 10 articles deal with the shaman itself. Typical shaman in Korea is woman. There are some male shamans, but they wear lady's costumes when performing shamanistic rituals. The most important element for becoming shaman is the initiation primarily after critical illness and the essence of shamanistic rituals is the ecstacy. From this criterion there are different opinions on Korean shaman, as one excludes those without ecstacy from shaman in southern part of Korean peninsula, while the other includes them in the category of shaman. There are some interesting works which deal with family organization, psychological characters and secret languages of shamans.

About 30 works belong to the ethnographical data of shamanistic rituals in different regions of different types. From these data we learn three types of shamanistic rituals, one for good luck of family, one against illness, and one for the spirit of the dead. There are regional differences as there exist northwestern, northeastern, southeastern, southwestern and middle part of Korean peninsula. Shamanistic rituals in Che-ju Island have special characteristics and there are about 10 reports about them.

More than 10 works deal with shaman's songs. All of these researches are on texts of songs. As mentioned already, there are countless original data on myths, legends, voices of people, values, concepts of future life, daily life, etc. Namely all possible lives of peoples are included in shaman's songs, so that texts of shaman's songs themselves are important data for anthropologists.

Theoretical studies of shamanism deal with shamanism in consideration of psychiatric heal of mental illness, philosophy, folk belief, folk drama, ancient novel, mythology, material culture, funeral and other religions.

Only in this area of shamanism there are 7 articles which review the studies of shamanism in Korea. That means there has been many discussions and criteria on the studies of shamanism. Important topics of discussion are origin of Korean shamanism, connection between Korean shamanism and those of Siberia and Southeast Asia, and the definition of Korean shaman as mentioned already. Some say that Korean shamanism belongs to the Siberian shamanism but some oppose to this and say it is so peculiar that it is not shamanism in Eliade's definition. Especially the two types of shamanism in the Korean peninsula, the northern type and the southern one, brought many discussions on the origin of Korean shamanism. It is also connected with the definition of shaman whether shaman should be limited to the person who passed initiation after special illness. Structure of shaman rituals is one of the items of debate. The more researches and studies are done, the more spaces of debate remain in Korean shamanism.

Newly-rising religion is one of interesting topics for anthropological research. There are more than 300 kinds of newly-rising religions, including Chon-do-kyo already recognized as established religion in Korea, and Moonism, now a world wide religion. Most of researches in such religions are currently ethnographical data explaining their history, theory, orgarnizations and influences. Recent studies of the newly-rising religions have concentrated on one religion called Chung-san-kyo.

Conclusion

For more than 30 years, since the end of the World War II, Korean anthropologists in wider sense have achieved steady progress in various areas of anthropology as mentioned above. Rendering a total evaluation, the research activities have been so far characterized by ethnographical data collection, and still it is main stream of anthropological studies in many subject areas.

When the ethnographical data are accumulated in subject areas there appears a tendency of historical studies even though there are some differences according to the subject itself, and historical data.

The next stage is theoretical approach building structural models of diffusion patterns. For example, there are some works of diffusion patterns in oral tradition. The most fruitful areas are kinship system and shamanism. Several issues and discussions about shamanistic ecstacy, origin of Korean shamanism and basic structure of shamanistic rituals are not only the problems but also the achievements of studies of shamanism in Korea.

One of important achievements in Korean anthropology is ethnohistorical studies of kinship. Ethnohistorical studies in this case mean the combination of two fields or two data into one subject. For example, the peculiar customs of inheritance of remote islands or mountainous areas considered abnormal type of inheritance become main issues of research and they are useful in reconstructing inheritance pattern in earlier period in the matching with historical data. The ethnohistorical method is different from the unilineal history of one subject.

Besides the general evaluation of anthropological studies, three more areas should be added, which have been developed very recently. One of new area or direction of study is application of new anthropological theories in research. For example, structuralism in kinship and religion, symbolism in religions and rites of passage, urban anthropology in urban studies, culture ecology in rural studies, linguistic anthropology, medical anthropology are being used.

The other area or direction of study is model building for Korean culture pattern or ethos. Some works are based on philosophical anthropology using inductive method which has been formed from the model of Yin and Yang theory. There is another direction which is based also on dualistic principle but emphasizes cultural mechanism dealing with conflict and harmony in cultural pattern based on psychological anthropology. It is characterized by deductive method.

Another area of studies is research in foreign countries. There are some studies on Taiwan aborigines, and Ryukyu culture. The studies of Korean minority in Japan and the United States also belong to this category.

References

Books in Korean

Chang, Dok-Soon
    1970 *Study of the Korean Oral Literature.* Seoul: Seoul National University Press.
Chang, Dok-Soon et al.
    1971 *Introduction to Oral Literature.* Seoul: Il-cho-kak.
Cho, Dong-Il
    1980 *The World of Folk Tales.* Seoul: Sae-mun-sa
Choi, Chung-yo & Su, Dae-Suk
    1974 *Shaman Song in East Coast.* Seoul: Hyong-sul Press.
Choi, Gil-Sung
    1978 *A Study of the Korean Shamanism.* Seoul: Asia Mun-wha-sa
Choi, Jai-Seuk
    1966 *A Study of Korean Family.* Seoul: Min-jung-so-kwan
    1975 *Studies on Korean Rural Community.* Seoul: Il-ji-sa
    1979 *Kinship Organization in Che-ju Island.* Seoul: Il-ji-sa
Im, Dong-Gwon
    1961 *Korean Folk Songs.* Seoul: Min-jung-so-kwan
    1971 *The Studies on the Korean Folklore.* Seoul: Sun-myong-mun-wha-sa
    1975 *Korean Folk songs, 4 vols.* Seoul: Chip-mun-dang
Kang, Shin-Pyo
    1980 *Dan-san Society and Korean Imigrants.* Seoul: Korean Research Center.
Kim, Du-Hun.
    1969 *The Study of Korean Family System.* Seoul: Seoul National University Press.
Kim, Tae-Gon
  1971-80 *Korean Shaman Song, 4 vols.* Iri: Won-kwang University
Kim, Taek-Kyu
    1979 *Study of Lineage Village Structure.* Seoul: Il-cho-kak
Kim, Yol-Kyu
    1971 *Studies on Korean Folklore and Literature.* Seoul: Il-cho-kak
    1977 *Korean Myths.* Seoul: Il-cho-kak
    1977 *Studies on Korean Myth and Shamanism.* Seoul: Il-cho-kak
Ko, Sung-Je
    1977 *A Study of Urban Society in Yi Dynasty.* Seoul: Il-ji-sa
Lee, Du-Hyun
    1966 *A Study of the History of Korean Modern Drama.* Seoul: Seoul National
          Unversity Press.
    1973 *History of Korean Drama.* Seoul: Min-jung-so-kwan
    1979 *Korean Mask Dances.* Seoul: Il-ji-sa

Lee, Du-Hyun, Chang, Chu-Keun & Lee, Kwang-Kyu
    1978   *Introduction to Korean Folkore.* Seoul: Bo-sung-mun-hwa-sa
Lee, Kwang-Kyu
    1975   *The Structural Analysis of the Korean Family.* Seoul: Il-ji-sa
    1977   *A Historical Study of the Korean Family.* Seoul: Il-ji-sa.
Lee, Man-Gap
    1973   *The Social Structure of Korean Village and Its Changes.* Seoul: Seoul
          National University Press.
Pak, *Kye*-Hong
    1973   *The Study on the Korean Folklore* Seoul: Hyong-sul Press.
Roh, Chang-Sub, Kim, Chong-Suh & Hahn, Sang-Joon
    1965   *A Study of Three Developing Rural Communities.* Seoul: Ewha Women's
          University Press.
Ryu, Tong-Shik
    1975   *History and Structure of the Korean Shamanism* Seoul: Yeon-sei University
          Press.
Son, Chin-Tae
    1948   *Korean Myths, Legends and Folktales: A Cultural-Historical Study.* Seoul:
          Eul-yoo Publishing Co.
    1948   *A General History of Korean Nation.* Seoul: Eul-yoo Publishing Co.
    1948   *A Study of Korean Ethnic Culture.* Seoul: Eul-yoo Publishing Co.
Son, Chung-Muk
    1977   *A Study of Urban Society in Yi Dynasty.* Seoul: Il-ji-sa.
Song, Suk-Ha
    1962   *The Study of Korean Folklore.* Seoul: Il-sin-sa.
Su, Dae-Suk
    1980   *A Study of the Korean Shaman Song.* Seoul: Mun-hak-sa-sang-sa.
Sung, Ki-Sul
    1976   *A Study of the Korea Oral Tradition.* Seoul: Il-cho-kak.
Yang, Hwae-Su
    1967   *A Study on the Structure of the Korean Farming Village.* Seoul: Korea
          University Press.
Yim, Hi-Sup & Kang, Shin-Pyo(eds.)
    1980   *Korean Society.* Seoul: Min-um-sa.
Yun, Tae-Rim
    1977   *Character of the Korean People.* Seoul: Hyun-dae-kyo-yuk Press.

Books in English
Brandt, Vincent S. R.
    1971   *A Korean Village: Between Farm and Sea.* Cambridge: Harvard Uni-
          versity Press.

Han, Sang-Bok

    1977 *Korean Fishermen: Ecological Adaptation in Three Communities*. Seoul: Seoul National University Press.

Harvey, Young-Sook Kim

    1979 *Six Korean Women: The Socialization of Shamans*. St. Paul: West Publishing Co.

Joe, Wanne J.

    1972 *Traditional Korea, A Cultural History*. Seoul: Chung-ang University Press.

Kang, Shin-Pyo

    1978 *The East Asian Culture and Its Transformation in the West*. Seoul: American Studies Institute, Seoul National University

Lee, Mun-Woong

    1976 *Rural North Korean under Communism*. Houston: William Marsh Rice University.

McCann, David et al. (eds.)

    1979 *Studies on Korea in Transition*. Honolulu: The Center for Korean Studies.

Osgood, Cornelius

    1951 *The Koreans and Their Culture*. N. Y.: Ronald Press

Pak, Ki-Hyuk et al.

    1975 *The Changing Korean Village*. Seoul: Shin-hung Press.

Journals in Korean

Korean Cultural Anthropology, vol. 1-11, 1968-1979.
Anthropological Study, vol. 1-5, 1975-1979
Anthropological Research, vol. 1, 1980
The Korean Folkore, vol. 1-12, 1969-1980

Journals in English

Korea Journal, vol. 1, No. 1-, 1960-
Korean Studies, vol. 1-2, 1977
The Journal of Korean Studies, vol. 1, 1979
Social Science Journal, vol. 1-6, 1978-1979

Journals in French

Revue de Corée, vol. 1-46, 1968-1980

8   Thai Studies in Transition: A Report on Origins, Problems, and Trends[1]

SRISAKRA VALLIBHOTAMA

Introduction

Among Thai scholars who are Western-oriented in their education, studies and research on social and cultural aspects, or "Thai studies" as carried on by native scholars and researchers, has developed only about a decade ago. Before this, knowledge of Thai history and culture was a prerogative of two groups of people, the traditional elites and foreign scholars.

For the first group, interest in collecting and recording historical and cultural accounts began from the reign of King Mongkut (1851-68) when ranking princes and bureaucrats were associating with Europeans and Americans, acquiring concepts and framework for examining their own society and culture. However, most of their works would by no means qualify as research in the modern sense. Furthermore, many of them took the form of local and dynastic chronicles, such as *The Dynastic Chronicles of the Bangkok Era*[2] by Chao Pharaya Thipakarawongsa (1961).

During the reign of King Chulalongkorn (1868-1910), there were many scholars whose studies and activities laid a foundation for the modern study of the present day. For example, King Chulalongkorn wrote *The Royal Ceremonies of the Twelve Months*(1971) discussing ancient and contemporary royal rituals practised in Thailand and another book *The Memoir of Princess Narinthara Devi*, accompanied by his own analysis and criticism (King Chulalongkorn 1958). These two books provide a great deal of social and cultural data for the later Ayuthya and early Bangkok periods. Further, the king's *Travelling Records** (Ministry of Education 1969) have provided information on cultural aspects of various localities in his day. These diaries set an example for the princes and high-ranking officals to record and later publish what they had seen and studied during their offcial tours to the provinces.

Prince Damrong Rajanupab, a half-brother of King Chulalongkorn, who was appointed the Minister of Interior, distinguished himself as the "father of Thai history and archaeology." His long descriptive and analytical book *War between Thailand and Burma** (1958), chronicling the war between Thailand and Burma during the Ayuthya and Bangkok periods, is regarded as the best historical study of his time. Another book, *Origins of Buddhist monuments** (1960), is basic to the study of Thai art and architecture, and *Ancient Administration in Siam** (1958), explaining the ancient government, is still listed among reference books today. After his retirement from the government, the prince took up residence in Penang, where he exchanged extended correspondence with his half-brother Prince Naris on Thai culture and society. This correspondence was subsequently published as *Correspondence** (Damrong and Narisara 1962). Another scholar, Phraya Prachakit Korachak, studied the northern chronicles and wrote *History of the North** (1955), which is useful for the study of the history of Northern Thailand. Phraya Anuman Rajadhon, who took, the lead in studying the history of the Thai people, wrote *Indochina in the Ancient Times** (1954); but later he turned to ethnology, writing about rituals and cultural traditions of many parts of the country, and his works such as *Thai Customs** (Satien Koset 1972) and *Record of Knowledge** (Satien Koset 1959) are of great use for those who want to undertake ethnographical study in rural Thailand.

To promote studies on Thai culture and history and also to create an awareness of the cultural heritage of the nation, these traditional elites, particularly Prince Damrong, helped to establish the National Museum in 1874 to collect and display art object and other archaeological materials gathered from various localities of the country. The other institution that followed was the Vajirayan Library, established in 1905, which later developed into the National Library and the National Archives. In addition, the Boran Kadi Samosorn (Archaeological Association) was established in 1907 to promote archaeological studies and research extensively. Through these institutions, various historical and cultural documents have been compiled and published in large numbers such as *A Collection of Ancient Chronicles,** which consists of seventy-eight parts altogether (Fine Arts Department 1964). The officials who were in charge of these institution were mostly students and followers of Prince Damrong and his colleagues, so they served also to spread the works of their forbears. Through the tradition of publishing historical and archaeological books to be distributed on the cremation of one recently deceased, the National Library became an influential centre for cultural studies, and this consequently helped to produce pioneering scholars such as Prince Damrong and others as authorities, and raised the level of the institutions.

Anyone who opposed these authorities and did not study along their lines was regarded as unorthodox, and his publications might even be banned, as in the case of a series of books entitled *War between Vietnam and Thailand** of K. S. R. Kulab (1903) that related the event of war among Thailand, Laos, Cambodia, and Vietnam during the nineteenth century. As a result, scholars of the following generation chiefly distinguished themselves by reading ancient documents widely, memorizing and applying what had been done and studied by the traditional authorities. Unlike their forbears, they were armchair-oriented; many of them became university lecturers and heads of cultural and historical institutions, having much influence in the studies of the culture and history of the country. So the period after Prince Damrong was rather stagnant, and new studies and approaches were not popularly accepted if they happened to go against the works of former authorities. Together with a persisting value that required the young to be docile and follow without criticism in the footsteps of their forbears, students and scholars of former decades took a passive attitude towards their studies and thus allowed what had been put forward by the traditional authorities to be assumed to be correct. This is of course inconsistent with modern educational philosophy and the critical attiutde developed among scholars and students of the present generation, and eventually leads to conflict in terms of the objective, scope, method, and techniques of study.

The second group of scholars of Thai society and culture were foreigners who came to Thailand as diplomats, technical advisors, businessmen, visiting lecturers, and graduate students. Many of these people began their studies as early as the seventeenth century when the kingdom of Ayuthya was in contact with the Europeans. The Dutch offcials such as Jeremias van Vliet (1910) and the French diplomat De la Loubère (1969) produced a good record of the history, geography, economics, and politics of the Thai kingdom. During the Bangkok period from the nineteenth century onward, British officials like John Crawfurd (1830), Henry Burney (1971), and John Bowring (1969) presented to their government numerous accounts of Thai culture and society which remain today as valuable sources for Thai studies. Other foreigners who took up residences in Bangkok, notably McFarland and Bradley (1896) also had a part in studying, compiling, and publishing ancient documents. From the reign of King Chulalongkorn, the Thai government allowed several French scholars to conduct archaeological studies and surveys in various parts of the country, and among them was the epigraphist George Cœdès who was invited to undertake research and translation work on ancient inscriptions found in Thailand. Cœdès was so closely associated with Prince Damrong that he greatly influenced the Prince's thought and writing on Thai archaeology and history. There were close association and interaction between traditional Thai elites and foreign scholars; the former received new ideas, theoretical frameworks, and research methods from the latter. This is probably the reason why traditional scholars could carry on their studies effectively and consequently establish themselves as authorities in various aspects of Thai culture. Interaction between these two groups of scholars that shared common interests in studies and research consequently led to the establishment of the Siam Society as the centre for research and study of Thai culture and society. Research from this centre was published in English in *the Journal of the Siam Society,* and as such the benefit was withheld from the Thai students whose command of foreign language is so limited.

Comparing modern standards of scholarship of the traditional Thai elites and foreign scholars, there was of course some disparity. The foreigners were academically trained, having scientific approaches and anthropological thinking in their studies which were dynamic and led to new discoveries and proposals. On the other hand, traditional Thai scholars clung to old theories and techniques, becoming very dogmatic and rather static. This is clearly evident from their writing on Thai history, many of which still adhered to racist concepts such as the struggle of the Thai race, nationalistic ideas to the effect that Thailand used to be a great nation, etc. So when their followers accepted these assumptions of their teachers as accurate and most reliable, further studies and research became limited and stagnant in many respects. Thai students of former decades seemed to take courses in culture and history as subjects to meet the requirements of the university curriculum without any interest in understanding social behaviour and the cultural values of contemporary society.

The concept of Thai studies is something new among the Thai and not closely connected with any study in culture and history of former generations. Instead, this concept seems to be linked with the Southeast Asian studies programmes initiated by American and European universities after the Second World War (Fifield 1976). Particularly, American scholars and researchers from universities like Yale, Cornell, Michigan, Hawaii, and Northern Illinois came in to carry on intensive and extensive field studies in Thailand many years before 1960 and published several stimulating books and monographs such as Blanchard's *Thailand: Its People, Its Society, Its Culture* (1957), Konrad Kingshill's *Ku Daeng: The Red Tomb* (1960), John E. de Young's *Village Life in Modern Thailand* (1963), Herbert P. Phillips' *Thai Peasant Personality* (1966), and Kaufman's *Bangkhand* (1960). These books appeared in several libraries, particularly in universities like Thammasat and Chulalongkorn. But still, interest in such studies was no widespread. Interest seemed to be confined to lecturers and students of certain disciplines, notably public administration and political science, which were oriented toward interdisciplinary approaches.

Also with the National Development Programme initiated during the term of office of Field Marshal Sarit Thanarat (1959-63), information and data on Thai society and culture became prerequisite for the planning and implementation of government programmes. New institutions were set up to promote studies and research in the field of social sciences such as the National Research Council, the National Economic Development Council, and the Institute of Public Administration. Foreign scholars were invited both as advisors and researchers to conduct field studies in various regions of the country, and many Thai students and researchers worked with them as research assistants.

As time went on, interest in social scientific study and research became widespread in the Thai universities. Sociology and anthropology were taught either as main courses or supplementary subjects. Furthermore, students and lecturers received government funds and support to study abroad, and of most importance, foreign aid was extended to Thai universities through the Southeast Asian studies centres of many universities in America and Europe such as Cornell, Hawaii, Michigan, Northern Illinois, and London universities. As a result, there were increasing numbers of the Thai social scientists both at the Ph. D. and M. A. levels to teach and work in the universities and other research institution. The period from 1966 saw a full consciousness among Thai scholars and students in the studies and interest in social and cultural aspects of their own country.

Catching up with such a growth of interest was the development of many institutions concerned. In the first place was the Social Science Association of Thailand which issued the quarterly journal —— *The Social Science Review* —— promoting the publication of articles and research papers written by Thai and foreign scholars. To the Thai, the publication of this journal marked a turning point in the history of education since it became the mouthpiece for Western-oriented Thai scholars. Various articles poured in from different directions within and without the country and departed completly from the previous trend of study, which was marked by nationalistic overtones. Other institutions that followed were the Institute of Asian Studies, Faculty of Political Sciences, Chulalongkorn University, The Lan Na Thai Research Centre, which is now attached to the Faculty of Social Sciences, Chiengmai University, and recently, the Institute of Thai Studies, Thammasat University. Apart from these institutions, there were also cultural studies programmes organized either by a team of lecturers or student clubs at the faculty or departmental level in many universities, both in Bangkok and the provinces. Such programmes, in some universities, later developed into voluntary programmes for students to study and work in rural areas.

As interest in Thai studies grew, there were several journals issued occasionally and monthly to publish the works of scholars both from within and without the university. The *Sam Thaharn,* sponsored by a government oil enterprise, and the *Cho Fa,* founded by Wat Maha Dhat, were two such publications. Recent journals of considerable value are the *Thammasat University Journal* which promotes a wider range of studies in the fields of social sciences, *The Archaeology,* the journal of the Faculty of Archaeology, Silpakorn University, and the *Muang Boran Journal* that promotes the studies on history, art, and culture. It seems that with growing concern for the development of the nation, interest in and study of social and cultural aspects of Thai society are no longer a prerogative of the traditional elites and scholars but are now spreading to the middle class who form a new intellectual group in the country. However, Thai studies as carried on among the Thai seem to be limited, that is, they are rather scattered and rarley written in English because of language problems and above all are not theoretically and methodologically sound. Judging in terms of historical backgroud, cultural values, and the social and political situation of the present day, most studies and research on social and cultural aspects of the country are connected with three major areas of study, namely, archaeology, history, and anthropology. Following is an outline of current problems and trends in each.

Archaeology

In a country like Thailand which abounds with ancient monuments and has a relatively homogeneous culture forming a highly integrated society, archaeology contributes to interest and pride in the nation's former glories. The establishment of the National Museum, Library, and the Boran Kadi Samosorn (Archaeology Association) which later developed into the Fine Arts Department in charge of the art and culture of the country, and finally the establishment of the Faculty of Archaeology in Silpakorn University to produce archaeology graduates and to conduct archaeological research and studies, shows the great concern of the government. However, archaeology as understood by the Thai of the former generations and many of the present generation is not archaeology in its accepted sense but rather *classical* archaeology which is more connected with the study of ancient civilization. Later, with the growing interest in prehistory brought about by foreign archaeologists and scholars, a split in the study of Thai archaeology into so-called archaeology of the prehistoric period and that of the historical period occurred. There is a disparity in scope of study and fieldwork methodology between these two "archaeologies." Prehistoric archaeology developed in association with foreign archaeologists who bring new theories and techniques and is far advanced. This is reflected in its use of systematic surveys, test excavation, stratigraphic digging and analysis of pottery sequences, and scientific dating techniques such as radio-carbon thermoluminescence, etc.

The archaeology of the historical period still maintains an art-historical approach developed by former French scholars like Cœdès (1928) and Dupont (1959), from the time of Prince Damrong. Such study is based on typological and style analysis of architectural monuments and art objects to determine their dates, cultural developments, and contacts and eventually leads to the reconstruction of cultural and political history (Cœdès 1968). However, the gap between the two archaeologies was partially bridged recently when a team of American archaeologists from the University of Pennsylvania excavated an ancient city of Chan Sen (Bronson n.d.) in the province of Nakhon Sawan. This resulted in the use of stratigraphic excavations and pottery sequence analysis in many historical sites such as the excavation of a Hindu shrine at Ayuthya by the Faculty of Archaeology, Silpakorn University, in 1969 (Maleipan 1969).

Concerning progress in archaeology in Thailand, one can state that it is proceeding well in the field of prehistory as Thailand is probably one of the most interesting prehistoric areas of Southeast Asia. Paleolithic tools were found and identified from 1932 (Sarasin 1933), and extensive surveys and intensive excavations of Mesolithic and Neolithic sites were carried out by a team of Thai-Danish archaeologists during 1962-63 (Chin 1969). The results of these excavations were published and distributed widely by both Thai scholars and foreign archaeologists (Saengwichien 1966). The excavation at a Metal Age site in the vicinity of the Artillery Center at Lop Buri by the Fine Arts Department (1964) has unearthed bronze and glass materials which are contemporary with those of the Dongson culture in Vietnam. Of even greater interest is the archaeological salvage programme in Northeastern Thailand started by the American archaeologists from the University of Hawaii in 1963 (Solheim 1966). The purpose is to conduct surveys and excavations in the areas to be flooded after the completion of irrigation dams which are to be constructed in connection with the Mekhong Valley Project of the United Nations. Many archaeologists from abroad came to take part in the fieldwork programme in collaboration with Thai archaeology officials from the Fine Arts Department and students from Silpakorn University. Their excavations unearthed some interesting sites of early bronze working in Southeast Asia such as the excavation at Non Nok Tha (Bayard 1971). Further, an American archaeologist, Gorman, has excavated a Paleolithic site in Northwest of Thailand and claimed that the earliest food producing people probably developed in this country, because rice grains of domestic origin are found dating back 10,000 years ago (Gorman, 1971). Although these proposals are perhaps premature, they are of course very stimulating.

Working with foreign archaeologists has increased the fieldwork experience and broadened the perspective of Thai archaeologists. They are able to conduct archaeological surveys and excavations of their own with confidence. As a result, excavation of the prehistoric site at Ban Chieng in the province of Udorn Thani was first started by Thai archaeologists from the Fine Arts Department (Kuakun 1975). Their work revealed a sequence of cultural materials ranging from the Neolithic, Bronze, and Iron Periods to the recent past. With the discovery in large numbers of bronze materials, stone and glass beads and ornaments, and painted pottery of high artistic value, Ban Chieng becomes a focus of interest for many people from within and without the country, ranging archaeologists and historians to antique collector. Interest in the study of Ban Chieng is also shared by lecturers and students from the Faculty of Archaeology, Silpakorn University, and the Department of Sociology and Anthropology, Thammasat University who carried on fieldwork studies at the village of Ban Chieng, resulting in both archaeological reports on the excavations and ethnographical accounts of Ban Chieng society of the present day. However, at present archaeological study at Ban Chieng has reached an integrative programme since the Fine Arts Department and the University of Pennsylvania cooperate to conduct a long-term research project in this site and other areas. Excavation and laboratory works are in progress both at Ban Chieng and in America, and a date of 3,600 B.C. for some objects, the earliest bronze development in the world, has been confirmed (Charoenwongsa 1976).

Another prehistoric site of equal interest is Ban Don Ta Petch in Amphur Phnom Tuan, Karnchanaburi, which has recently been excavated by the Fine Arts Department. Large amounts of bronze and iron objects of advanced technology and of high artistic quality have been recovered; particularly, bronze works cast and decorated with incised designs and figures of women and animals. Other objects such as beads of glass and stone, many of which show similar shapes and patterns to those found in India and the Middle East, have also been found (Chin 1976). Apart from archaeological excavations, progress in studies of prehistoric paintings and engravings has been achieved also. Archaeology officials from the Fine Arts Department in the past discovered geometrical patterns, animal and human figures painted or engraved in certain caves in the central, south, and northeast parts of the country. Particularly in the Northeast, figures of human hands and scroll designs were found in many localities in the provinces of Nakhon Phnom and Kalasin (Saengwichien 1974). In addition, the Faculty of Archaeology, Silpakorn University has recently discovered a number of rock paintings in the Phu Pan Range in Amphur Ban

Phu, Udorn Thani. These show a variety of patterns of geometrical designs and figures of men and animals (Karnchanakom 1969).

In reviewing progress in the field of historical archaeology, there is a difference from prehistoric archaeology in that the scope of interest is not global but rather confined to Thailand, or in some cases, extended to a regional area like Southeast Asia. However, it seems to mobilize more people inside the country to participate in these studies, such as scholars and researchers from other fields notably history, anthropology, architecture, and political science, and below the academic level, there are also other individuals such as learned monks and local scholars. The Fine Arts Department has done considerable work in survey, excavation, and restoration of archaeolgical monuments in various areas, but unfortunately, most of their report and studies have not yet been published. Distinguished reports that have been published recently are surveys and excavations of ancient monuments in the Northeast (1960 and 1967), of the ancient towns of Muang Bon, Nakhon Sawan (1965), and Muang U Thong, Supanburi (1966). These reports deal with the periods from the seventh to the twelfth century which of course contain data for the study of society and culture before the foundation of the kingdoms of Sukhothai and Ayuthya. Other reports that have just come out are those of the excavations and restorations of ancient monuments in Sukhothai, Kampaeng Petch, and Sri Satchanalai (1969) which deal with the kingdom of Sukhothai; and the excavation of Phra Dhat Phnom, one of the most sacred shrines in the Northeast, which collapsed in 1975. Valuable documents such as inscriptions on the gold and silver leaves telling the social events during the early eighteenth century in the Northeast (Chiachanpongsa 1976) were recovered. Excavation in progress at Prasat Muang Singha, Karnchanaburi, which is one of the historical sites during the thirteenth century (Fine Art Department 1977), reflects technical advancement on the part of the Fine Arts Department.

Turning to the Faculty of Archaeology, Silpakorn University, it has also made a considerable contribution to new discoveries of historical sites. From 1965 onward there have been large-scale extensive surveys in different parts of the country by teams of lecturers and students making aerial photographs to map out ancient earthworks, such as old cities and towns, roads, and water reservoirs. Reports of these surveys have been published in the journal of the Faculty of Archaeology, *Cho Fa Journal,* etc. Results of these surveys stimulate archaeology lecturers and officials more and more to pay attention to earthworks instead of focusing on religious monuments like stupas and temples alone. Outstanding excavations of ancient towns by the Faculty of Archaeology have been conducted at Sab Champa, Lop Buri, revealing a sequence of occupation from the late Neolithic Period to the Dvaravati Period of around the seventh century. At the moment, another excavation is in progress at the ancient city of Indra Buri; it is so far unearthing living floors, bases of stupas, and cultural materials of considerable numbers.

In addition, the Fine Arts Department and the Faculty of Archaeology, Silpakorn University and scholars from related fields have shared the contribution. The studies of Buddhist folk tales depicted in stucco reliefs at the base of a Dvaravati stupa in Nakhon Pathom, in the Khao Ngu caves in Rajburi, and also the study of the Jataka stories depicted on upright stones found in many localities in the Northeast, by Piriya Krairiksh (1974), all present a new trend of development. These studies go beyond the boundary of art styles and dating to the explanation of cultural events and contact among Thailand, Burma, and Cambodia prior to the eleventh century. In Northern Thailand, and archaeological survey has been conducted by researchers for the Department of Anthropology and Sociology Chiengmai University, the result of which is the discovery of a group of ancient cities and towns of the old kingdom of Haripunjaya (Vallibhotama 1974). Further new methods and techniques have been invented to analyse the architectural styles and dating of archaeological monuments shown in such works as "The Study of Structure and Brick-Laying of Ancient Monument" by Anuwit Charoensupkul (1974). Apparently there are some disagreements and conflicts between the traditional scholars who claim to be archaeologists and amateur archaeologists who come from other fields. But as far as the present situation is concerned, historical archaeology is becoming an interdisciplinary subject as more and more people from other fields of study become involved.

Recently, with the discoveries of sunken ships in the Gulf of Siam which yielded a large quantity of glazed pottery of Sukhothai, China, and Vietam, many Thai archaeologists have begun to study underwater archaeology. At the moment, the Fine Arts Department and Silpakorn University are considering teaching underwater archaeology.

History

Interest in the study of Thai history is as old as that of archaeology, and it is hard to separate the two since they share the same founding father, Prince Damrong Rajanupab. The difference between Thai history and historical archaeology, as it is conceived by traditional scholars, is only that history deals with data and evidence proved accurate and reliable by archaeologists, and that any reconstructions which are based on controversial accounts and information fall not within history but within archaeology. Thai history became a subject of study in the university and college long before archaeology, but as the university system in the past decade was highly specialized at the first degree level, this subject of study seemed to be confined to the Faculty of Arts, Chulalongkorn University. The study of Thai history there developed along the lines laid down by Prince Damrong, so consequently, most history teachers who graduated from this faculty and work in other institutions both at the university and high school levels have limited their teaching to (1) the origins and the movements of the Thai race prior to the establishment of the kingdom of Sukhothai in the thirteenth century and (2) the historical accounts of the royal dynasties, emphasizing the deeds of the kings and great men.

The reconstruction of the history of the Thai race relies on data from linguistic accounts and materials collected by foreign missionaries and ethnologists. They proposed the existence of Thai states and kingdoms outside Thailand such as the kingdom of Nan Chao in Yunan Province of Southern China, but at the same time excluded the original people and kingdoms existing in the present-day Thai territory before the kingdom of Sukhothai by classifying them as the Mon and the Khmer, the history of which are treated in courses on Southeast Asian history. Further, such an approach is motivated by racism and nationalism and also adopts an approach inspired by ethnocentric feelings among the Thai of the Central Plain, who regard those who set up the kingdom of Sukhothai as the direct line of Thai ancestors. Other contemporary kingdoms such as Lan Na to the North and Lan Chang to the Northeast which formed by other Thai speaking groups are classified as the Lao; they have not been considered legitimate subjects of study until the present decade.

As for the trend to study the history of the royal dynasties, the reason

behind this is that knowlege of Thai history from the Sukhothai to Bangkok periods is mainly based on sources and materials from the dynastic
chronicles, inscriptions, and official notes, and this seems to be congruent
with the "great man" theory of history which was widely accepted at that
time. Study along this line persists and is supported by the government.

Two committees were set up in the term of office of Field Marshal
Sarit Thanarat to be responsible for the writing of the national history and
revising and publishing valuable historical and cultural accounts of the
country. The first is the Committee for Revising Thai History and the latter
the Committee for Publishing Historical, Cultural, and Archaeological
Documents. The committee members are recruited from among retired
experts, university lecturers, and officials from the Fine Arts Department
and other institutions concerned. The works of the former committee,
published in its journal, *Thalaeng Ngan Prawatisat Ekasan Boran Kadi*
[Report on History Records and Archaeology], are still oriented towards
dynastic history such as history of Ayuthya (Sayamanonda 1967) and
history of Bangkok (Kasemsri and Wimon Pongsapipat 1967). There are
also other articles such as a translation of history of Southeast Asia before
the thirteenth century (Diskul 1967), some proposals and speculations on
the development of the Thai states during the tenth century (Sukhapanich
1967), etc. In contrast to the works of the former committee, the Committee of Publishing Historical, Cultural, and Archaeological Documents has
more to contribute to Thai studies since it serves to revise, compile, and
publish some rare and valuable documents such as a series of inscriptions
found in Thailand, Cambodia, and Burma (The Office of the Prime Minister 1965, 1970).

Since 1965, with the impact of a change from a highly specialized
system to a general liberal arts programme at the first degree level as well
as developments in social science research, Thai history is taught as main
and supplementary subjects in many other universities outside Chulalongkorn. More trained historians and other social scientists in related fields
such as anthropology, sociology, economics, and political science came
back to teach in the universities. Many of them discussed the philosophy of
history, historical theories, methods, and techniques, and even conducted
studies on Thai history themselves. Articles and writings on philosophy and
theories of history are compiled and published as *Philosophy of History**
(Kasetsiri and Suchart Swatdisri 1975).

This caused two trends of change in the study of Thai history. The first is that many academically trained historians prefer to confine their studies to the period from the eighteenth century onward because of the availability of reliable sources and data. Moreover, some of them have narrowed themselves to an area like foreign relations, for which ample data exist both in Thailand and abroad, for example, Thamsook Numnonda's "First American Advisers in Thai History"*(1973). In so doing they leave the period before the eighteenth century to amateur historians and archaeologists to work out from reliable sources of old chronicles, stone inscriptions, archaeological monuments and objects. One work of by an amateur historian, Prasert Na Nagara's "Researches in Sukhothai History"*(1966) deals with the kingdom of Sukhothai.

The second trend of study is an interdisciplinary approach applied recently by most social scientists. It challenges the historians to undertake social and intellectural history. Scholars who follow this line of study do not limit themselves to any specific period or area in which primary data are available, but rather use a wider range of materials, particularly chronicles and folk tales which are often rejected by professional historians as unreliable and irrelevant. There are discussions on the use of chronicles for the study of Thai history by David K. Wyatt (1976) and Anan Karnchanaphan (1976). With this approach, many professional historians study the history of the early and even the pre-Ayuthya periods. For example, Charnvit Kasetsiri wrote "The Rise of Ayuthya: A History of Siam in the Fourteenth and Fifteenth Centuries" for his Ph. D. dissertation at Cornell University (1973), and Anan Karnchanaphan in his M.A. thesis presented at the same university, "Early Lan Na Thai Historiography: An Analysis of the Fifteenth and Sixteenth Century Chronicles."

Apart from professional historians, scholars from other fields also approach Thai hisotry. Akin Rabibhadana in his thesis for M.A. in anthropology, *The Organization of Thai Society in the Early Bangkok Period, 1782-1873* (1969), used a wider range of data on Thai sources and chronicles. This book provided a new insight into the Thai society and culture of the past. Another scholar, Likhit Dhiravegin wrote *Siam and Colonialism (1855-1909): An Analysis of Diplomatic Relations* (1975) which is also a contribution to Thai history from the politics.

It seems that with the development of an interdisciplinary approach, history teachers and students of the present generation have departed completely from the traditional interest and old trend of study. They ignore the concept of Thai race and reject the nationalistic view of the former historians (Suvarnatat Pierre 1976) and at the same time utilize structural and functional viewpoints to analyse and criticize historical events and social institutions in Thai society. Another development along this line is the study of local history. Many institutions such as Thammasat University have encouraged students to conduct fieldwork on the social and economic history of a district or town (Srihiran 1975).

However, the use of an interdisciplinary approach to study Thai history in many cases leads to an overemphasis on Marxist theory. This often results in viewing past events through the eyes of the present. Many books and articles published sometime after 14 October 1973 have indicated such a trend, for example, a book entitled *Image of the Thai Ruling Class** by Somsamaj Srisuthrapan (1974) which criticizes the bureaucrats in the past. Consequently, such writings lead to a conflict with scholars of former generations, many of whom still cherish the idea of evolution and the "great man" theory of history.

Anthropology

Unlike archaeology and history which are established subjects of interest and study, anthropological study of Thai culture and society is a recent development of past ten years. It is greatly inspired by the Southeast Asian studies programme of the American and European universities, which brought about the development of the fields of social sciences in Thailand. Most Thai students who receive training abroad realize the need for anthropological fieldwork and study in their own society. But they cannot carry out such study because of various limitations, notably the availability of time and research funds. And as the university system in Thailand admits no sabbatical leave, the majority of anthropology teachers have no other choice but teaching. So anthropological research on Thai society is left to foreign scholars. Thus, each year there are numbers of Ph. D. candidates and post-doctorate researchers coming in to conduct studies and surveys in various localities in the country. Recent works and monographs are, for example, Michael Moerman's *Agricultural Change and Peasant Choice in a Thai Village* (1968), Mulders' *Monks, Merit, and Motivation: An Exploratory Study of the Social Functions of Buddhism in Thailand in Processes of Guided Social Change* (1969), Wijeyewardene's *Some Aspects of Rural Life in Thailand* (1967), Tambiah's *Buddhism and the Spirit Cults in North-East Thailand* (1970), and Jane Bunnag's *Buddhist Monk, Buddhist Layman* (1973), etc.

Having few chances to conduct field research of their own, most Thai anthropologists spend their time, apart from teaching, in (1) preparing and translating lecture notes. Translating textbooks is of great importance in the Thai situation, since anthropology and sociology are such new subject with complex theories and moreover written in the foreign languages so difficult for Thai students whose command of English is very poor, and (2) studying and summarizing works and monographs on Thai society which have been written by foreign scholars to use in their teaching. So at present, most of the Thai know of their own culture and society through the studies and research of foreigners. There are, at present, several books on anthropology and sociology of Thai society compiled and translated and edited by Thai anthropologists such as *The Sociology of Village Community in the Northeast** (Sunthronpesatch 1968), and a recently published book on the society and culture of Lan Na Thai (Sunthornpesatch 1970) which is composed of various articles by foreign scholars.

However, at the moment there are many Thai students studying anthropology abroad and some of them are likely to come back to conduct fieldwork in Thailand for several months before going back to write a thesis later. But these are few compared to those who have no chance. There is another way to get a chance to do research work, which is to ask for research funds from foreign foundations, universities, governments, and other institutions that are interested in solving certain social, economic, or political problems. This is why most anthropological field research conducted by university teachers and students up to the present time are problem-oriented. Moreover, with the need for social and cultural data for the national development programme of the country, the trend in anthropological research inclines more and more towards applied anthropology and sociology. Thammasat University set up the Graduate Volunteer Programme in 1969 to train graduates from various fields for six months, and after that they work in a village for a period of time. Students who complete the training course and fieldwork are likely to be hired or recruited as community development personnel in some other institution, such as the Mae Klong Integrated Rural Development Project which initiated by Thammasat University in 1974.

Anthropology and sociology tend to merge into one and unseparable subject in the Thai universities. No anthropological fieldwork has been conducted at any village community by Thai scholars except a few in the past which were done for an M. A. thesis (Vallibhotama 1971). Other field studies that exist are chiefly short-term ethnographical studies often conducted by university students to write up a term paper or report submitted to the department as partial requirements for completing a course. Many of these works, particularly those of anthropology students in the Department of Anthropology, Silpakorn University, have come out very well, for example, a study on a Lao Puan village at Ban Nong Hua Ling, Nakhon Nayok (Department of Anthropology 1976) that described in detail a belief system and rituals practised among the villagers. Apart from ethnographical studies, there is an increasing interest in studying and collecting local tales and myths. Teams of lecturers and students go out to various regions and localities interviewing and recording what they can elicit from aged informants. Many of these local tales are published in separate volumes such as Prateep Chumpol's *Literature of Southern Thailand** (1976) which deals with regional literature of the South. Unfortunately, there is no attempt at the present time by any scholar to carry on anthropological study on myths and folk tales to see how they are related to the social structure of the village or locality.

Conclusion

To sum up, Thai studies, as it developed from about 1966 along with scientific thinking and social scientific study introduced from the Western societies, can be viewed at this juncture as having reached a transitional stage. When evaluating it against the social and cultural environments and backgrounds in the Thai society, one can see a pattern which consists of at least three characteristic features. The first is cultural lag, that is, the fact that the attempt to study cultural and social aspects in order to understand and to gain an insight into Thai society is chiefly confined to the younger generation of the middle class who form a new intellectual group of the country. These people want change and development, and all their studies and viewpoints are geared towards a structural and functional approach. The upper class and the older generations prefer to maintain the old views and ideas towards their study, and this is reflected in their interest in the remote past or strange and exotic traditions and customs in the studies of Thai history and archaeology. At the same time, the lower class, most of whom do not receive academic training, tend to share with the upper class pride in the country's long and independent history. Phenomena like this often lead to conflicts between the old and the new intellectuals and as such inhibit the progress of Thai studies.

The second feature of the transitional stage is the lack of integration among the various fields of Thai studies, for example, the study of Thai archaeology which subdivided into prehistoric and historical periods. The first is more developed in terms of scientific methods and techniques but pays less interest to interpretation and generalization, while the latter, which is technically lagging behind, enjoys a broader range of generalization that easily leads to the reconstruction of conjectural history.

The third characteristic is perhaps overemphasis on an interdisciplinary approach among the new intellectual scholars who conduct Thai studies for applied purposes, that is, to create a better society. This causes them to overlook the differences in the frames of references of each field of study involved. For example, social and cultural studies in the field of anthropology are by nature micro-studies of a certain given area at a given time, but anthropological study among the Thai is more likely to take a macro-approach as seen in many problem-oriented researches conducted to feed in data for the community or regional development programme. Such discrepancies are likely to create a superficial view to overemphasize one or two social theories, for example, Marxist theory. It is likely that conflicts and different viewpoints and approaches in Thai studies as viewed from the three areas archaeology, history, and anthropology will persist for a long period of time.

Notes

1) This paper has been published in *East Asian Cultural Studies,* Vol. XIX, Nos. 1-4, 1980, pp. 1-19.
2) In the text, works written in Thai are listed by their English renderings marked with an asterisk. For their original Thai titles, see *References.*

References

Akin Rabibhadana
   1969 *The Organization of Thai Society in the Early Bangkok Period,*
          1782-1873. Cornell Southeast Asia Program Data Paper no. 74, Ithaca,
          N. Y.: Cornell University Southeast Asia Program.
Anuman Rajadhon, Phraya
   1954 *Lhaem Indo Chin Boran* [Indochina in the Ancient Times]. Bangkok:
          Klang Withaya.
Bayard, D. T.
   1971 *Non Nok Tha: The 1968 Excavation.* Dunedin, New Zealand: Universi-
          ty of Otago.
Blanchard, Wendell
   1957 *Thailand: Its People, Its Society, Its Culure.* New Haven, Conn.: HRAF
          Press.
Bowring, John
   1969 *The Kingdom and People of Siam.* London: Oxford University Press.
Bradley, George
   1896 *Kodmai Muang Thai Lem 1* [Siamese Law, volume 1]. Bangkok: Rim
          Pak Klong Bangkok Yai Press.
Bronson, Bennet and Dales, F. George
   1970 "Excavations at Chansen, 1968-1969," *Silpakorn Journal* XIV, no. 1
          (May): 41-46.
Bunnag, Jane
   1973 *Buddhist Monk, Buddhist Layman,* Cambridge at the University Press.
The Burney Papers
   1971 5 vols., Reprint edition, Farnborough: Gregg Press International.
Charoensupkul, Anuwit
   1974 "The Study of Structure and Brick-Laying of Ancient Monument,"
          Archaeology V, no. 3 (August):283-301.
Charoenwongsa, Pisit
   1976 "Early Southeast Asian Bronze in the Light of Excavation in Thailand,"
          Paper read at Symposium on Bronze Culture in East and South-East
          Asia, Bangkok, 5-9 July 1976.
Chiachanpongsa, Piset
   1976 "Report on Archaeological Fieldwork at Phra Dhat Phnom," *Silpakorn
          Jurnal* XX, nos. 1-2 (July-August): 51-73.
Chin, Yudi
   1969 *Kon Kaun Prawatisat Nai Prades Thai* [Prehistoric Man in Thailand].
          Bangkok: Fine Arts Department.

1976 *Ban Don Ta Petch: A Report on Archaeological Excavation at Ban Don Ta Petch, 1975-76*. Bangkok: Fine Arts Department.

Chulalongkorn, King

1958 *Chotmalihet Kwam Song Cham Khong Kromluang Narindhra Devi Lae Phra Rajawicharn Nai Rajkarn Thi 5* [The Memoir of Princess Narindhra Devi with Critique by King Chulalongkorn]. Bangkok: Tha Phra Chan Press.

Chulalongkorn, Phra Bat Somdet Phra Chao Yu Hua

1971 *Phra Rajphithi Sib Song Duan* [The Royal Ceremonies of the Twleve Months]. Bangkok: Klang Withays.

Chumpol, Prateep, ed.

1976 *Wana Kam Pak Taj* [Literature of Southern Thailand]. Bangkok: Department of Eastern Languages, Faculty of Archaeology, Silpakorn University.

Cœdès, George

1928 "The Excavations at P'ong Tük and Their Importance for the Ancient History of Siam," *The Journal of the Siam Society* XXI, pt. 3 (March): 195-209.

1968 *The Indianized States of Southeast Asia*. Canberra: Australian National University Press.

Crawfurd, John

1830 *Journal of an Embassy ·from the Governor General of India to the Courts of Siam and Cochin China, Exhibiting a View of the Actual State of Those Kingdoms*. London: Henry Colburn and Richard Bentley.

Damrong Rajanupab

1958 *Thai Rob Phama* [War between Thailand and Burma]. Bangkok: Klang Withaya.

1960 *Tamnan Buddha Chedi* [Origins of Buddhist Monuments]. Bangkok: Sivaphorn Press.

1959 *Laksana Karn Pok Krong Prated Syam Tae Boran* [Ancient Administration of Siam]. Bangkok, Printed on the occasion of the cremation of Sawaeng Thimthong with the permission of the Fine Arts Department.

Damrong Rajanupab and Narisara Nuwatiwongsa

1962 *San Somdet* [Correspondence between Prince Damrong and Prince Naris]. Bangkok: Khuru Sapha.

De la Loubère, Simon

1969 *The Kingdom of Siam*. London: Oxford University Press.

De Young, John E

1963 *Village Life in Modern Thailand*. Berkeley and Los Angeles: University of California Press.

Department of Anthropology, Silpakorn University

1976   *Ban Nong Hua Ling: A Village Study.* Bangkok.
Dhiravegin, Likhit
1975   *Siam and Colonialism (1855-1909): An Analysis of Diplomatic Re-latons.* Bangkok: Thai Wathana Press.
Diskul, Subhadradis, M. C
1967   "Sapab Karn Pak Asia Arkanae Kon Po Sor 1800" [History of Southeast Asia before 1257], *Thalaeng Ngan Prawatisat Ekasan Boran Kadi* [Report on History Records and Archaeology] I, no. 2 (May): 16-38.
Dupant, Pierre.
1959   *L'Archéologie mone de Dvaravati* [The Archaeology of the Mon of the Kingdom of Dvaravati]. Paris.
Fifield, Russell H.
1976   "Southeast Asian Studies: Origins, Development, Future," *Journal of Southeast Asian Studies* VII, no. 2 (September): 151-61.
Fine Arts Department
1960   *Plan and Report of Survey and Excavations of Ancient Monuments in Northeastern Thailand, 1959.* Bangkok: Sivaphorn Press.
1964   *Excavation of Prehistoric Site at Artillery Centre, Lop Buri.* Bangkok.
1964   *Prachum Phong Sawadan* [A Collection of Ancient Chronicles]. Bangkok: Sam Nak Phim Kao Na.
1965   *Some Recent Discovered Sites of Dvaravati Period.* Bangkok: Sivaphorn Press.
1966   *Report of the Survey and Excavations of Ancient Monuments in the Ancient City of U Thong.* Bangkok: Sivaphorn Press.
1967   *Report of the Survey and Excavations of Ancient Monuments in Northeastern Thailand, Part Two:1960-1961.* Bangkok: Sivaphorn Press.
1969   *Report of the Survey, Excavations, and Restorations of Ancient Monuments in the Ancient City of Sukhothai, 1965-1969.* Bangkok: Khuru Sapha.
1977   *Prasat Muang Singha* [Ancient Sanctuary of the Ancient City of Muang]. Bangkok.
Gorman, Chester F.
1971   "Excavation at Spirit Cave, North Thailand: Some Interim Interpretations," *Asian Perspectives* XIII.
K. S. R., Kulab
1903   *Anam Syam Yuth* [War between Vietnam and Thailand]. Bangkok: Syam Prapet Sunthrarowat Piset.
Karnchanakom, Precha
1969   "Preliminary Report on Archaeological Survey of Prehistoric Paintings and Engravings in Udorn Thani between 10th-23rd May 1969," *Archaeology* III, no. 1 (July-September): 20-42.

Karnchanaphan Anan

1974 "Early Lan Na Thai Historiography: An Analysis of the Fifteenth and Sixteenth Century Chronicles," M. A. thesis, Cornell University.

1976 "Tam Nan Lae Laksana Kwamkit Thang Prawatisat Nai Lan Na Rawang Buddha Satawat Thi 20 Lae 21" [Chronicles and Mode of Thought in History of Lan Na between the Fourteenth and Fifteenth Centuries], *Thammasat University Journal* VI, no. 1 (June-September): 9-21.

Kasemsri and Wimon Pongsapipat

1967 "Prawatisat Smai Krung Ratana Kosin" [History of Bangkok], *Thalaeng Ngan Prawatisat Ekasan Boran Kadi* [Report on History Records and Archaeology] I, no. 2 (May): 93-119.

Kasetsiri, Charnvit

1973 "The Rise of Ayuthya: A Hisotry of Siam in the Fourteenth and Fifteenth Centuries," Ph. D. dissertation, Cornell University.

Kasetsiri and Suchart Swatdisri eds.

1975 *Prajaya Prawatisat* [Philosophy of History]. Bangkok: Social Science Association.

Kaufman, Howard Keva

1960 *Bangkhnad: A Community Study in Thailand.* Monographs of the Association for Asian Studies, no. 10, Locust Valley, N. Y.: J. J. Augustin Incorporated Publisher.

Kingshill, Konrad

1960 *Ku Daeng: The Red Tomb.* Chiengmai: The Prince Royal's College.

Krairiksh, Piriya

1974 "Semas with Scenes from the Mahānipātā-Jātakas in the National Museum at Kohon Kaen," In *Art and Archaeology in Thailand,* Bangkok: Fine Arts Department, pp. 35-65.

Kuakun, Pote

1975 "Ban Chieng Kon Prawatisat" [The Village of Ban Chieng in Prehistoric Period], *Muang Boran Journal* I, no. 3 (April-June): 79-91.

Maleipan, Viraphan

1969 "Technique Karn Khud Khong Boranstan Thi Thevasatan Doem, Ayuthya" [Excavation of an Old Hindu Sanctuary in Ayuthya], *Archaeology* III, no. 2 (October-December): 26-54.

Ministry of Education

1969 *Sadet Prapat Ton Nai Ratchakarn Thi Ha* [Travelling Records of King Chulalongkorn]. Bangkok: Khuru Sapha.

Moerman, Michael

1968 *Agricultural Change and Peasant Choice in a Thai Village.* Berkely and Los Angeles: University of California Press.

Mulder, J. A. Niels
  1969 *Monks, Merit, and Motivation: An Exploratory Study of the Social Functions of Buddhism in Thailand in Processes of Guided Social Change.* Special Report Series no. 1. De Kalb, Illinois: Center for Southeast Asian Studies, Northern Illinois University.

Numnonda, Thamsook
  1973 "Thi Prüksa Rajakarn Phaen Din Chao American Nai Prawatisat Thai" [The First American Advisers in Thai History], *Thalaeng Ngan Prawatisat Ekasan Boran Kadi* [Report on History Records and Archaeology] VII, no. 3 (September): 50-66.

The Office of the Prime Minister
  1965 *Prachum Sila Charuk Pak Thi Sam* [A Collection of Inscriptions, vol. 3]. Bangkok.
  1970 *Prachum Sila Charuk Pak Thi Si* [A Collection of Inscriptions, vol. 4]. Bangkok.

Phillips, Herbert P
  1966 *Thai Peasant Personality: The Patterning of Interpersonal Behavior in the Village of Bang Chan.* Berkeley and Los Angeles: University of California Press.

Prachakit Korachak, Phraya
  1955 *Phong Sawadan Yo Nok* [History of the North]. Bangkok: Chusin Press.

Prasert Na Nagara
  1966 "Karn Chamru Prawatisat Sukhothai" [Researches in Sukhothai History], *Sangkhomsat Parilhat*, special volume, no. 3(June).

Saengwichien, Sood
  1966 "Laksana Krong Kraduk Manut Thi Ban Kao" [Skeletal Remains at Ban Kao], *The Journal of the Social Science Review*, June: 32-38.
  1974 *Prehistory in Thailand.* Bangkok: Krom Saraban Thaharn Rua.

Sarasin, F.
  1933 "Prehistoric Researches in Siam," *The Journal of the Siam Society* XXVI, pt. 2 (October): 171-202.

Satien Koset
  1972 *Prapenee Tang Tang Khong Thai* [Thai Customs]. Bangkok: Khuru Sapha.
  1959 *Bantük Kwam Ru* [Record of Knowledge]. Bangkok: Rung Rnangrat Press.

Sayamanonda, Rong
  1967 "Prawatisat Thai Samai Krung Sri Ayuthaya, Paendin Somdet Phra Ramathibodi Thi 1—Somdet Phra Barom Trai Lokanat" [History of Ayuthya from the Reign of King Rama I to That of King Trai Lok],

162

Thalaeng Ngan Prawatisat Ekasan Boran Kadi [Report on History Records and Archaeology] I, no. 2 (May): 64-89.

Solheim, Wilhelm G., II, and Gorman, Chester F.

1966 "Archaeological Salvage Program: Northeastern Thailand—First Season," *The Journal of the Siam Society* LIV, pt. 2 (July): 111-209.

Somsamaj Srisuthrapan

1974 *Chom Na Sakdi Na Thai* [Image of the Thai Ruling Class]. Bangkok: Aksaranukun Karnphim.

Srihiran, Suthon

1975 "Prawatisat Setakit Lum Mae Nam Nakhon Chai Sri" [Economic History of the Nakhon Chai Sri River Basin], *Thammasat University Journal* IV, no. 3 (February-May): 60-76.

Sukhapanich, Khachorn

1967 "Krung Yasothorn——Nakhon Thom Nai Prawatisat Thai" [The City of Yasothorn and Nakhon Thom in Thai History], *Thalaeng Ngan Prawatisat Ekasan Boran Kadi* [Report on History Records and Archaeology] I, no. 2 (May): 47-61.

Sunthornpesatch, Suthep ed.

1968 *Sangkom Withya Khong Mu-Ban Tawan Org Chieng Nua* [The Sociology of Village Community in the Northeast]. Bangkok: Social Science Association Press.

1970 *Sangkom Iae Watanatam Lan Na Thai, Ruam Pon Ngan Wichaj Thang Sangkomsat Nai Pak Nua Khong Prades Thai* [Lan Na Thai Society and Culture: A Collection of Research Papers]. Chiengmai: Faculty of Social Science, Chiengmai University.

Suvarnatat Pierre, Kobkna

1976 "Karn Khien Prawatisat Baeb Chati Niyom Picharana Luang Vichitwatakarn" [Nationalism and the Writing of History by Luang Vichitwatakarn], *Thammasat Universtiy Jounal* VI, no. 1 (June-September): 149-80.

Tambiah, S. J.

1970 *Buddhism and the Spirit Cults in North-East Thailand.* Cambridge: Cambridge Universtiy Press.

Thipakarawongsa, Chao Phraya

1961 *Phraraj Pongsawadan Krung Rattana Kosin, Ratchakarn Thi Sam* [The Dynastic Chronicles, Bangkok Era, the Third Reign], 2 vols. Bangkok: Khuru Sapha.

Vallibhotama, Srisakra

1971 "Ban Muang Khao: The Village and the Wat," M. A. thesis, The University of Western Australia.

1974 "The Kingdom of Haripunjaya," In *Art and Archaeology in Thailand,*

Bangkok: Fine Arts Department, pp. 247-85.

Van Vliet, Jeremias
    1910 "Description of the Kingdom of Siam," *The Journal of the Siam Society* VII, pt. 1 (July): 1-105.

Wijeyewardene, G.
    1967 "Some Aspects of Rural Life in Thailand," In *Thailand: Social and Economic Studies in Development,* ed. by T. H. Silcock, Canberra: Australian National University Press.

Wyatt, David K.
    1976 "Chronicle Tradition in Thai Historiography," *Thammasat University Journal* VI, no. 1 (June-September): 2-8.

Part II

Asian Peoples and Their Cultures

9 Continuity and Change of Ancestor Worship in East Asia: A Comparative Study of Memorial Tablet

MICHIO SUENARI

Introduction

In this paper[1] I would like to discuss some very limited aspects of ancestor worship[2] as found in the custom of memorial tablets. Examples are taken from four societies which have some common geographical and historical backgrounds and for which I have some field data.[3] While we may interpret the varieties found in the four societies in many ways, I will note the structural continuity found in them.

Though the custom of memorial tablets may be studied from many angles, I will concern myself in this paper only with the following points:

(1) Who are the people represented by the tablets?
(2) Who takes charge of the tablets and of its rituals?
(3) Who takes part in the ritual of death anniversaries?

I want to make a comparison of the tablet custom in three civilized societies in part I, to consider the process of the introduction of the tablet system among an aboriginal group of Taiwan in part II, and to discuss on the two types of continuity in part III.

Korea

Nowadays paper tablets are widely used in Korea.[4] The Koreans writes on them only the words which denote the kinship relation to the main worshipper. In case of males they add the official title and in case of females family name plus the local name of the lineage origin. No personal name nor date of birth or of death is written on the surface of the tablet.[5]

(1) Koreans worship their patrilineal ascendants and their spouses for four generations[6] (until the great great grand parents) at the domestic level on the death anniversaries and on seasonal festivals according to the Confucian manner. They exclude from the worship in the Confucian way those who died before adulthood nor daughters who died in their natal household, even though they may pacify these souls by shamanistic rituals. Brothers who died without sons may sometimes be remembered and worshipped by brothers on the death anniversaries for one or two generations. I suppose, however, it would be unthinkable for Koreans to worship the souls of "the others", for example, the deceased parents of wife at her husband's household.

(2) In Korea two patterns of ritual responsibility are reported. One is the orthodox one found in most of the country. According to this, a descendant of the senior line (the line of the eldest son) takes charge of the rituals for the ancestors and junior descendants gather at his house to share in the celebration. The responsibility of the ritual may move to the household of the junior line temporarily, when the descendant of the fourth generation has died out in the main household and old men of that generation still survive in other household.[7] The other pattern is found in marginal mountain areas, coastal areas or remote islands.[8] There they distribute the tablest among sons. This practice seems to be contrastive to the former by neglecting the senior line, but it should be noted that they nontheless conform to patrilineal ideology.

(3) Descendants of junior lines and some of the collateral kin (usually within the range of third cousin) gather at the house of the eldest line for the ritual. Besides the patrikin, some non-patrilineal relative (for example, a daughter's husband or her son) may take part in it.[9] Women also gather to the house and help in the preparation of the offering, but do not take part in the ritual with men in the same room.[10] They sit next door or look from the court yards at the men who are worshipping, and they also eat the food distributed after the ritual.

In short, Korean memorial tablet worship is based on a strict patrilineal principle, is comparatively uniform, and is coloured with Confucian formalism.

China(Taiwan)

Compared with Korea, regional varieties in Taiwan seem to be greater. Though a box type of tablet[11] is also reported, the Chinese (Fukien origin) in Central Taiwan put a large wooden tablet board on a altar in the central room of the compound.[12] They also put talbets of the same style for the remote ancestors in the ancestral hall.[13] The ritual of death anniversary is held in daytime in contrast to that of Korean which is held at midnight of the previous day.

(1) They put the name of the apical ancestor who came to Taiwan or who started the compound on the center of the tablet and the names of his descendants on either side of it. The number of generations increases as time goes on, because they do not switch the worship of an ancestor at domestic level into that of the ancestral hall at a regular interval as Freedman (1958) writes. It should be noted all the ancestors whose names are on the tablet are not necessarily commemorated on their individual death anniversaries. So, a table of the death anniversary which is hung in the corner of the central room is helpful to know which ancestors are actually worshipped.[14] For example, a table in one household shows that the ancestors of the past eight generations are still worshipped on the domestic level.

Sometimes non-patrikin are worshipped at the domestic level. An inmarrying husband may bring the tablets of his natal household and put them on the altar but separat from the tablets of his wife's ancestors.[15] An inmarrying wife may bring the tablets of her kin if she is the only child. She may put them and worship in the corner of the kitchen or on the eaves.[16] There is a strong norm that the tablets of a daughter should not be put on the altar of her natal family, so temples often provide a tablet hall for such souls.[17]

In the ancestral hall male descendants worship only the apical or focal ancestors with their wives and those who made contributions at the time of construction of the hall. There, worship is conducted in the Confucian manners[18] in contrast with bowing with incense in hand as done at the level of domestic worship. The expense are paid usually from the common property endowed to the hall or sometimes from the donation evenly allotted to each branch of the lineage.

There seems to be a strong sense of obligation to worship for those from whom one gets property.[19]

(2) Ancestral tablets and the central room are usually not divided even a few generations after the division of other property. There are a few obligations and rights concerning ancestor worship that are committed to a single son. Each household is the unit which must prepare, bring, take back and consume the offerings.

A wife or a child may offer the tea every morning and they may worship on the death anniversary if the head of the household is busy.[20] This is in contrast with the worship at the ancestral hall where only male adults can take part.

(3) For patrilineal ancestors the descendants and often their spouses take part in the ritual at domestic level. It is the custom for a bride to worship the ancestors of her husband when she enters his house at wedding. For the non-patrikin the related persons may worship on the days of seasonal events.

In short, among the Chinese in Taiwan the patrilineal principle is a little attenuated to permit some range of deviation. We find a strong sense of reciprocity between the ancestors and descendants. The Confucian process of the ritual is found only at the level of the ancestral hall.

Japan

The presence of wide variation is one of the characteristics of Japanese religion.[21] For example, all tablets are buried in the yard of a temple after the 33rd years of the death anniversary in a village of Tsushima island, while talbets are supposed to be kept in the altar of family for ever in a village of Shimane district. In spite of these regional variations, it is a common feature that ie is closely associated with Japanese relgion. So ancestor worship is best understood in the context of ie.

An ie corresponds to a household when it conforms to a corporate residential unit. Ideally it is composed of a stem family. One of its most prominent feature is its continuity: only one child each generation remains in the parent's ie, while other children leave their natal household, so that ideally the ie continunes through an infinite number of generations. The household property is inherited by the child who remains in the natal household. There arises a distinction of status between the successor and non-successor or marginal members.[22]

Tablet rituals are influenced with Buddhism in Japan. Tablets are often put on the altar with the statue of Buddha. The monk chooses the posthumous name and recites a sutra on the death anniversary or during the seasonal rituals for the deceased. Compared to Confucian way of Korea, the process of offering is simple and brief. It is not necessarily practised on the date of death and sometimes rituals for several ancestors are combined in one day for the sake of convenience. In a village of Tsushima the villagers hold a joint ritual by which all ancestors who had death anniversaries during the year worshipped in the temple on a day during the farmers' slack season.

(1) It is the successor of *ie* and his wife who are worshipped as the regular ancestors of the *ie*. It should be noted that Japanese primarily worship ancestors of their own *ie* and this does not extend to the ascendants beyond the founder of one's own *ie*. For example, one whose father branched off from the main *ie* worship the dead father, but does not worship the grand father as the ancestor of his own *ie*, though he may participate in the ceremony of the death anniversary in the main *ie* as a guest.

The marginal members who died at the natal *ie* may be worshipped but in less splendid manner. In some districts they are put in separate boxes, or treated as *muen botoke* (literally, the dead to whom the living have no direct relationships).

Japanese ancestral altars may also include those who have no lineal relation with the *ie*, that is, kin of inmarrying or of adopted members of the *ie*. R. Smith (1976: 44-45) reports 5.9% of 3,050 cases in his census of memorial tablets belonged to this category and 0.8% of them were of strangers.

(2) Since an ancestral altar is one of the important parts of the properties of *ie*, it is the right and responsibility of the successor of *ie* to keep the tablets and to officiate at the commemorative rituals. The daily offering is usually made by the hands of wife.

(3) At death anniversary close relatives are invited. They include both male and female. Since it is the event of *ie*, they also invite such guests as the members of the wife's natal *ie*.

In short, Japanese tablet worship is closely related with *ie* institution, it has wide varieties and non-kin members are included more widely than is done by the Chinese in Taiwan.

To sum up, if we look at these three societies of Korea, Taiwan and Japan, we find these differences. Patrilineal descent is stressed in the tablets of the Koreans and Chinese, while the latter admits some exceptions. In the generational limit of worship the former is more punctual than the latter. In Japan ancestors are, as it were, *ie* lineal: the successors of *ie* and their spouses are the regular members to be worshipped, even though talbets of non-kin members and even a stranger may be included on the altar of *ie*. The responsibility of the ancestral ritual at the domestic level is assigned to a single child in Korea (orthodox pattern) and in Japan, while it is evenly shared among all the sons in China. While only the patrilineal descendants and their spouses participate in the death anniversary in China, some non patrikin or their spouses are added to them in Korea. This is a reflection of the Korean zeal in ancestral rituals, rather than a deviation of patrilineal principle. In Japan relatives bilaterally traced from the members of the *ie* participate. On the other hand, in Korea and in the ancestral hall of Chinese only males play the major role, while females can participate in the ancestral ritual of domestic level in China and in Japan.

What is the meaning of these varieties found in a cursory look at the tablet systems of the three societies? If we consider the classical Chinese memorial tablet system as a means of worship of the patrilineal ancestor in Confucian manner, we cannot help but being struck with the contrast of Korean formalism and Japanese looseness. Koreans observe the classical rules faithfully while some diversions from the norm are found even among the Chinese. It was only in Japan that the material elements in the custom of the ancestral tablet was introduced, while dropping the patrilineal element and Confucian ritualism.

Though it would be interesting to know the process by which such an elastic introduction was made, we have few historical records. The following Puyuma example may be of some help for understanding this issue, though conditions might have been very much different.

The Puyuma

The Puyuma is one of the aboriginal groups of Taiwan speaking a Malayo-Polynesian language. Their population is about six thousand and they live on the southeast coast. As late as eighty years ago they were head-hunters living by shifting cultivation of millet. Their age grade system centering around the men's house, was efficient enough to dominate over rival tribes in their neighbourhood.[23]

There was a strong tendency towards village endogamy. Dominant residence pattern was uxorilocal which gave their kinship a tinge of "matrilineal". But closer investigation shows their descent system ambilineal or optional. The kindred is functionally important in ordinary social activities.

Because of their small population (six thousand) they have been deeply influenced by contact with the majority group, the Chinese. Let us see the case of R village of the Puyuma.[24]

The History of Contact with a Larger Society

The Puyuma had contact with the Japanese troops as early as 1897. In 1905 primary school education was initiated in the R village, and paddy rice cultivation was introduced from the neighbouring aboriginal group of the Ami with an irrigation system. Around 1930 their men's house and the cult house of the village were abolished. Thus, their traditional way of life was considerably undermined during the period of Japanese control (1895-1945).

After the end of the Second World War the Puyuma became citizens of the Republic of China, and experienced improved hygenic conditions, increased chances for higher education, participation in voting, but they also faced severe economic competition with the Chinese whose population increased rapidly in the east coast after the end of the Second World War. They had sold two thirds of their arable land to Chinese by 1967.

Another conspicuous event was their Christianization after the end of the Second World War. A third of total households in R village were converted. The peak was 1957 for Catholics and 1962 for Presbyterians respectively. But a considerable number of them lost their zeal and reverted to their traditional religion or to Buddhism in Chinese style, with the suspension of the distribution of the rehabilitation aid goods from abroad.[25]

The following words of an informant are to the point on these changes: "We aborigines discarded our traditional religion during Japanese rule under which we were guided to think that the *Karomaan* (cult house)was superstitious and after the end of the Second World War we adopted Christianity. But now we face toward Buddhism,[26] the religion of the majority group of the Chinese."

Compared with the past Japanization and the fluctuating Christianization, the Sinicization has taken a slow but steady course because it is the custom of the majority people of the island. The Puyuma feel that they have to get on well with the Chinese. In other words, the Chinese way of life is attaining the position of a standard for the villagers in proportion to the decline of their traditional ways. The introduction of the custom of memorial tablets should be considered in this context. A third of 156 households of the Puyuma in the R village call themselves "Buddhist", and 37 have memorial tablets on their altars in the central room. They make board type or box type of tablets imitating Chinese neighbours.

Table 1
Religious Sect of the Puyuma in R Village (household)

"native"	"Buddhist"	Christian		Total
		Catholic	Presbyterian	
44	54	21	31	156

The following table shows the types of ancestors in the memorial tablets of 28 housholds in which I could check the genealogical relations. Classifications are based on generation and the residence at the time of marriage.

Table 2
Types of Ancestors in the Tablet

gene-ration	cases that include virilocal marriage			cases of only uxorilocal marriage			total
	Ancestor of household	Ancestor of the inmarrying member	Ancestor of both sides	Ancestor of household	Ancestor of the inmarrying member	Ancestor of both sides	
1	3	1		9	1		14
2				4	1	3	8
3	2			3			5
4				1			1
total	5	1	0	17	2	3	28

From these data we may note the following points.
(1) The generation depth of tablets is shallow, which may be interpreted

either as the result of the Puyuma's recent introduction to the use of the tablet or as a reflection of the shallow depth of tracing ancestors in their native system.

(2) Usually the ancestors of the household are more often worshipped than those of the natal household of inmarrying members.

(3) Sometimes ancestors of the inmarrying members are also worshipped with the tablets of the household ancestors. Though this seems to be contrary to the ideal pattern of Chinese, such cases are also reported among some group of Chinese in Taiwan.

(4) There is a norm that the responsibility of tablet worship is closely related to the inheritance of property. This is also in line with the Chinese case in Taiwan.

Then we come to a question of whether the similarity of their tablet system with the Chinese is caused by their acceptance of the Chinese system or it is the result of their native structure. Some observation on the behavioural level would be necessary in order to check this issue. The New Year's Eve is a good occasion for that purpose.[27]

On New Year's Eve the Chinese worship gods and ancestors offering the gorgeous dishes. After this the family take dinner together. This dinner is thought to be the climax when the solidarity of the family is strengthened during the year. Those who have left home for work or study in the city come home as far as possible. Married women spend the night at their husband's because women are regarded to be members of their husband's family once they marry.

The Puyuma are also busy in preparing dishes on New Year's Eve. Though some earnest Christians try to be indifferent to the event, others are invited to their relatives to take part in the worship or to share the dinner. Let us see in whose household they worship, and who take part in the worship.

There is a norm that the eldest daughter should keep the tablets and have the responsibility to make the ritual for the ancestors. Actually, half of the cases conform to the norm out of 12 cases in which the genealogical relations are clear and ego is not a single child.

The follwoing two examples show clearly the pattern of the participants of the ritual among them.

Five brothers gather at the eldest's house. B is a Christian and does not take part in the ritual but shares the dinner after it. C made a uxorilocal marriage, so his wife and her children worship at her household. D is the same case. *E*'s wife goes to her natal household by herself. *A*'s wife does not return to her natal household which is in another village.

Ex. 1.

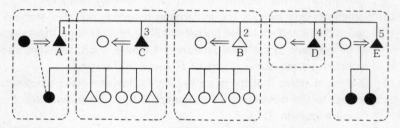

F is the eldest daughter and keeps the tablets of ancestors. *F*'s husband does not return to his natal household because its members believe in native religion, and he attends the ceremony of his wife's ancestors without offering the incense. *G* comes to worship with her children. *H* does not come to her natal household though she lives within the village, because her husband knows the Chinese language and customs well, having lived outside the village for a long time. *I* came with her daughter who helped for preparation of offerings. She prepares two sets of offering, one for her own ancestors at *F* and the other for her husband's ancestor which are kept on the altar of her household. She may worship her husband's ancestor if she is in time for the ritual, after finishing worship at *F*. *J* came with his wife and children until last year though he is a type of a rationalist saying "There are no *biruwa* (gods and souls). If one hehaves righteously it is unnecessary to rely on gods." That year *J*'s wife's mother made a tablet of her ancestors and the family worshipped them.

Ex. 2.

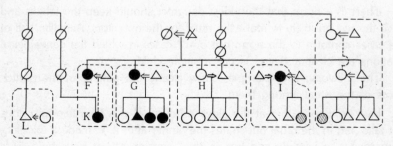

Though this example shows some influence of the Chinese pattern it also reflects native patterns strongly. *F*'s foster daughter's case is typical. Though she came to worship her foster mother's ancestor recently, she used to go to the main household of her grand mother. The reason was that her eye had pained her from the time she was three years old and it did not get well until she worshipped there following the advice of a shaman. This method of finding which ancestor to worship by the divination of a shaman is parallel to the native pattern of deciding one's membership in a cult group.

I's present husband commented that his wife's siblings should gather at their natal household for worship, since they had gotten property from their ancestor even when they married out. Such a norm of obligation to worship in compensation for the inheritance of property is also found in cases of native ancestor worship. Out of these data we may find the following features in the worship of memorial tablets among the Puyuma on New Year's Eve.

(1) There are many inmarrying members of the household who go back to their natal household to worship. Some of them also worship the ancestors of their present household out of courtesy when they have time to do so.

(2) When the natal household keep no tablets they worship at the main household from which the natal household divided off.

(3) An adopted child is supposed to worship the ancestors of the foster parents, but in some cases he worships those of the natal family.

(4) Inheritance is recognized to be an important factor in maintaining ancestral tablets.

(5) The ancestor may urge his descendants traced bilaterally to worship him by inflicting illness.

All of the above customs except # 4 deviate from the Chinese example. Especially # 5 is coincident with the native mode of the Puyuma in deciding the members of the cult group. So we may conclude that they keep their own mode of worship in tracing their ancestors though they introduced the memorial tablet system from Chinese. What I want to stress is that the Puyuma may have felt no confusion in the process of introduction of the tablet custom, so far. They have been able to worship their ancestors in the Chinese manner using their own principles of descent. The reason why they could do so, is, I think, a result of the elasticity of their native system of kinship. Their traditional way of descent is optional: they can trace it patrilineally, for example, if the rule of residence at marriage change into 100% virilocal, without making a conscious effort for the change.

I infer that a similar continuity might have been possible in the introduction of the Chinese tablet system into Japan.

Conclusion

We may find two types of continuity in the adoption of the tablet system in Korea and Japan. They are concerned about its content and frame.

In Korea the content is very clear for most of it conforms to principles. For example, the principle of patrilineal descent defines who should be represented by the tablets, who should take charge of them, and who should gather at the ritual. The Confucian manual designates how the ritual should proceed in detail: for example, what kinds of dishes and in what order they should be offered, what kinds of bows and how many times they should be made, etc. Of course there does exist variations as is expressed in the phrase of common use "*Kagalie* (Each family has its own manner)". But these variations are not against the principles and come within a narrow range. In such a situation continuity takes the form of a faithful preservation of the original form or even of an elaboration of it into purer form according to orthodoxy.

On the other hand, in Japan a kind of chaotic diversity comes to the fore, where practices may be mutually contradictory. It is true that there is *ie* principle, but its membership is open to situational factors. For example, even under the rule of primogeniture, the eldest may lose his right on the *ie*, if he leaves his natal *ie*. The treatment of marginal members varies greatly according to informants, for there is no specific rule and emotional factors intervene. Without such a manual as that of Confucian ritual, the procedure of the ritual is simple and has variations. The Buddhist monk officiates only for clergical matters and the rest is mostly left to local customs. In such a situation continuity takes the form of the preservation of indigenous elements in a framework or material that is imported. The content can be accommodated with the change of time[28] or of environmental conditions. So it can be elastic to outer influences. For example, with the influences of Buddhism the tablet came to be associated with

Buddhist temple, which never happened in Korea.

The example of Chinese in Central Taiwan shows a considerable deviation from the classical pattern. The tablet system of Taiwan may be put inbetween on the continuum of the two extremes mentioned above. I think it is closer to the Korean type, since basic principles are still clear though it amalgamated some outer elements.

Then there arises the question of where this difference comes from. Though there may be many ways of explanations possible, one of the most plausible would be the presence or absence of a central authority which seeks orthodoxy. The three countries have had a long history of central governments. The Korean government was eager to guide and to control the manners of the ritual, while the Japanese authority did not intervene in the content of ancestor worship even at the time of persecution of the Christian in seventeenth century or at the height of military nationalism during World War II. The Chinese government encouraged the exercise of local autonomy provided that enough taxes were collected and public peace was maintained,[29] even though there might have been influences on the ancestor worship through the high esteem of the Confucian Classic in the official examinations. But this explanation is not decisive, since it does not elucidate the cause of the difference between Japan and China nor it leaves room for the question of why the Koreans still keep essentially similar rituals even after the central authroity ceased to be concerned with the family ritual with the fall of Yi dynasty. Is it clarified only by historical factors, or rooted in the difference of the basic structures of these societies? Such a question might not be answered either by anthropologists nor historians alone. In this paper I used few hitorical data. This is not because I regard historical treatment unimportant, but because I hesitate in handling with the records of such a long time span on this issue without ample trainning of historical method. I think collaboration[30] with historians is indispensable if we are to challenge the issue of continuity and change of these societies. A synchronic study as is tried in this paper would be of some help also as a starting point for such an exploration.

Notes

1) I am much indebted to Prof. Taik-Kyoo Kim of the Yeongnam University and Prof. Sakurai Tokutaro of Komazawa University for their comments on this topic. Prof. Bourret of University of the Sacred Heart kindly helped in polishing my English.
2) Freedman (1958:81-91) makes a distinction between ancestor worship and memorialism. Though I admit the distinction may be useful in some cases, I feel it rather difficult to sort out the data of these Asian societies into a strict dichotomy. For example, Janelli (1973) strenghthens the similarity between the behaviour towards ancestors and that toward the living elders in Korea. But to the eye of a Japanese observer the element of formalism is so strong that makes him hesitate to lable it as "memorialism" in the same sense that Plath (1964) applied this term to Japanese case. The same can be said of the distinction between ancestor worship and the cult of the dead. While the distinction of the two concepts may be fruitful in other societies (for example, in Africa), one of characteristic of the Japanese case lies in the combination of both elements. So in this paper I use the term ancestor worship in a broad sense to cover some of the element of "memorialism" and the cult of the dead.
3) The data for Korea were collected at two farm villages of Songju-gun (March-April and August-October, 1972) and of Andong-gun (October-November, 1973) and at a fishing village in Yongduk-gun (March, 1979-March, 1980), for Chinese of Central Taiwan at a farm village (January-April, 1976, December, 1976-January, 1977, August-September, 1977), for Japan at a fishing village of Tsushima (August, 1980).
4) Among some upper class families wooden tablets are still used. In this case personal names are written inside the tablets. Cf. Kwang-Kyu Lee (1977:10-12).
5) Cf. Suenari 1975:60. This is contrastive with the Chinese tablets in Taiwan on which personal names are inscribed on the surface. A manual book of home rituals contains the form for a child's tablet on which the personal name is written. This may be a modern example, for the soul of the junior generation is not worshipped according to the traditional norm.
6) In Yi dynasty the king admitted some great scholars and meritorious retainers to the privilege of being commemorated for ever. On the other hand three generation worship is customary in some districts including the fishing village on the east coast where I did this research.
7) Suenari 1973:71-72, Kwang-Kyu Lee 1977:5-8.
8) Yeo (1980) is an extensive and detailed work on this issue. I think it is necessary to divide further these cases into the two sub-types. One is the sub-type in which the tablet division coexists with the orthodox pattern. For example, in the fishing village of the east coast, sometimes younger son takes charge of the tablet of his mother. But this is an exceptional case to orthodox pattern (only 7 out of 142 cases). According to the other sub-type, no definite line of descendants is supposed to take charge of the tablet as is reported in Che-ju island (Sato 1973:135-137). There the distinction between the senior and junior lines is minimal or absent. It sometimes accompanies the joint management of worship by rotation that is usually found in China.

9) In my observation at the fishing village, 15 out of 44 cases include at least one person of non patrikin. The presence of non-patrilineal relatives is not necessarily an evidence of the existence of the bilateral descent. They would rather be interpreted as guests invited to the ritual.

10) A wife or a daughter without her brother may offer the wine to her deceased husband or her deceased father respectively.

11) There is also a new box type of tablet that contains small slips of wood on which names of the deceased are written individually. I suspect it is introduced from Japan.

12) Suenari 1978b: 15-16.

13) Suenari 1977:113-146.

14) Suenari 1978b:19-22.

15) A. Wolf 1974:157

16) A. Wolf 1974:154

17) A. Wolf 1974:154, Suenari 1978b:16-17.

18) Suenari 1977:121-145.

19) Sung-Hsing Wang 1974:370.

20) In a ritual of death anniversary I observed in Central Taiwan, only two out of thirteen were male heads, while the rest of participants were nine wives, one school boy and a girl.

21) R. Smith (1974b) also points out the chaotic diversity of Japanese religion.

22) For more detail see Nakane 1967.

23) For general back ground see Mabuchi 1960.

24) Suenari 1968, Chiao 1972.

25) Shih (1975) reports the same phenomenon in another Puyuma village.

26) The Puyuma call the religion of neighbouring Chinese "Buddhism" though it include much elements of Confucianism and Taoism. Buddhistic element is found only in an image of the *Kannon* (The Goddess of Mercy) in a picture of gods of the altar, and in the participation of Buddhist monks in some of their funerals.

27) Sueneri 1968.

28) I got this idea from R. Smith (1974b).

29) Freedman 1958:114.

30) Freedman 1963.

References

Ahern, Emily M.
   1973   *The Cult of the Dead in a Chinese Village*. Stanford University Press.
Chiao, Chien
   1972   "Ambilineal Descent and Identity Problem of the Rikavon Puyuma" (in
          Chinese), *Bulletin of the Institute of Ethnology, Academia Sinica,* 34:
          1-21.
Fortes, Meyer
   1965   "Some Relfections on Ancestor Worship in Africa," *African Systems of
          Thought,* edited by M. Fortes and G. Dieterlen, Oxford University Press.
Freedman, Maurice
   1958   *Lineage Organization in Southeastern China*. London: Athlone Press.
   1963   "A Chinese Phase in Social Anthropology," *British Journal of Sociolo-
          gy,* 14: 1-19.
   1966   *Chinese Lineage and Society: Fukien and Kwangtung*. London:
          Athlone Press.
   1967   "Ancestor Worship: Two Facets of the Chinese Case," *Social Organiza-
          tion: Essays Presented to Raymond Firth,* edited by M. Freedman.
   1979   *The Study of Chinese Society*. Stanford University Press.
Harrell, C. Stevan
   1976   "The Ancestors at Home: Domestic Worship in a Land-Poor
          Taiwanese Village," *Ancestors,* edited by W. H. Newell.
Hyun, Yong-Joon
   1977   "Funeral and Ritual for Ancestor Worship of Che-ju Island" (in
          Japanese), *The Japanese Journal of Ethnology,* 42-3: 249-266.
Ito, Abito
   1973   "A Sketch on the Village-life in Chindo Island" (in Japanese), *Oriental
          Culture* (University of Tokyo), 53:147-159.
Janelli, Roger L.
   1973   "Anthropology, Folklore and Korean Ancestor Worship," *Cultural
          Anthropology* (Korean Society for Cultural Anthropology), 6:175-190.
Lee, Kwang-Kyu
   1977   "Descent Group and Ancestor Worship" (in Korean), *Korean Cultural
          Anthropology,* 9:1-124.
Li, Yih-Yuan
   1976   "Chinese Geomancy and Ancestor Worship: A Further Discussion,"
          Ancestors, edited by W. H. Newell.
Mabuchi, Toichi

1960 "The Aboriginal Peoples of Formosa," *Social Structure in Southeast Asia*, edited by G. P. Murdock, Chicago: Quadrangle Books.

1976a "Optional Cult Group Affiliation among the Puyuma and the Miyako Islanders," *Ancestors*, edited by W. H. Newell.

1976b "A Note on Ancestor Worship in 'Cognatic' Societies," *Ancestors*, edited by W. H. Newell.

Nakane, Chie

1967 *Kinship and Economic Organization in Rural Japan*. London. Athlone Press.

Newell, W. H.

1968 "Chinese and Japanese Ancestor Worship," *Proceedings of VIIIth International Congress of Anthropology and Ethnological Sciences*, 3:300-301.

1970 "Memorialism and Ancestor Worship in Japanese and Chinese Society" (in Japanese), *Sha* 3-1:1-9.

1976 "Good and Bad Ancestors," *Ancestors*, edited by W. H. Newell, The Hague:Mouton.

Ooms, Herman

1976 "A Structural Analysis of Japanese Ancestral Rites and Belieff," *Ancestors*, edited by W. H. Newell.

Plath, D. W.

1964 "Where the Family of God Is the Family: The Role of the Dead in Japanese Households," *American Anthropologist*, 66:300-317.

Sato, Nobuyuki

1973 "Family and Kinship in Che-ju Island" (in Japanese), *Oriental Culture* (University of Tokyo), 53:109-145.

Shih, Lei

1975 "Social Change of the Puyuma in Kasavakan" (in Chinese), *Bulletin of the Institute of Ethnology, Academia Sinica*, 40:119-142.

Smith, Robert

1974a *Ancestor Worship in Contemporary Japan*. Stanford University Press.

1974b "Afterword," *Religion and Ritual in Chinese Society*, edited by A. P. Wolf, Stanford University Press.

1976 "Who Are the 'Ancestors' in Japan?—A Census of Memorial Tablets," *Ancestors*, edited by W. H. Newell.

Suenari, Michio

1968 "Affinal Relationships among the Puyuma of Taiwan," *Proceedings of VIIIth Congress of Anthropological and Ethnological Sciences*, 3:134-137.

1969 "A Preliminary Report on Puyuma Language," *Bulletin of the Institute of Ethnology, Academia Sinica*, 27:141-164.

1970   "Cognatic Kinship System among the Puyuma, Taiwan" (in Japanese), *The Japanese Journal of Ethnology*, 35-2:87-123.

1973   (Coauthor with Kwang-Kyu Lee) "A Preliminary Report on Two Villages in Kyong-sang-puk-do" (in Japanese), *Oriental Culture* (University of Tokyo), 53:41-78.

1977   "The Cult of the Ancestors in Taiwan (1)" (in Japanese), *Seishin Studies*(University of the Sacred Heart), 50:85-153.

1978a "The Cult of the Dead at the Grave in Andong District of Korea" (in Korean), *The Journal of the Institute for Shilla Kaya Culture* (Yeongnam University), 9-10:151-163.

1978b "The Cult of the Ancestors in Taiwan (2)" (in Jpanese), *Seishin Studies*(University of the Sacred Heart), 52:5-55.

Takeda, Choshu
1976   " 'Family Religion' in Japan: *Ie* and Its Religious Faith," *Ancestors,* edited by W. H. Newell.

Wang, Sung-Hsing
1971   "Comparative Study of Ancestor Worship of the Chinese and the Japanese" (in Chinse), *Bulletin of the Institute of Ehtnology, Academia Sinica,* 31:235-252.

1974   "Taiwanese Architecture and the Supernatural," *Religion and Ritual in Chinese Society,* edited by Arthur Wolf.

Wolf, Arthur
1974   "Gods, Ghosts, and Ancestors," *Religion and Ritual in Chinese Society,* edited by A. Wolf, Stanford University Press.

Yeo, Joong-Chul
1980   "A Study on Divided Inheritance of the Ritual Service of the Ancestor Worship" (in Korean), *Anthropological Research* (Yeongnam University), 1:25-54.

10　The System of Belief in Korean Rural Communities[1)]

OAK-LA CHO

Introduction

The practice of religion in Korean rural communities is one of the most striking areas which show continuity with the past despite the dramatic socio-economic transforamtion of modern Korea. During the last dynasty when Confucianism became the ethical doctrine in the society, most folk religion had been denounced as superstition. Since 1948 the government of the Republic has also followed this traditional policy to discourage the practice of folk religion. In spite of this constant discouragement by the authorities throughout the history of Korea, folk religion in a rural community with their basic function of relieving the sufferings of the villagers, continues quite unaffected by modern influences. Religious activity is at the very center of the life of the villagers; it is the single most important element in their lives and it controls and influences their behavior and hopes at every turn. It is difficult to achieve a perspective on rural Korean life and tradition without a sound understanding of their religious beliefs and practices.

Korean rural villagers are exposed to daily problems due to their meager economy and marginality as a peasantry. Lack of sufficient means of relieving their difficulties enforces them depend upon traditional treatment through folk religion. Confucian ethics, official doctrine since the Yi dynasty, hardly encourage the worship of spiritual beings, but at the same time it does not exclude the possibility of a spiritual world which influences human destiny. The folk religion, in fact does not cause conflict directly with Confucianism, because its emphasis on the power of the dead per-

son's spirits can be the common ground with the ancestor worship ceremonies which are the core of Confucian rituals.

This paper will deal with the common elements among various religious forms and activities among Korean peasants. Special attention will be
given to folk way of thinking expressed in Confucian rituals and others.
Finally, the paper will attempt to interpret this way of belief in terms of
social relationship among Korean rural villagers.

Folk Religion

The villagers believe in or assume the existence of spiritual beings in
various aspects of the objective world. Rural villagers whose economy
traditionally depends upon the nature, grant the power of natural spirits
and show respects or fears toward them. Spirits in natural objects seem to
be able to influence the daily life of human beings. Well-beings of whole
village are often conceptualized in relation to the functionings of these
animistic spirits.

Natural symbols like mountains, trees and rocks around their residence represent long life, fertility, and power. A mountain is considered to
have a deity. A tree has a spirit too; an old or strangely shaped one is
supposed to have an especially unique spirit.

Many traditional rural villages have their patron deity who resides in
its shrine located near a big tree or at the top of a mountain near their
residential area. These villages offer communal ceremonies for their patron
deities once or twice a year.[2] The ceremonies are carried on by *chekwan*
who are selected from elders. They are the domain of males who are the
heads of each household. Their procedure is very similar to the one in
Confucian rituals. Each household shares the expenses of ceremonies
depending upon its economic condition and petitions. The formal ritual for
the patron deity is usually followed by another ceremonies for various
spirits functioning in meticulous daily life of villagers.[3] These ceremonies
are open to most villagers, even to outsiders. Formerly before the land
reform, some rich *yangban* (Korean gentry) landlords entertained other
peasant villagers by financing them generously.[4] Traditional ideology of
good neighborliness plays major role in these rituals. Through these communal occasions villagers strengthen solidarity as a territorial unit (Chang
1975:53).

A house and each of its parts have their guiding spirits also. The direction of house construction,doors and walls is also viewed as being related to the well-being of its household members. The main guiding spirit resides in the central part of the house. On every special occassion in the family such as ancestor worship ceremony, a house warming ceremony or the first harvest, an offering is made to him. The kitchen god, next in importance and favorite of the women who work in the kitchen, gets special offerings at least twice a year. The women who have special petitions to her place a symbolic jar of clean water outside the kitchen and pray to it and replenish it every night, sometimes for a whole month.

In order to cast away bad spirits who may sneak into the house a wife sometimes worships and appeals to a special deity for the well-being of her family. This special deity is officially invited through shamanic performance. Usually this deity is supposed to live in a pottery jar which is full of raw rice. Once it settles in a certain position of the house, it is not easily removed, and receives hot cooked rice at each family celebration. This special family deity can be bequeathed from a mother-in-law to her daughter-in-law who resides in the same house. It is never handed down from a mother to her own daughter. When an old woman who had lived with her daughter's family, died in 1978, her jar which contains the deity was destroyed during the funeral.

A family sometimes performs a shamanic ceremony to these guiding spirits of each parts of the house for the particular purpose such as curing a sick family member or having a son. This ceremony is often arranged by the wife of a family. Some families regularly conduct shamanic ceremony for various spirits residing in their house.

Because they believe that the destiny of human life lies beyond human powers, they consult shamans, usually women, regarding the destiny of a new-born child. If the destiny of the baby is seen by the shaman to be bad, she may recommend its parents to perform a special ceremony in order to obtain a spiritual protector by ritually offering the baby to a natural being like a rock or a nearby mountain. The baby's parents are expected to offer a small gift of food to his natural protector several times a year to continue this contract (the local term to offer in this ceremony is 'to sell' instead of offering).[5]

Most figures surrounding a human life are understood to be interconnected through an unseen string. Each spirit of a natural object is a tangible part of the present world. Most villagers who are believers in folk religion firmly subscribe to the notion that an individual's unique destiny is determined and influenced by many elements in his or her world; the time of his (her) birth, the position of tree in relation to his (her) house, a benign or maleficient ancestral spirits etc.

Ancestor Worship

Even though Confucianists do not clearly define the future world after death, the ancestor worship ceremony is performed under the assumption that the ancestral spirits can visit their descendants through this formal occassions.

One of the important ritual processes in an ancestor worship ceremony is to offer food and wine, and let the spirit of the ancestor receive it at the table. After the ceremony, all food, especially the cooked rice offered to the ancestor, has to be mixed thoroughly with the other rice, because its nutrition has already been consumed by the ancestral spirit. An old *yangban* in Kyegokch'on[6] told me on the day of an ancestor worship ceremony that he had to stay up after the ceremony in case the spirit of his sister-in-law dropped by his room. He explained to me that if what is believed about spirits after death is true, his sister-in-law ought to stop by his place after such a ceremony.

Filial piety expressed in performing ancestor worship ceremonies is the core of relationships among family members. The greatest virtue of a human being, according to Confucianism, is filial piety, the obligation of a son to take care of his parents in their old age and to perform or participate in ancestor worship ceremony after they die. By fulfilling these duties, a man reassures his social status as a full member of the family, sublineage, lineage and clan.

When I asked the villagers the reason why they have to perform ancestor worship ceremonies, twenty four out of forty-five questioned responded that they did it to keep the traditional law. One *yangban* villagers who was sixty-seven years old said that a human being has to perform *chesa* (ancestor worship ceremony) "because he cannot forget his debt to his parents," and that "human beings cannot survive without their parents. Therefore, we wear a mourner's garb for three years and serve them even after their death as a filial duty."

Rural villagers view the ideal death as the peaceful transition from its present world to another one leaving descendants behind at home. The abrupt sudden death resulting from accidents outside the house cannot make up this peaceful transition.

According to local belief when a person dies outside the house, the spirit of the dead body cannot find its home. Thus the house has to have a special ceremony to lead the spirit back to its original home. This kind of ceremony is considered to be the most emotional one since through it the sorrow of the dead person's family can publicly and vividly expressed. Its purpose is to reenact the death and then to let the dead person's spirit leave peacefully for the eternal world.

Strenghthened by the authority of Confucian ethics, the neglected ancestral spirits are the most troublesome ones. Unsatisfied ancestral spirits are often accused to cause illness which do not respond to repeated modern medication. The wife or mother of the sick person may try to identify the spirit on her own or do it with the aid of a shaman. When the spirit is identified they perform a ceremony which has two potential objects; to appease the spirit by offering it food or threaten it against invading the sick body again. A shaman explains most serious cases as the results of neglecting certain ancestors.

Children are usually considered vulnerable to the attack of displeased wandering spirits. When a child suffers from an illness, one performs a ceremony to find out the spirit who might be causing it. The celebrant tries to stand a spoon in a bowl of rice while reciting the names of the potential, intervening spirits. If the spoon stands up at the mention of a name, the evil spirit is identified. Next, a bowl of rice, water, and a dried fish are offered to the spirit. The spirit dwelling in the sick child's body is supposed to be attracted to food and is expected to leave the sick body to partake of the offering. Once it has left the body, through a succession of offerings of food and water, the spirit is carefully led outside the house. At this ritual, a cutting knife used in the kitchen is employed to indicate the path to the spirit. During the last stage, a perfomer throws the knife on the ground. If the sharp end of the knife points toward the gate of the house, it is generally accepted as a sign that the spirit has left the house.

In short, ancestral spirits are divided according to "whether or not they are worshipped" as the case of China (Feuchtwang 1974:118). Officially recognized ancestors are worshipped through *chesa* by a surviving son or descendants. The ancestors or dead persons who died accidently and are not worshipped properly, cannot settle peacefully in *chŏsŭng* (the world of dead persons). They wonder around human settlements. These neglected spirits are the most feared and receive shamanic performance occasionally from women.

A man operates formal ancestor worship ceremonies for his direct ancestors within the context of family system. A woman worships neglected ancestral spirits who are excluded from the official seance of family ceremonies. While a man holds the backbone of family relationship by performing *chesa,* a woman counterbalances the spiritual structure by pleasing neglected ancestral spirits in order to prevent from unpredicted misfortune among family.

The belief in geomancy is one of the distinctive features of the religious practices of the villagers (Janelli 1980). Since the villagers believe in the power of ancestral spirits, they accept that the location of the grave site of the ancestors can influence the well-being of the descendants. In order to receive the good favor of the ancestral spirits, the villagers are eager to find the best site for their dead parents. The villagers hire a geomancer to choose the site. When a family has been in constant trouble, usually it asks a geomancer to recheck the grave site newly built for the dead family member. If the site is later decided to be the main cause of the family's misfortune, the family changes the grave site to another place. "So and so became wealthy because of his parent's good grave site," is a common saying. Even though some villagers question the possibility of the existence of ancestral spirits, most villagers seem to be concerned about the possible fortune or misfortune resulting from the location of the grave site. This geomancy also indicates their way of thinking which is marked by the belief that human destiny is determined by its connection with the spiritual world.

Shamanism

Shamans play a significant role in folk religion. When a family has suffered continuously from various misfortunes, it is common to consult a shaman, because illness and misfortunes are often viewed as the result by angers of spirits who govern functionings of human daily life. A shaman usually recommends that the wife of the household perform a shamanic casting away ceremony in order to relieve the anger of bad spirits. The date of the performance is set for one of the "clean" days according to the lunar calendar.[7] On the day of the ceremony, the wife of a household cleans the whole house. The ceremony starts at dinner time before the sunset and lasts until one or two o'clock in the morning. The most important items of food offered to the various spirits which govern all aspects of human life are rice, raw and cooked, vegetables, dried fish and pork. Rice especially symbolizes the wealth of the family. It is constantly offered on the temporary altar arranged in the main living room of the house. The shaman who is invited to this ceremony (*kut*) sets the table for all the spirits including the ancestral spirits. After the table is set, she starts singing, inviting the spirits to the feast offered by the wife of the household. Next, she tries to talk personally with each ancestral spirit related to the wife of the household. In this case, ancestors who died outside their home or women who died without a surviving son, receive the most attention because unhappy ancestors might be the cause of the bad luck of the household.

One ceremony that was performed in 1977 was carried out in order to help the wife of the household who constantly suffered from economic and family problems. She was once the mistress of the present husband, and later became a legal wife to him after his former wife committed suicide. The recent troubles that she suffered brought back all her old guilt feelings. She had been worried about the stained relationship with her husband and step sons. The shaman in charge of that ceremony invoked her family problems in public in the presence of her husband and her step sons. The troubled wife acknowledged her fault in public, asked the dead former wife of her husband to forgive her fault and promised to offer the ancestor worship ceremony to the spirit of the dead former wife of her husband sincerely. the wife of the household carried on that shamanic performance and invited as many guests as possible because it is generally thought that the more people participate in the ceremony the more benefit the sponsoring person can derive from it. The shaman also liked to have many guests. During the ceremony, food was freely offered to all the participants. Therefore, it turned out to be a feast in that settlement. Most of the participants were expected to respond vocally to the sharman's invitation in order to increase the dramatic effect of the ceremony. All in all, it was a very emotional exposing of the family's problems in public. After the ceremony, the conflicts in the family were fully understood by most participants. The troubled relationship of the woman to her family was supposed to be repaired through the help of ancestral spirits. This kind of special shamanic performance is also conducted when a person has died outisde the house.

In Kyegokch'on the villagers most often bring their problems to an old women who lives in a nearby hamlet. She has been conducting her shamanic practice for the last fifty years. She is considered a very effective shaman whom the villagers can consult for a reasonable fee. Her clients include both the *yangban* and the *sangmin* (commoner) of that area. She has her own shrine for her sponsor deity. Most of her treatment is carried on in the house of her clients, because it is thought that most spirits responsible for influencing a person reside in the house of the afflicted person. The general attitude to the villagers toward her is that she may be close to the spirit world. They feel that spirits may receive her requests and be influenced by her more easily than by an ordinary person. Therefore, even though her social status around Kyegokoh'on is not as high as that of the *yangban* women, the villagers have a certain respect for her. By the authority of spirits and ancestors a shaman provides comprehensive solution to the misfortunes and illness of villagers. Her explanation is close to the belief system of rural communities. It strengthens the connection between human life and spiritual beings. Her activities, though, are mostly bounded to an individual household.

Women and Religion

Among the organized religion such as Christianity, and Buddhism, Buddhism has the highest practicing population — about ten women in Kyegokch'on. Only three or four women, however, go to a temple regularly. Sometimes they stay in a temple for a few days to say special prayers. They told me that if they repeat a chant a thousand times, they will keep good health, and gain peace of mind, and after death, they will go to heaven (*Kŭnrak*). When they go to the temple which is located in mountain about two miles away from the community, they stay in one of the branch houses attached to the main building of the temple. In the branch house (*amja*) a woman who is called Kim *bosal* (a potential or future Budda) keeps her own shrine and receives her own clients. Sometimes, women come to ask her a special prayer for the troubled members of their family. And Kim *bosal* also treats people, especially neurotic patients. Her connection with the main temple is very ambiguous. One of the monks in the temple expressed to me that her practices could not be directly related to the main functioning of a Buddhist temple. As long as Kim *bosal* accepts the authority of the main temple, the main temple can get many followers, through her. All of the three regularly practicing village women identify themselves as devoted Buddhists. All of them go to Kim *bosal* and receive advice from her with regard to their family, financial matters and health problems. Some other Buddhists in that area told me that one of the main reason to be a Buddhist is the advice of a fortune-teller who claims that their destiny is tied to Buddhism. They go to a temple irregularly. Somehow the basic attitude toward Buddhism is similar to the one toward shamanistic performances. A a matter of fact, a shaman who performed a shamanistic ritual in that area is called Kye *Bosal,* even though she worships all kinds of natural spirits. Her followers in that area consider themselves Buddhists.

There is a small church branch run by a young missionary on the main street of Kyegokch'on. There are four practicing Christians in that area: one is old woman whose son and husband died one after another during the two previous years, another is a girl who is the only daughter of a small shop keeper, and the last one is a clerk and his wife in the Agricultural Cooperative branch who is staying around there temporarily. Most villagers are a bit suspicious of them. Two of them are considered to be caught by the "spirit" of Jesus and the clerk's family is totally isolated from the rest. His family rarely communicates with other villagers, which only reinforces their suspicion about Christianity. In short, the influece of Christianity in that community is almost negligible, even though some villagers accept the spiritual power of Jesus over other spirits. One wife told me that when she found out about her son's stomachache, she asked her daughter to sing a hymn that her daughter learnt from Sunday School in order to cast away a bad spirit which caused the stomachache. For her, Christianity which worships Jesus is one among many kinds of spiritual worships.

As the matter of fact, the direct reaction of villagers toward this spiritual world varies; even the same person has different beliefs from time to time. Most villagers, however, implicitly accept the existence of spirits and their power over human beings. According to my general survey in Kyegokch'on, most villagers vaguely accepted the possibility of a spiritual world. Villagers often say, "it is very hard to accept the existence of deity or to deny it." This is the basic attitude toward the spiritual world of the average man in that area (Andong) regardless of their *sinbun* (estate).[8] Most villagers seem not to have any organized religious practice. Their belief in various spirits is one of the ways to view their surrounding world. Most religious rituals including that of Buddhism are practiced irregularly and the observance of these rituals depends on the situation or the problems that the villagers face in their daily life. In a way, the villagers cannot construct a logical framework for their world in terms of their ideal Confucianism. Women, especially, who occupy the lowest social position in a rural society regardless of their *sinbun* search for explanations of their unknown future through shamanic performance. Generally the spiritual world is considered to be the domain of the women. All shamans around Kyegokch'on area are women. Villagers regard a religious man as slightly abnormal. Although men also accept the spiritual world, they barely participate in the performance of shamanic ceremonies directly, even though they agree to have the ceremony and meet its expenses.

Conclusion

The system of belief in Korean rural communities is a view of interaction between human life and spiritual world. The above mentioned religious aspects among rural villagers help them to cope with the crises of life, of failure, of sickness, of death. It is peasant religion which is both utilitarian and moralistic, but not ethical and questioning (Wolf, 1966:99)

Most villagers seem to believe that a man who is in charge of social system, controls the secular world with Confucian ethics, and that a woman listens to the spiritual world. This folk concept confirms the traditional notion about oriental rural society especially in China that "the educated people are indifferent to religion" (Hu 1948, Gallin 1966, Yang 1961). Men hold responsibility of the worship ceremonies for ancestors and for village patron deity, while women take charge of spiritual matters influencing daily and future life. Through the ancestor worship ceremonies men reconfirm the blood-tied family which succeeds indefinitely. The village patron deity ceremonies contribute to strengthening the solidarity among villagers as members of a village community.

In short, men's rituals are closely related to the formal structure of rural society. Women concentrate their rituals on family matters such as the well-being of their household.

Through the help of a shaman, women often attempt to communicate with spirits which affect daily life of human beings, and comprehend their sufferings. A shaman who is an intermediate between the present world and the another world, employs the authority of various spirits including ancestral one to solve her client's problems. Men, with a few exception, never engage directly in folk religious activities conducted by a shaman or a wife.

As far as religion is concerned, there is no sharp divergence in the beliefs of the two major estate groups, *yangban* and *sangmin*, as we can see in Kyegokch'on. Among ninety-three households in that area, regardless of their occupation or *sinbun*, there is not particular religious form involving all members of each household except the case of a clerk's family who is temporal resident.

Confucianism seems to replace the ethical function of religion. The utilitarian beliefs of folk religion do not conflict with the Confucion ideology. They explain the spiritual objects whose function is not clarified by Confucianism. By accepting the existence of ancestral spirits and their power, folk religion rather strengthens the Confucian model. Since the position of ancestor spirits in folk religion is superior to other various spirits which influence daily life in detail, folk religion contributes to the continuity of traditional social system, such as lineage organization, various kinship rituals including ancestor worship ceremonies, and *sinbun* (estate) system. On the other hand, by providing the functional spiritual beings who influence each area of the villagers' daily needs, folk religion merges these spiritual objects into a harmonious whole.

Since Confucianism has been so closely connected with the traditional social stratification system, the other major religions whose ethics may be in conflict with that of Confucianism cannot develop in the conservative rural areas like Kyegokch'on.

Thus it becomes clear that in the belief system of Korean rural communities, the elements of Taoism, Buddhism, Confucian teaching and even animistic belief have been combined into a plastic, accomodating, single loose system. As in the case of principle behind neighborliness, the belief in this loosely constructed spiritual world enables the villagers to face the problems of daily living. As in their general acceptance of the concept of harmony among neighbors, the villagers, in their belief in folk religion, share the idea of a spiritual world. By providing the path to relieve the pressure imposed by the hierarchical social system such as distinction on the basis of *sinbun,* sex, age, and generation, and their limited economic condition, the belief system in Korean rural communities functions to put all villagers together as the relationship of neighborhood does.

Notes

1) Field research was conducted from Sept., 1977 to May, 1978. It was financed by the State University of New York at Stony Brook. I would like to give thanks to Dr. Pedro Carrasco, SUNY at Stony Brook and Dr. Sang-Bok Han, Seoul National University for their valuable advice for this paper. All names of place and persons in this paper are fictive ones.
2) Chu-Gun Chang (1975:49) says that around half of rural villages might have conducted these ceremonies until several years ago.
3) Shamans used to be invited for these low-level ceremonies (Chang 1975, Chung 1979).
4) See Taek-Kyoo Kim 1964, pp. 236-254.
5) In some other parts of Korea such as Kyung'gi province, a baby ritually becomes a fosterchild to a shaman according to Chang and Kwang-Kyu Lee.
6) Kyegokch'on is pseudonym for a peasant village located near Andong city, Kyong-sangbuk-do.
7) Most families in rural villages keep a booklet that indicates what activities are good or bad each day. This booklet is based on the oriental *yi* and *yen* philosophy. It is not true, though, that people always follow the advice of the almanac, as Fei (1939) reports for China. But they do consult the booklet on such activities as building houses, arranging marriages, starting long trips, etc. They avoid undertaking any important and adventurous activities on inauspicious days especially those that are explicitly stated as "good for nothing." They pay more attention to bad days than to good days.
8) Hereditary hierarchical social strata translated to the estate (Bergel 1962).

References

Bergel, Egon Ernest
  1962   *Social Stratification.* New York: McGraw-Hill.
Brandt, Vincent
  1971   *A Korean Village: Between Farm and Sea.* Cambridge: Harvard University Press.
Brunner
  1928   *Rural Korea: A Preliminary Survey of Economic, Social and Religious Condition.* New York: International Missionary Council.
Cancien, Frank
  1976   "Social Stratification," In *Annual Review of Anthropology* 5: 227-48.
Carrasco, Pedro
  1959   *Land and Polity in Tibet.* American Ethnological Society Publication, Seattle: University of Washington Press.
  1952   *Tarascan Folk Religion: An Analysis of Economic, Social and Religious Interactions* (Middle American Reserch Institute, Publication no. 17)
Chang, Chu-Gun
  1975   *Hanguk ŭi Hyangt'o Sinang.* Seoul: Ul-yu Mungo.
Cho, Oak-La
  1979   *Social Stratification in a Korean Peasant Village.* Ph. D. Dissertation, State University of New York at Stony Brook.
Choe, Kil-Sŏng
  1980   "Communal Ritual and Social Structure in Village Korea," Paper presented at Conference on Korean Religion and Society, Aug. 1980, Mackinac Island.
Chung, Sŭng-Mo
  1979   "Uirye esŏ Nat'anaŭn Ŭimi ŭi Sangjingjŏk Pyohyŏn e Kwanhan Il Yŏn-gu," *Ilryuhaknonjip* 5:49-89.
Deschamps, Christian (Cha, Ki-Son)
  1972   "Mingan Sinang ŭi Hyŏngt'ai wa T'ŭksong," M. A. thesis, Seoul National University.
Dix, Griffin
  1980   "Folk Confucianism, Shamanism and the Symbolic Resolution of Fundamental Oppositions in Korean Social Structure," Paper presented at AAS Annual Meeting, March 1980, Washington, D. C.
Elliade, Mircea
  1964   *Shamanism: Archaic Techniques of Ecstacy.* New York: Pantheon.
Fei, Hsiao-T'ung
  1939   *Peasant Life in China: A Field Study of Country Life in the Yang-tze*

198

Valley. London: Kegan Paul.

Feuchtwang, Stephan
    1974 "Domestic and Communal Worship in Taiwan," In *Religion and Ritural in Chinese Society,* ed. by A. Wolf, Stanford: Stanford Univ. Press.

Freedamn, Maurice
    1974 "On the Sociological Study of Chinese Religion," In *Religion and Ritual in Chinese Society,* ed. by A. Wolf, Stanford: Stanford Univ. Press.

Gallin, Bernard
    1966 *Hsin Hsing, Taiwan: A Chinese Village in Change.* Berkeley: Univ. of California Press.

Han, Sang-Bok
    1977 *Korean Fishermen.* Seoul: Seoul National Univ. Press.

Hu, Hsien-Chin
    1948 *The Common Descent Group in China and Its Functions.* New York: Viking Fund Publication in Anthropolgy.

Janelli, Roger and Dawnhee Yim Janelli
    1980 "The Effects of a Grave: Geomancy and Ancestral Affliction in a Korean Village," Paper presented at Conference on Korean Religion and Society.

Kendall, Laurell
    1980 "House Persons and Women's Sites," Paper presented at Conference on Korean Religion and Society.

Kim, Eugene and Chang-Boh Chee (eds.)
    1969 *Aspects of Social Change in Korea.* Kalamazoo: The Korea Research and Publications, Inc.

Kim, Taek-Kyoo
    1964 *The Cultural Stucture of a Consanguinous Village,* (in Korean with English summary). Tae-gu: Chong-gu University Press.

Lee, Sang-il et al. (eds.)
    1976 *Hanguk Sasang ui Kunwon.* Seoul: Bak-young mungo.

Norbeck, Edward
    1970 "Continuities in Japanese Social Stratification," In *Essays in Comparative Social Striatification,* eds. by Plotniv and Tude, Pittsburgh: Univ. of Pittsburgh Press.

Osgood, Cornelius
    1951 *The Koreans and Their Culture.* New York: Ronald Press.

Wolf, Arthur
    1974 "Gods, Ghosts, and Ancestros," In *Religion and Ritual in Chinese Society.* ed. by A. Wolf.

Wolf, Eric
    1966   *Peasants*. Englewood Cliffs: Prentice Hall.
Yang, C. K.
    1961   *Religion in Chinese Society*. Berkeley: University of California Press.

11   Meru: A Symbol of Continuity and Change in Thai Society

SRISAKRA VALLIBHOTAMA

Introduction

Ritual is a symbolic representation of human society. It is a part of the human culture that reflects the hopes, fears, joys and sorrows of mankind. Among various rituals, the funeral rite, which is classified as a rite of passage, comes out as the most universal. Analytically, it can be viewed as two faces of the coin by taking the deceased as the focus. On one face is a psychological dimension concerning the relationship between the dead person and the supernatural world and thus it welcomes speculation on religious belief and practice to separate the dead from the living. On the other face is a social dimension regarding the deceased as a member of the society. His death causes a loss to his immediate family and thus upsets the economic and social equilibrium requiring both a re-adjustment and a re-integration.

Archaeologically speaking, funeral practices and beliefs about death were of central importance to the early development of the study of human evolution, of the rise of ancient civilizations and of cultural and social institutions. This is because data concerning the emergence of human kind has relied heavily on two kinds of evidence: tools and grave assemblages. It is at the burial site that one finds the remains of symbolic activity of both psychological and social dimensions. Outstanding anthropologists of the past like Durkheim, Van Gennep, Hertz and Radcliffe-Brown paid much attention to the study of death ritual in forming up their social theories. Durkheim and Radcliffe-Brown emphasized the emotional aspect of ritual and suggested that it was accountable for the social solidarity and social integration of a society (Huntington and Metcalf, 1979: 28). Van Gennep and Hertz on the contrary were more specific in treating funeral ritual as a symbolic representation of the ambiguous ("liminal") state of the deceased while in passage from life toward some fixed eternal condition. It is a transition that begins with the separation of the deceased from life and ends with his or her incorporation into the world of the dead. Thus it involves tripartite analytical scheme —— separation, liminality and reincorporation (Huntington and Metcalf, 1979: 97-98).

From various viewpoints emphasizing the social and cultural significance of the funeral ritual as mentioned above, I accept the universality of this ritual and see that its essence continues beyond space and time in the human society while its form of practice may change according to social situation. Therefore, it is worthwhile to investigate the funeral ritual in Thai society in order to see how, and to what extent, it reflects cultural continuity and change in Thai society.

At the present time funeral ritual among the Thai in general is more conspicuous and is not tied to a specific period of time of the year as is ordination which is regarded as another important rite of passage. From my observations, I see an increasing similarity in the process and pattern of funeral rites as practiced in the urban and the rural areas. Such a phenomenon has never occurred in the past. Central in this similarity is the presence of the funeral pyre known as the Meru. It is characterized by an elevated square concrete structure, open from all four sides and has a pyramidal roof and spire on top. A flight of staircases exists at each of the three sides leading to the place where the coffin is. The fourth side of the building is associated with a passage to the cremating chamber which is topped with an imposing chimney. The Meru is found in an open space in the compound of the *wat* (a Thai Buddhist monastery) and is often associated with another buildings serving as the funeral halls. The imposing character of its spire and chimney can be seen from afar and seems to tone down the significance of the steep gabled roof of the *bod* (ordination hall) and the lofty *stupa* that were formerly regarded as the landmarks of the monastery.

In the past there was no such permanent concrete building of a Meru constructed in the *wat* compound, since cremation of the deceased always took place in the cemetery, a separate area either at the back of the *wat* on the outskirts of the village. Only the corpses of nobles and monks and the rich were allowed to be cremated in the *wat* by setting up a temporary funeral pyre of wooden structure. This required big expense beyond which ordinary people could afford. That the Meru or the funeral pyre is present in the *wat* compound today is clearly indicative of a changing in the funeral pattern which does, no doubt, affect the socio-economic status of both the *wat* and the people who sponsor the cremation. Here, by taking the Meru as the focus, I shall attempt to explore its symbolic meaning in relation to the cremation ritual of the past and the present. Finally, I shall delineate its socio-economic implications so far as they are felt by the *wat* and the people who sponsor cremation.

The Origin and Symbolic Meaning of the Meru

The term Meru is, in fact, an abbreviation of Phra Sumerumat which means the golden Mount Meru, the pillar of the universe according to Hindu-Buddhist conception. We do not know for certain when the Thai derived such a concept but, judging from archaeological evidences found in Thailand, we could say that this country as well as other Southeast Asian states had been enormously influenced by Indian civilization from the 2nd century A.D. Buddhist and Hindu monuments and objects have been found in various parts of the country since the 7th century A.D. Relevant to the concept of Mount Meru are the Khmer and Khmer-like temples called *prasada* which were either devoted to the Hindu gods or to Mahayana Buddhist deities. As a general practice, the *prasada* was erected either on a mountain or at the centre of a city or town to represent a microcosm of the universe. To the Khmer, the *prasada* as the representation of Mount Meru is connected with kingship in two ways: one as the abode of the god of whom the king is the incarnation, and other, as the seat of the *cakravartin*—the world ruler who moves the wheel of righteousness to revolve round the centre of the universe.

Although the ancient Hinayana Buddhist states of Thailand, and particularly those in the Central Plain, accepted the relation between *cakravartin* and Mount Meru, they did not built their religious monuments in relation to the physical centre of the city or town as did the Khmer. They were simply big or small *stupas* erected either within or without the city or town. Around the 13th century A.D., they began to incorporate the Khmer concept of Mount Meru as being the centre of the city and town into their society. From this period we see that the main *stupa* containing the relics of the Lord Buddha known as Phra Maha That was erected at the centre of the city, thus connecting more profoundly religion to kingship However, as the Buddhist kings at that time had never been regarded as the incarnation of a god but only as the Dharmaraja who was the patron of the Buddhist Faith, we see no grand construction of the royal residence as the abode of the god like those of the Khmer. The royal palace and living quarters were built of perishable materials, were lower in status and prestige than those of the *wat*, particularly the Wat Maha That which was the spiritual centre of the kingdom (Tambiah, 1977: 86).

It was around the 15th century A.D., when the state of Ayudhya under King Trailok gained political control over wider territory of the country, that the role of kingship began to be equal to that of the religion. Divine kingship together with the concept of the *cakravartin* was heavily emphasized and this is manifest from the incorporation of Brahmanic rituals to kingship and state ceremonies and the Khmer and Sanskrit words were used to enhance royal prestige. The royal palace was enlarged and encircled with three concentric walls. The innermost was for the living quarters of the king and his family and here, according to the palatial law, no man was allowed to enter. Within the middle wall were groups of stately buildings like the audience hall where the king carried out the business of government as a daily routine, and the throne halls where important state ceremonies such as coronation and the royal funeral ritual were performed. These royal buildings were called *prasada* imitating the abodes of the gods on Mount Meru. Many of them were named after the abode of Indra, the chief god who resides in the Tavatimsa Heaven above Mount Meru. They were, for example, the Chakawat Phaichayon Maha Prasada and the Suriyat Amarindra Maha Prasada. The outer wall of the royal palace was very well fortified for the safety of the royalty and within it was the royal chapel — Wat Phra Sri Sanphet, built up to replace the former Wat Maha That in importance. It was exclusively for the use of royalty and some religious rituals of the state such as the biannual ceremony of drinking the water of allegiance. Here, large *stupas* were erected to house the relics of the Lord Buddha. The two sacred images of the famous Phra Sri Sanphet and Phra Lokanat were also installed here, and religious halls of various kinds were built. Also this *wat* served as the royal cemetery since it was recorded in the royal chronicles of Ayudhya that after the royal cremation, the remains of the king was taken to be enshrined in its *stupas*.

No doubt, the incorporation of the royal *wat* into the compound of royal palace had marked not only the rising power of the god-like monarch of Ayudhya, but also a shift from the spiritual centre of the kingdom of Wat Maha That to the materialistic one of the royal throne halls in the palace. This is attested from the praise of beauty and richness of the royal palace of Ayudhya in foreign notes and in the Thai poem from the 17th century A.D. (Vallibhotama, 1977:67-77). In the latter period, the royal palace of Ayudhya is the model of the royal palace of Bangkok indicating from the presence of the three concentric walls in which the Temple of the Emerald Buddha is included. There exist in the second inner wall, lofty throne halls like the Tusita Maha Prasada, the Amarindra Vinichai Hall, etc., all connected with the name and abode of Indra on Mount Meru— the centre of the universe.

Judging from the development of the royal palace of Ayudhya to its connections with that of Bangkok, I would say that the pattern is the Thai innovation. It is created from mixing the Hindu and Buddhist ingredients for the materialistic pursuit of the royalty, i.e., political power and social distance on the one hand and the loyalty and stability of the state on the other. Brahmanic rituals and the concept of Mount Meru are a rationale to sustain it. This is obvious through Brahmanic ceremonies performed in the Thai court. Here, I shall cite the coronation and royal cremation as the case in point. At coronation the king is stately crowned in the Maha Prasada which represents the abode of Indra above Mount Meru and this implies that the king is the *cakravartin* — the universal monarch. For the great king when he considers that his earthly power entitled him to the rank as an emperor, he has himself consecrated again with the rites of Indra, king of the gods known as Indrabhiseka. This royal ritual was described in the palatial law of Ayudhya and Quaritch Wales (1931:122-123) mentions it in his *Ancient Siamese State Ceremonies* as follows:

> For the royal ceremony of Indrabhiseka a Meru, of a height of 1 *sen* 5 *va* is built in the middle of an open space. There Indra sits on the Meru surrounded by Isindhra and Yugundhara mountains, one *sen* high; and there stand Karavika Mountain 15 *va* high and Mount Kailasa 10 *va* high. On the inside are golden umbrellas, in the middle are red gold umbrellas, and those of silver are outside. Outside these again is a *rajavat* fence with umbrellas of five colours. Within the umbrellas stand figures of *devata,* and outside them is *rajavat* fence. Paper umbrellas and figures of giants *(yaksa, gandharba, raksasa)* stand at the foot of the Meru, and there are figures of various kinds of lions

(*gajasiha, rajsiha, sinto, kilen*), goat-antelopes, cows, buffaloes, tigers, bears and *devata*. On Kailasa sits a figure of Siva and graceful Uma. On the top of Meru is a figure of Indra. Figures of *asuras* are in the middle of the Meru; Vishnu sleeps on the water at the foot of the Meru, and a seven-headed *naga* encircles the Meru. Outside the open space stand *asuras,* and outside the wall are dancing halls where lictors are dressed as 100 *asuras* and pages represent 100 *devata*. There are Bali, Sugriva, Mahajambhu, and a train of 103 monkeys. They pull the ancient *naga;* the *asuras* pull the head, the *devata* pull the tail, and the monkeys are at the end of the tail. One side of Meru is gold, one side is red gold, one side crystal, one side silver, the Yugundhra mountain is gold, the Isindhara is red gold, the Karavika and Kailasa are silver. On the surrounding space outside are elephants, horses and the four divisions of the army. Officials of 10,000 marks of dignity wear precious stones and put on coats and silk *phanun* of honour. Those of 5,000 grades wear golden hats and put on coats and splendid silk *phanun*. Those of 2400-1200 marks of dignity carry silver and golden flowers according to rank, with flowers and pop corn to pay homage. Brahmans of various sects sit within the enclosure. On the first day there is *kardhibhasa* (a discourse?), on the second *rapvan* (all is quiet?); on the third day *sranvan* (the building goes on?); and on the fourth day *capsamiddha* (?) and on the fifth day they puɪɪ u.e ancient *naga*. On the sixth day they make three pools of angelic water, a three headed elephant, a white horse and a king of oxen. They take arms, elephants, weapons, and ropes for catching elephants and steep them in water. They take on hundred figures of Siva, Vishnu, Indra and Visukarma, and bear utensils for following the custom of entering to offer a blessing *(thvay brahbar)*. On the seventh day the Brahmans offer a blessing and on the eighth day the king offers a blessing; on the ninth day they offer the elephants and horses and the four divisions of the army; on the tenth day they offer the twelve treasuries; on the eleventh day they offer the taxes; on the twelfth day they offer the city; on the thirteenth day they offer the consecrated water; on the fourteenth day they make offering to the *devata;* on the fifteenth day they make offerings to the king; on the sixteenth day they make offerings to the prince; on the seventeenth day the king rewards the Brahmans; on the eighteenth day there are offerings of *kalpavrksa* fruits; on the ninteenth, twentieth and twenty-first days gold and silver flowers are scattered. For a month theatrical is performed. They build a standing effigy of a giant 1 *sen* high. The pages represent monkeys and go out through openning in its ears, nose, eyes and mouth, and drive a royal car scattering alms about the city. This is the end of Indrabhiseka.

While coronation and the Indrabhiseka ceremonies are connecting the living king to Indra and his abode —— Mount Meru, the royal cremation has done so to the dead king. Actually the cremation of ordinary Thai is almost entirely Buddhist but that of the royalty is Buddhist superimposed on a Hindu basis and accompanied by the survival of much Brahmanic ritual (Wales, 1931:137). As a Buddhist, the king does not imagine himself an incarnation of the god and this is reflected from his death bed. It is recorded that when King Maniwongsa of Cambodia was about to die he was placed on a death bed underneath tiered umbrella in the throne hall surrounding with Buddhist altars and offerings. The royal family, monks and nobles were attending. On the ceiling and at the altar near the bed were hanging the paintings of the Chulamani Stupa in the Tavatimsa Heaven where Indra is ruling. This *stupa* enshrining the Lord Buddha's hair is where the soul of the dying king will go. A set of offerings consisting of betel nuts, joss sticks and candle was inserted into his hand for offering to the *stupa* and meanwhile the monks gave a chanting to send the king's soul to heaven (Department of Fine Arts, 1972:574). Such a record confirms that the Buddhist king is connected to Mount Meru through the belief that his soul will go to pay homage to the Chulamani Stupa there.

On the contrary to Buddhist belief, the Brahmanic ritual gives another ground to explain relationship between the dead king and Mount Meru. Quaritch Wales (1931:162) sees the resemblance between the coronation and cremation ceremonies and then puts forward the term "Spiritual Coronation" as found among the ancient Khmer. He explains:

"...most religions connect death with rebirth in another world and to secure that rebirth in a happy state is the raison d'etre of all funeral ceremonies (except those primitive ones designed to prevent the dead from worrying the living, which comes to practically the same thing). We have seen that according to Hocart, the theory of coronation is, or was, that the king (a) dies (b) is reborn (c) as a god; and if in Siam (a) and (b) are not definitely expressed at least they are understood when the king takes on the divine attributes of the Hindu god at his coronation ..."

The term "Spiritual Coronation" as applied to funeral ritual of the ancient Khmer fits very well to some religious monuments in Ankor notably Ankor Wat which was a special shrine devoted to the cult of Deva-ra-ja. The ancient legend current among the modern Cambodians says that it was supernaturally built as palace of a king who was miraculously reborn a second time on earth after a short stay in Indra's paradise. Ta-Kouan Chou, a Chinese envoy who visited Cambodia in the 13th century A.D., supposed that it was the tomb of a dead monarch. Finally George Cœdes, the most prominent among French scholars has shown that it was indeed the palace of a king, but of dead one, under the name of Paramavisnulo-ka, who was supposed to inhibit the central tower of the temple (Wales, 1931:170). What is so impressive is that the temple of Ankor Wat assumes a square plan and the central tower of which is surrounded by lesser towers in the lower basements representing mythical mountains that are around Mount Meru. Thus, Ankor Wat is the replica of Mount Meru on earth, so it is where the dead king receives his spiritual coronation. The presence of Ankor Wat and others of the same nature is a manifestation of how grand and significant the funeral ritual of the ancient Khmer was. Mortuary rite for the Thai royalty since Ayudhya period was quite similar. Its scale is actually bigger than that of the coronation but instead of con-structing stone temples for the dead king as the Khmer who were inspired by their faith in Hinduism, the Thai were emphasizing the social and political prestige of the living king and built up a big stately funeral pyre called Phra Meru to cremate the deceased king in open space at the heart of the city.

To construct the Meru for royal cremation is a state activity. Soon after the death of the king, work begins on erection of the Meru which assumes an imposing structure with a series of concentric terraces from which emerge four tall columns supporting a conical spire. These columns are fashioned from massive teak trunks from 200 to 250 feet in length and each with 12 feet in circumference. These logs were obtained by royal order from four different provinces in the North and were selected from virgin jungle. They were embedded in the ground 30 feet deep, their bases forming a square and the trunks were made to lean slightly together to form a truncated pyramid. At the top they were joined by a roof upon which was erected a gilded *prasada* spire. The pyre proper is prepared on the top terrace, under the spire. The whole structure is magnificently car-ved and gilded and it represents the sacred mountain of Meru.[1]

When the proper time comes for cremation, the deceased king's body, which is retained in the urn (*phra kaud*) in the Lying-in-State in a throne hall of the royal palace, is removed to the big funeral car dragged by two hundred soldiers in a state procession to the Phra Meru Ground. This funeral procession is escorted by a high ranking monk who sits on a small car chanting Buddhist stanza. There are series of religious rites per-formed by the monks and Brahmans during the royal corpse is waiting for cremation on the Phra Meru. The new king presides over the ceremony amid the attendance of the royal family, nobles and members of the

Diplomatic Corps. Before the cremation, people are allowed to pay homage to the deceased king. The cremation takes place late in the afternoon and continues the whole evening. The next morning the king comes again to perform the rite of collecting the remains; a part of them is enshrined in the royal temple and the rest is taken to be jettisoned in mid river. Every night throughout the cremation ceremony, there are entertainments of various kinds in the cremation ground around the Meru. As a rule it is after this royal cremation that the coronation of the new king can take place; he is not regarded as the rightful monarch if the cremation of his predecessor has not been done.

Clearly as already mentioned, the royal cremation on the Meru enables us not only to understand the cosmological implication of the funeral rite itself, but also to gain a perspective on its social aspect which is considerably emphasized. This practice means a great deal to the living as it involves what has been paralleled in Bali which Huntington and Metcalf (1979: 132) put it, "The carefully staged cremation of kings were a principal weapon to which their successors maintained or advanced their standing". Looking at the grandeur of the Meru in which the urn of the dead king is put in state, one can not help speculating that it is the centre of the world where the *cakravartin* is installed. Thinking in terms of devout Buddhist, the funeral attendance paid by people from all categories means to pay a last homage to the dead who is returning to heaven. Politically, it has another meaning in that it is an obligation for the subject to express their loyalty to the new monarch as well as representatives from allied states to confirm their friendship. The absence on part of the vassal states is interpreted as an act of rebellion and often leads to the war of suppression.

Further, in reviewing the royal cremation of both Ayudhya and Bangkok, I would add another significance in that it functions to uphold the central bureaucracy initiated by King Trailok of Ayudhya from the 15th century A.D. This bureaucracy consisted of the members of the royal family and royal officials of both civil and military. Each person had a position attached with appropriate rank and specific name together with *sakdina* or the mark of dignity attached to it. These were the ruling class and below them were commoners and slaves. People in the ruling strata were entitled with previleges according to their rank, position and marks of dignity. The most conspicuous among them was that at death they were inserted in the urns or coffins provided by the government. For example, the corpses of the high ranking princes and princesses were retained in the urns under tiered umbrellas; the ranking bureaucrats also in the urns and cremated in special Meru assigned by the government; and the ordinary officials were given decorative coffins.

The previleges and dignity the royal officials receive from the king served not only to mark the ruling class of the commoners but also to set an incentive for people in general to crave for becoming the royal official. There is an old saying that states "sib chao koh mai thao phraya liang", meaning to work for ten masters can not be compared with serving under the king. This craving desire to become a bureaucrat has consequently contributed to (1) the persistence of the central bureaucracy which owed its allegiance to the king and (2) the prevalence of class consciousness among the Thai in general.

Socio-Political Change and the Persistence of Cremation on the Meru

Historically speaking, Thailand experienced large scale socio-economic change around the 19th century A.D. during the reign of King Mongkut. Political pressure from the West leading to the signing of the Bowring Treaty with the British, in 1855 had put an end to the government's monopoly of trade with foreigners. Free trade developed and wage labour resulting from hiring the Chinese replaced the traditional corvee system of the government. The digging of canals and water ways for transportation in the Central Plain during King Chulalongkorn's reign had favoured the spread of irrigation network for large scale rice cultivation. Large numbers of people moved out to settle down in the farming areas. Later with the abolishment of slave by King Chulalongkorn in 1905, Thailand was full of freemen ready for various kinds of occupations. This period saw the emergence of a new socio-economic strata, i.e., the middle class consisting of merchants, middlemen, landlords and well-to-do government officials. Finally, the coup d'etat of 1932 has replaced the absolute monarchy with a democratic government with the king under the constitution. There were rearrangements in the structures of the upper and middle classes. More channels have been open for vertical mobility. Education, wealth and marriage with the upper class are among effective means for climbing up social ladder. In order to integrate the new classes of people, both official and non-official, the government grant them some previleges and dignity that it had done to the bureaucrats in the past. The most obvious and most desirable are decorations conferred by the king. They are expressed through wearing of uniforms adorned with decorations during royal rituals and state ceremonies. At death these previleged people are given the urns or coffins to retain their corpses and also cremated on the Meru assigned by the government.

To grant a death ritual to the upper class, the government still continues what had been practiced during the absolute monarchy. That is, to grant them the right to use the urns or coffins for their corpses according to the grades of decorations conferred by the king. As a rule, those who receive the urn are people conferred with high order illustrating with a decorative stripe on the uniform. At cremation their corpses are taken to a special Meru of Wat Dhebsirindhra which is regarded as the royal cemetery (Prince Damrongrajanuphab, 1972: 309-315). It is a replica of the royal Meru but in a smaller scale and constructed of concrete for its permanent use. For convenience and hygienic reasons, a firing chamber with lofty chimney is connected to it through a passage from the pyre proper which is used only for mock cremation. People without decorative stripes obtain only decorative coffin from the royal palace. They are cremated on any *wat* ground by erecting a temporary Meru, the size of which depends on their economic status. Later permanent concrete Meru modelled after that of Wat Dhebsirindhra are built in many *wat* around Bangkok to facilitate the cremation of the rich and middle class who are of increasing size consisting of merchants, businessmen and government officials of medium grade. As a result cremation in Bangkok developed into a pattern possessing some reminiscence of the funeral rite of the nobles in the past.

As a general practice, soon after a person dies his body is immediately taken to the *wat* and put up in the funeral hall for a ritual bathing attended by close friends and relatives. After that it is put into a coffin which is, in its turn, inserted in an outer coffin decorated with gilded designs. If the deceased is a high ranking person, an urn or outer coffin is sent from the royal palace to retain the corpse. It is then raised on a platform surrounded with wreaths and flowers and a stand of the dead man's portrait, waiting for ritual chanting officiated by a chapter of monks in the evening. This religious rites is attended by big gatherings of relatives, friends and guests from far and near and is likely to continue for seven nights if the deceased is very well known. In general, chanting rite goes on for three nights before the coffin is removed to keep in the cemetery. Cremation does not take place immediately, unless the sponsor has an urgent need, but rather waits for several months or over a year for readiness which depends on social and economic status of the bereaved family.

When the appointed time comes for cremation, the coffin is taken from the cemetery to put up in the funeral hall close to the Meru. Chanting services by the monks is done again in the evening and on the day of cremation, the monks are invited to give a preaching and partaking food. Early in the afternoon the coffin is lifted to the pyre proper in the middle of the Meru waiting for last religious services and social gathering. Later around 4: 30 p.m. friends, relatives and guests arrive at the funeral halls in front of the Meru to witness the cremation. Among the attendants, a person is specially invited as the guest of honour to initiate the funeral fire. If the deceased is a ranking bureaucrat, the guest of honour is likely to be the representative of the king. Cremation begins with the *pangsukula* rite; the sponsor invites a senior monk and the guest of honour to the Meru and a yellow robe is offered to the monk who touches it with his hand and reflects that the life of human is not permanent and then pulls it from the hand of the guest of honour. This is an act of transferring merit to the deceased. As soon as the *pangsukula* cloth is pulled the mock cremation or the rite of offering sandal-wood and candles at the pyre follows. The guest of honour lights the sacred fire, conferred by the king, to the pyre and this is accompanied by mournful music that requires all the attendants below to stand up in honour of the deceased. When the guest of honour descends from the Meru, the attendants go up to take their turn to offer lighted sandal-wood and candles at the pyre. The giver asks forgiveness for any wrong that he may have done the deceased during his life time.

Actual cremation starts in the presence of the bereaved family as soon as the guests leave. The coffin is removed from the funeral pyre to the firing chamber; a coconut water is poured into the corpse to bathe its face for final purification and after that it is left to be consumed by the fire. Next morning they come again to collect the remains of which a small amount is taken to keep in the *wat* shrine; the rest are thrown into the river. This often follows by a series of religious rites officiated by monks at the house and the *wat* where the relics of the deceased are enshrined.

The funeral pattern, the highlight of which is cremation on the Meru initiated by the guest of honour who is the representative of the royalty, has rendered social prestige to both the deceased and the living. Moreover, to consider in terms of convenience and economy on part of the sponsor and of sanitation of the *wat* and living areas, the permanent structure of the Meru which is equipped with firing chamber and high chimney to prevent disgusting smell of the corpse, has done away with the reluctance to erect a permanent funeral pyre in the *wat* of the past. It results in a wide-spreading construction of concrete Meru in the *wats* in Bangkok and in urban areas in the provinces. Many *wats* in Bangkok do not only give a cremation service to local people but also to the members of specific government organizations. For example, the Army has assigned Wat Somanat for the funeral of its members, the Navy has Wat Krua Wan and the Police has Wat Tritotsadhep. Wat Phra Sri Ratana Maha That near Don Muang air port is selected by the Air Force and also for granting grand cremation for those who die in heroic death as fighting with the communists.

Among the many *wat* that are popular for their cremation services in Bangkok today, Wat That Thong in the east of the city is the most eminent, owing to its location in the upper class area. About 30 years ago, it was only a local *wat* of a low populated area scattered by slums of the lower class. With the expansion of roads and urban facilities from Bangkapi, the area was rapidly encroached by the rich and soon became urbanized. Wat That Thong then served as the sole religious centre of the rich who overwhelmingly supported it. Its major income derives from cremation fee, religious services and donation, which enable it to develop into a very large monastery in Bangkok, having huge buildings of the *bod, viharn,* library and comfortable, residential quarters of the monks. The *wat* compound is enlarged to cover a local school and playground serving as parking place whenever there are social gathering and funeral rituals in the *wat*.

In Wat That Thong, the most outstanding structures uncomparable elsewhere are those of funeral buildings which are built in a large compound separated from the *bod* and *viharn*. Here, three rows of funeral halls are put up to render many funeral services at the same time. In the middle of the compound amid funeral halls a space is provided for erecting a twin Meru equipped with up-to-date firing chambers that can cremate more than one corpse at a time. With the exception of the Meru of Wat Dhebsirindhra, the rich and upper class in Bangkok look for sponsoring cremation at Wat That Thong because it is so grand and respectable worthy of their social status. Everyday, at least one or two funeral rites are held in Wat That Thong according to local newspapers. Its funeral services, particularly cremation cut accross its local boundary to various parts of Bangkok. Very often cremation of an important person causes an hour of traffic jam on the street.

The Meru and Village Society

From Bangkok, the construction of permanent Meru spread to urban *wat* in the provinces and the incentive behind it is social prestige, economy and convenience on part of the sponsor of cremation, while on part of the *wat*, a major income is obtained. It became popular first in the *changwat* (provincial city) and *amphur* (district centre) where the rich and well-to-do can afford to back it up. To my own observation, cremation on the Meru found its way to village society at the *tambon* (commune) and *mu-ban* (hamlet) about a decade ago, when the socio-economic condition was undergoing a big change. This is due to the improvement of communication, notably construction of roads and highways that bring isolated areas into contact with urban centres. Cultivation of upland crops has expanded economic frontier into the village and this results in the development of market area occupied by merchants and the rich. Class consciousness gradually develops observable from the presence of concrete house, television, car and other luxury goods. It is emphasized by the arrangement of large scale rites of passage particularly ordination and cremation. The Meru is, in many respects, serving as a symbol of class distinction.

In the village of Ban Muang Khao in the province of Prachinburi to the east of Bangkok, I have observed, during my fieldwork study in 1969, that there appeared a difference in opinions and ideas concerning funeral ritual among villagers. This village was among a few at that time in the Central Plain that had cemetery and cremation place located at the outskirts, separating from the village *wat*. Here villagers did not like to hold cremation in the *wat* compound and explained that it was disgusting and aweful to children, so they preferred to do it in the cemetery where a rich woman had built a small brick pyre for the communal use. Funeral practices among them is simple and similar to most places in the Central Plain.

Usually when a person dies of natural death, his body is undergone a ritual bathing by close friends, relatives and neighbours who come to help at the house without any invitation. After bathing rite, the body is wrapped with white cloth and inserted into coffin prepared by kin and neighbours; it is kept for a night or at most three days to wait for those coming from afar. At night a chapter of monks is invited to perform chanting service and on the cremation day, the coffin is removed from the house through an unusual door passing an artificial jungle gate in a procession escorted by monks and elder to the cemetery. Magic rite has been performed or observed at times for fear of the dead to return to the house. At the cremation only Buddhist rites officiated by monks have been observed. It starts with the rite of pulling the *pangsukula* cloth in front of the coffin and when finished, the coffin is open and coconut juice is used to bathe the face of the corpse and the body is raised on to the pyre. While cremation is going on, the sponsor is likely to have invited the monks to chant the Buddhist stanza. All attendants help to put fire sticks to cremate the corpse. Bones and ashes of the deceased are collected in the next morning and as a usual practice, a part of the remains is kept on the household altar or enshrined in a reliquary located in the periphery of the *wat*.

There was no sign of class consciousness in Ban Muang Khao but in an immediate village of Ban Kok Peep which was the commune centre, there was a new *wat* established by rich people in addition to the old village *wat*. Class disparity is obvious from the presence of these two *wat*; the former is for the rich and well-to-do who help to put up a concrete Meru equipped with cremation chamber and chimney; and the latter is village *wat* supported by local people who cremated their dead on simple pyre in the cemetery at the back of the *wat*. Many Muang Khao villagers often gossipped about cremation of the rich in Ban Kok Peep; some said that it was very expensive and not necessary, while many others appreciated its convenience and wished to have a Meru built in their own *wat*. This was frequently raised for discussion whenever there was a meeting concerning the future development of the *wat*.

Next to Ban Muang Khao about 1 kilometre to the south is Wat Ton Po, a regional *wat* which is shared by three adjacent villages of Ban Ton Po, Ban Dan and Ban Cham Wa for their daily religious affairs. It is a big *wat* owing to the fame of its sacred Bodhi Tree which is, according to local scholar, believed to derive from Ceylon over a thousand years ago when the district was then part of the ancient city. Large amount of donation to the *wat* came from within and outside the locality, rendering the abbot to look ambitiously for big construction. It was revealed that, in addition to the new *bod* and *sala-karn-parien* (teaching hall), a big concrete Meru and funeral halls were to be erected to render funeral service in the same manner as those of the city *wat*. The rich and well-to-do in Ban Muang Khao, particularly those who were living in the market came and supported Wat Ton Po.

A year ago I made a trip to Ban Muang Khao again and saw a change in this village as well as the others nearby. The entire *tambon* (commune) has been raised to *amphur* (district) of which the centre is located at Ban Kok Peep. Every village is open to each other through better roads and electricity. Wat Muang Khao has already built up concrete buildings and the *wat* fence to replace the old ones of wooden structures. Among the new buildings is a Meru of small size looking so impressive from its high chimney. With the cremation performed more and more within the *wat* compound is consequently reduced the function of the cemetery at the outskirt to a sheer burial ground for those who die of unnatural death. The Meru at Wat Ton Po was then under construction requiring more than a year to complete since the abbot wanted it to be a big place. On the contrary, the new *wat* at Ban Kok Peep is established as the cremation centre of the district owing to its Meru and funeral service.

Elsewhere at the present time I have seen that the Meru with its high chimney has already been incorporated into the village society. It is a part of the *wat* that can be seen from afar, reflecting symbolically a departure from old pattern of cremation to a new one that is greatly inspired by the urban culture.

Conclusion

Cremation is the major means of disposal of the remains of the deceased in Thailand. It is the most conspicuous part of funeral ritual, articulating through the presence of the Meru—the funeral pyre topped with *prasada* spire. It represents Mount Meru which is the centre of the universe according to Hindu-Buddhist mythology. This funeral structure, as it spreads from Bangkok to the provinces and incorporated into the village society, is a new cultural phenomenon reflecting continuity and change in the culture of Thailand of the present day. In the past under the absolute monarchy, there was social disparity between the ruling class and the commoners. The former with the king at the top had a very elaborate funeral ritual that was Buddhist superimposed on a Hindu basis and accompanied by the survival of much Brahmanic ritual; while the latter was simply based on Buddhist rites and magical observation.

Ordinary Buddhists simply believe that after death the soul either goes to heaven or hell depending on the merit they have made; while the king and nobles will go to the Tavatimsa Heaven to pay homage to the relics of the Lord Buddha at the Chulamani Stupa. The Tavatimsa Heaven is located on top of Mount Meru and it is also the abode of Indra. Ritualistically, the Brahmanic cult of the dead king probably derived from the ancient Khmer made the Thai king of Ayudhya god-like through the installation of the royal corpse in the urn and cremation on the Meru. This practice had political and social implications; firstly it was a barometer to measure the degree of loyalty of all the subject offering to the soveriegn. Secondly, it was serving as a means to express social status and prestige among the ruling stratà since their funeral pattern was modelled after the royalty.

Cremation of the royalty and nobles on the Meru continues in specific *wat* in Bangkok despite the end of the absolute monarchy. It is more proliferated than the past as permanent Meru have been constructed in most *wat* of Bangkok and also spreading into urban areas of the provinces for the cremation of the rich and well-to-do. Concrete Meru with its modern facilities, particularly firing chamber and its high chimney have done away with the unhealthy smell of cremating corpse and big expense in erecting temporary funeral pyre. Moreover, it enables the *wat* to earn more income through cremation fee, religious services and donation, thus helping it to survive the heavy maintenance and construction costs of today.

At the present time, socio-economic change, brought about by the integration of rural areas to urban centres through improving communication and administration, has been striping the village society of its egalitarian character. Urban values and class consciousness develop and are strikingly discerned from the presence of the Meru with its high chimney standing in competition with the traditional steep-gabled roof of the *bod* (ordination hall) to mark the existence of the Buddhist *wat* from afar.

Notes

1) Checking with reliable records, the construction of such a grand Meru for royal cremation appeared during the reign of King Phra Narayana (1657-1688). It was first built for the funeral of King Prasat Thong (1636-1657) who was King Phra Narayana's father (Somphob Bhirom, 1978: 57).

References

Bhirom, Somphob
  1978 *Phra Merumat Samai Krung Ratanakosindhra.* Bangkok: Aksornsyam Karn-
         phim Press.
Damrongrajanuphab, Prince
  1972 "Taman Susan Hlvan" (History of the Royal Cemetery), in *Anusorn Nai
         Ngan Phra Raj Than Ploengsob Nai Panjitta Anekavanich* (In Memory of the
         Cremation of Mr. Panjitta Anekavanich). Bangkok: Thai Anukroh Press.
Department of Fine Arts
  1972 "Raj Kamnod Krung Kambhuja" (Royal Regulation of Cambodia), in *Ladhi
         Thamnium Tang Tang Lem Chob* (A Collection of Different Customs and
         Practices). Bangkok: Klang Widhaya Press.
Huntington, R. and P. Metcalf
  1979 *Celebrations of Death.* London: Cambridge University Press.
Quaritch Wales, H. G.
  1931 *Ancient Siamese State Ceremonies.* London: Bernard Quaritch, Ltd.
Tambiah, S. J.
  1977 *World Conqueror and World Renouncer.* London: Cambridge University
         Press.
Vallibhotama, Srisakra
  1977 "Wieng and Wang during the Ayudhya Period," *Muang Boran Journal.* Vol.
         3, No. 3 (April-June): 67-77.

12 Spiritual Movements in Javanese Culture

KOENTJARANINGRAT

Introduction

Before I engage in my presentation on Spiritual Movements in Javanese Culture it is necessary to present some information on the various religions in Indonesia, and more specifically on Indonesian Islam. It is also necessary to define more specifically what is meant by Javanese Culture.

As you all know, unlike Korea Indonesia is an extremely diversified country, with a large population which, according to recent estimations, has passed the 130,000,000 figure.[1] Those millions of Indonesians, eighty-seven percent of whom are rural peasants, are diversified into more than three hundred and fifty different ethnic groups, each with its own cultural identity, while an almost equal number of mutually unintelligible languages are spoken throughout this vast archipelago. In the western part of the country are large ethnic groups and language communities with millions of people (50 million Javanese, 16 million Sundanese, 6 million Madurese, 6 Million Batak, 6.5 million East and South Sumatran Malays, 5 million Buginese, and over 2 million Balinese). When we move to the eastern part of the archipelago we get smaller ethnic groups of less than one million, e.g. those who inhabit the eastern Nusa Tenggara or Lesser Sunda, Islands, or those who inhabit the Moluccas. On the coastal areas of West Irian small bands of sago gatnerers have separate languages, spoken by not more than 100 to 150 people.

Like the diversity in ethnic cultures and languages, Indonesia also has a diversity in religions. All the great religions: Islam, Protestantism, Roman Catholicism, Hinduism, Buddhism and Confucianism are present, while those various religions known within their own communities, a large number of local varieties, sects and churches, which are sometimes quite distinct one from the other, and which do not always relate on very friendly terms. Accurate figures on the adherence of the various religions and religious sects in Indonesia are not available except for some areas, such as the area of Greater Jakarta,or for certain religions like Catholicism. However, it can be stated that the dominant religion in Indonesia is the Sunnah or Sunnite branch of Islam, which is followed by Protestantism, Catholicism, Hinduism, Buddhism, and finally Confucianism. The Jakarta percentage of religious followers presented in Table 1 more or less reflect the national proportions.

Table 1
Percentage of Followers in the Main Religions
in the Greater Jakarta Area (1970)

Religion		Total population of:
Islam	88.1	
Protestantism	5.2	
Roman-Catholicism	2.9	Greater Jakarta in 1970:
Hinduism	2.0	4,437,135
Buddhism	1.3	
Confucianism	0.5	

Source:*Statistical Year Book of Djakarta, 1971,* Kantor Sensus dan
Statistik D.C.I. 1971: pp. 10, 100.

The domination of the various above-mentioned religions in Indonesia varies according to region. The islands of Java, Medura and Sumatra, the coastal areas of Kalimantan, and the southern and southwestern areas of Sulawesi are dominated by Islam. Protestantism dominates the smaller East Indonesian islands and Sulawesi, while the Batak ethnic group of North Sumatra are also dominantly Protestants. Catholicism dominates the southern part of West Irian and the islands Timor and Flores in East Indonesia, while large enclaves of the urban population in Java and Sumatra are also followers of the Catholic religion. Hinduism in its unique localized form dominates the island of Bali, while in Central Java recent large-scale conversions to Hinduism are taking place. Buddhism and Confucianism of course dominate the Indonesian population of Chinese descent, while again in Central Java recent conversion to Buddhism have occurred.

It is obvious that I have to make a selection out of the great variety of religious and ethnic groups in Indonesia. I shall therefore concentrate on only one religion of one ethnic group in Indonesia: Javanese Islam. Likewise, I shall limit myself only on the discussion of religious movements in that religion. However, allow me to make some remarks on Javanese Islam in general first.

Javanese Islam

The Javanese, world's third largest Muslim ethnic group (after the Arabs and the Bengalis), occupy the central and eastern parts of the island of Java, a small island of the island-nation of Indonesia. The Javanese call themselves *Wong Jawa,* and despite their relatively small island among larger islands of the Indonesian Archipelago, they form the largest ethnic group (61 million in 1971) of the extremely plural population of the Indonesian Republic.

There are also Javanese on other islands of Indonesia, e.g. in South Kalimantan and North Sulawesi. Additional large Javanese populations are to be found in South and East Sumatra, and because Dutch colonialists had for two centuries moved Javanese laborers overseas, there are also Javanese communities in South Africa, Surinam, South America, and New Caledonia in Melanesia.

Nearly all Javanese (about 99%) consider themselves officially as Muslims. In the earliest stages of conversion to Islam in the thirteenth century, the commercial aristocracy in the port towns of Northern Java had also adopted many elements of mysticism, which seemed to have characterized South Indian Islam. As mysticism had long played an important role in the Hindu-Buddhist Javanese religion during the pre-Islamic period, it stimulated the easy acceptance of Islam among the Javanese. More orthodox Sunni teachings of the Shafi'i School of Law were acquired at a later period by Javanese pilgrims on their return from Mecca.

During the fifteenth century Islam penetrated into the interior regions of East and Central Java through zealous activities of Muslim missionaries who later became holy men *(wali)* in Javanese folklore. In the interior regions of Java where pre-Islamic Hindu and Buddhist Javanese cultural and religious tradition were strongest, the influence of Islam was less strong, and the religion was modified into a syncretistic Javanese kind of

Islam, which combines Hindu–Buddhist Javanese religious concepts with Muslim beliefs. The Javanese themselves continued to call this Javanese version of Islam *Agama Jawa* (Javanese religion), and those who adhere to a more puritan kind of Islam are called the *Santri* Muslim.[2]

To the Javanese the two categories of people really adhere to two different world views and live two different styles of life. The *Agama Jawa* Muslims ridicule the strong dogmatic concern of the *Santri* Muslims for Muslim learnings and doctrines, and consider their own life style to be far more flexible and tolerant. The ritual system of the *Agama Jawa* variant of Javanese Islam indeed mainly focus on recurrent communal sacred meals called *slametan,* or small offerings called *sesajen,* at fixed periods on particular places or spots, and on routine visits of graves and holy places. On the other hand, the *Santri* Muslims look down upon the *Agama Jawa* Muslims, when they accuse of neglecting the doctrines of Islam. They disdain the fact that the *Agama Jawa* Muslims seldom perform the five daily *salat* or Muslim incantations, that they are usually absent at communal *salat* in the mosque on Fridays, that they only occasionally fast during the month Ramadhan, that they have no desire to go on pilgrimage to Mecca, and they especially despise the fact that *Agama Jawa* Muslims used to violate the otherwise strong Muslim prohibition to eat pork.

It is difficult to estimate the proportion of the Javanese population who belong to the *Agama Jawa* religious variant, and those who belong to the category of *Santri* Muslims. Though the former seems to be more dominant in the interior regions of the Island of Java, and the latter in the coastal regions, there are no two geographically distinct areas which either category of Javanese Muslim can consider to be their homeland. Neither are there social classes where either one of the two variants of Javanese Islam dominate, and both may exist among the rural peasants as well as among the population of the towns and cities of Java.

As mentioned earlier, this presentation will limit itself to religious movements or organized activities based on certain trends and aiming at specific goals within a religious system, in this case within Javanese Islam of the *Agama Jawa* as well as *Santri* variant.

Agama Jawa Religious Movements

Kebatinan Kejawen Movements

There have always been followers of the *Agama Jawa* Islam who find a religious life that only focus on the afore-mentioned recurrent sacred communal meals, the routine preparations of offerings, the routine visits to graves and holy places, superficial, meaningless, and therefore unsatisfac- tory. They therefore search for a deeper understanding of the essence of life and the spiritual existence of man. Numerous movements, called the *kebatinan kejawen*[3] movements, which respond to the demand of many Javanese for a more spiritually meaningful life, have emerged and dis- appeared again in the course of the history of Javanese culture. The name *Kebatinan* refers to the similar fact in all these movements in that their members search for the truth of the inner-self, or *batin,*[4] of the human being, and it is a striking fact that during the past 25 years the number of these movements has increased tremendously.

On August 19 and 20 of 1955 a convention of representatives of dozens of *kebatinan* organizations from many parts of Java have convened in the capital of the Province of Central Java, Semarang, in an attempt to unite all the organizations which existed at that time. Another convention, held on August 7 to 9, the following year in the Central Javanese court city Surakarta, as a follow-up of the first one, was attended by over 2,000 participants, representing one hundred organizatopns.[5] The conventions succeeded in establishing a nationwide federal organization called *Badan Kongres Kebatinan Indonesi* (BKKI), or the Indonesian Congress of Kebati- nan (Badan 1956). Two other congresses and also seminars on particular topics concerning problems of *kebatinan* were organized by the BKKI in 1959, 1961, and 1962 (Pakan 1978: p.98).

The Bureau for the Supervision of Religious Movements, or *Pengawas Aliran Kepercayaan Masyarakat* (PAKEM) of the Ministry of Religious Affairs of the Republic of Indonesia has registered 360 movements in 1964. However, after the September 30, 1965 Affair many movements that sympathized with the Indonesian Communist Party disappeared, so that another PAKEM list only included 217 movements in 1971, 117 of which being in Central Java. Of these 117 movements, 13 were located in Surakarta (Jong 1973: pp. 10-12; Pakan 1978: p. 98).[6]

Most of the Javanese *kebatinan* movements have a local base with only a limited number of adherents, of only about 200 people. Such are officially called small movements, which is in Indonesian called *aliran kecil,* such as the *Panunggalan, Pirukunan Kawula Manembah Gusti, Jiwa Ayu, Pancasila Handayaningratan* from Surakarta; *Ilmu Kebatinan Kasunyatan* from Jogyakarta; *Ilmu Sejati* from Madiun; and *Trimurti Naluri Majapahit* from Majakerta.

A limited number of *kebatinan* movements, however, have over 200, and sometimes even up to thousands of followers, dispersed over many towns and cities in Java and organized in branches of the mother organization. They are officially called large movements, or *aliran besar* (Indonesian), five of which are considered to be the largest ones. They are: *Hardapusara* which originated in Purwaraja, a small town in the Bagelen area; *Susila Budi Darma* (SUBUD), originally from Semarang; *Paguyuban Ngesti Tunggal (Pangestu),* originally from Surakarta; *Paguyuban Sumarah,* originally from Jogyakarta; and *Sapta Darma,* originally from Jogyakarta.

Hardapusara is the oldest movement among the big five and is initiated in 1895 by Ki Kusumawicitra, a peasant of the village Kemanukan (near the town Purwareja) who was believed to have received a divine inspiration. In its early stages he called his learnings *Kawruh Kasunyataan Gaib* and his first fellows were *priyayi's* from Purwareja and a number of other towns in the Bagelen area. Today the organization has branches in various towns and cities in Central as well as in East Java, but also in Jakarta, where it has several thousand members.[7] Its learnings and doctrines are included in two books which are considered almost sacred by its followers, i.e. Buku *Kawula Gusti* and *Wigati.*

Susila Budhi Dharma (recently better known by its acronym SUBUD) was established in 1925 in Semarang, the capital of the Province of Central Java. Today, however, its headquarters are located in Jakarta. It refuses to be considered as a *kebatinan* movement, and prefers to call itself a *pusat latihan kejiwaan,* i. e. a training center for spiritual exercises. It has several thousand members dispersed over many towns and cities throughout Indonesia, and has even 87 overseas branches. Among its members are many non-Javanese, and even non-Indonesians, such as Asians, Europeans, Australians, as well as Americans. The principles, learnings, and doctrines of the organization are included in a book called *Susila Budhi Dharma,* and the organization also publishes a journal called *Perwata Kejiwaan Subud.*

Pacuyuban Ngesti Tunggal, or better known by its acronym *Pangestu,* is another large *kebatinan* movement, initiated by Soenarto, who has received a series of divine messages during the period between 1932 and 1933, and which were written down by two of his early followers, which are published as a book called *Sasangka Djati.* As an official organization, however, *Pangestu* was only established in May 1949 in Surakarta. Its 50,000 members are spread over numerous towns and cities in Java, and are mainly from *priyayi* circles. Quite a number, however, are peasants, for instance those who live in the Javanese resettlement areas in Sumatra and Kalimantan. A Journal called *Owijawara* maintains contact between the dispersed members of *Pangestu.*[9]

Paguyuban Sumarah is also a large organization, which started as a movement when its first teacher, R.Ng. Sukirno Hartond from Jogyakarta received a prophecy in 1935. After a decline in the late 19 century a revival of the movement occurred in 1950 in Jogyakarta, and today it has over the 115,000 members, who come from the *priyayi* class as well as from other social categories of the population of many towns and cities throughout Java.[10]

Sapta Darmo, the youngest of the five large *kebatinan* movements of Java is established in 1955 by a religious teacher, Hardjosaputro, who has subsequently changed his name to become Panuntun Sri Gutomo.[11] He came from Koplakan near Pare.[12] Unlike the other four movements *Sapta Darmo* has among its members people from the rural peasant category and the urban blue collar workers. All the leaders, however, are almost exclusively *priyayi. Sapta Darmo* has a book called *Kitab Pewarah Sapta Darmo,* which includes all its principal ideas and learnings.

Although *kebatinan* movements are all over the Javanese area, but Surakarta as the center of Javanese civilization indeed still seems to be the most important location of many of the most important *kebatinan* organizations. In 1970 there were 13 such organizations listed to have members in Surakarta. Five of them are small local organizations with only 30 to 70 members, although one has about 500 members in 1970. Ten others are large organizations with headquarters in other places, e.g. Jakarta, Jogyakarta, Madiun, Kediri etc. (Jong 1973: pp. 10-12).

S. de Jong, who has studied Javanese *kebatinan* movements in Central Java, reported that in the Province of Central Java alone 117 *kebatinan* organizations are registered in 1970, with the possibility that there are still more unregistered small organizations in the area.

The adherents and important participants of the movements, many of whom with an educational background in psychology, tend to explain the existence of the numerous movements by the fact that the greater part of the Javanese people tend to have a need for the individual search for the essence of the universe, the essence of life, and the essence of God (Prasadia 1969; Honggowongso, Tedjopramono n.d.; Kartoatmodjo 1976; Kartosutedjo 1977). The Javanese sociologist Selosoemardjan (1973), however, thinks that most Javanese tend to seek harmony with their environment and their own consciousness, very often through metaphysical means.

According to J. A. Niels Mulder, who studied *kebatinan* movements particularly in the city of Jogyakarta, the emergence of so many of such movements is a *kejawen* Javanese cultural awakening and that "....at least part of the *Abangan* cultural awakening has been brought about by the vehement pursuit of organized Islam to push its views and ways of life upon the syncretist majority of the Javanese population" (Niels Mulder 1975: p. 3).

I cannot agree with Niels Mulder's opinion, and think that the increasingly rapid socio-cultural changes which have occurred in the period of transformation, the extreme hardships, poverty, and insecurity suffered by the people during the period of the Pacific War, the Japanese occupation, the Indonesian Revolution, and the unsettled conditions during the first decades of Indonesia's independence, account for the recent increased emergence of Javanese *kebatinan* movements.[13]

Another limitation of Niels Mulder's dissertation which especially concerns Chapter IV is that mysticism is considered to be the main theme in most Javanese *kebatinan* movements. This is naturally not true. M. M. Djojodigoeno, for example, has stated that there are at least four kinds of Javanese *kebatinan* movements: (1) with a focus on mysticism; (2) with a focus on theosophy; (3) moralistic and ethical movements which focus on the purification of the soul; and (4) movements which focus on magical practices and occultism (Subagya 1970: pp. 39-45). To those four types of *kebatinan* movements I add a fifth type, the messianic *Ratu Adil* movements. Except the one which focuses on theosophy, they will be discussed in the following paragraphs.

Kebatinan Mysticism

Information on the Nawaruci poem, one of the original sources of present-day Javanese mysticism for an adequate, brief, but comprehensive description on the Javanese mystical concept of God and its basic pantheistic and monistic variants, are discussed on another place, whereas an excellent, elaborated, and extensively documented description of five variants of presentday Javanese mysticism, their enactment and recent influences from Christianity, modern science, and political ideas, is written by H. Hadiwijono (1967).

Javanese *kebatinan* mysticism views human existence in a wide cosmological context and as only a small part of an eternal cosmic life, representing only "a brief stop to have a drink"[14] along an endless road, in search of the ultimate unification with the Creator.

The correct attitudes, life style, ceremonial activities, and exercises, which under guidance of spiritual teachers and leaders (*guru, panuntun*), the Javanese mystically inclined individual has to adopt and to enact, are basically similar throughout all the various *kebatinan* movements. Imperative are the willingness and capacity to distantiate and to detach the individual self from the material world which involves the spiritual attitude of *rila*, the voluntary total surrender of possessions, the thoughts and feeling of possessing, and the need to possess. Through this spiritual attitude one frees the individual self from forces and influences of the external world of matter. This attitude of total surrender must not be conceived of as a sign of weakness; it should on the contrary be conceived of as the inner strenghth and stability of the soul. The detachment from the material world also involves the spiritual attitude of *narima*, the total acceptance of one's fate, and another spiritual attitude called *sabar,* which means "patience," "endurance," and the "state of being in total harmony with one's fate." The capability of assuming those attitudes can be acquired by assuming a life-style of genuine plainness, purity, simplicity and modesty, but also by certain ceremonial activities and by the development of a capacity to concentrate through self-restrain and exercises in meditation (*semedi*),[15] through which one attempts to turn one's self inwardly, turning off all bodily functions and physical desires. This may lead to total clarity (*hening*) and understanding of the essence of life and to the harmony (*selaras*) between the internal spiritual life and the external physical reality of life. When this release from the burden of this worldly life (*pamudaran*) has been achieved, the individual will, after passing a number of subsequent stages, eventually experience the unification with God (*jumbuhing kawula-Gusti, or manungaling kawula-Gusti*).

The achievement of *pamudaran,* however, in which the individual has the capability to exist detached from the physical reality of life, does not release man from his duties in real life. It even obliges him to endeavor *amemayu ayuning bawana,* i.e. to work for the beautification and salvation of the world by good works and by living an ethically responsible life.

Ethical Movements for the Purification of the Soul

Except SUBUD, all the afore-mentioned big *kebatinan* organizations have indeed a mystical character. Many Javanese *kebatinan* movements, especially the small ones, indeed only search for the purification of the soul without having the ultimate objective of experiencing the unification with God. They only want to achieve a spiritually secure life, free from fears and uncertainties. This is what the Javanese call a liberated human being (*kamanungsan, kasunyatan*).

The way to achieve *kamanungsan* is basically similar to the way to achieve the mystical state of *pamudaran.* Apart from detailed variations, the way to achieve purification of the soul basically consists of leading an ethically responsible, morally good, plain, simple, and modest life, detaching the individual self from the material world, adopting the correct attitudes towards life, fate and death, and exercising meditation disciplinarily. Since this type of *kebatinan* movements seek individual spiritual liberation, it is easy to understand that they have a rather individualistic character, at least it attracts people who want to fulfill their religious needs without, however, being forced upon by habit, custom, or formal religious rules (Said 1972-a: pp. 153-154).

Kebatinan Magic

There are plenty of *kebatinan* movements with only a few dozen members each throughout Java. Most of them are urban based, and often have a secret character; they may originally have mystical, moralistic, or ethical objectives under the leadership of a teacher, or *guru.* To achieve the desired goals they make extensive use of magical practices besides study and meditation. Many such movements were originally also organizations for learning the Javanese art of self defence (*pencak*). Except teaching physical exercises the teachers of such groups also instruct their students the practice of meditation; and to create a sacred atmosphere extensive use is made of secret magical rituals which should make the students invulnerable and magically potent. As such, the groups have turned into secret organizations in which magical rituals are practiced to achieve magical power instead of being organizations to practice physical exercises to learn the Javanese *pencak* art of self defence.

Messianic Movements

A brief but excellent and comprehensive over-all view of Messianic, or *Ratu Adil,* movements in rural Java which includes a review of earlier studies on the subject is included in Sartono Kartodirdjo's book, *Protest Movements in Rural Java* (1973: pp. 64-105). Most of the 15 Javanese messianic movements that have occurred in the past three centuries[16] have, according to Sartono's analysis, similar features. Unlike *kebatinan* movements, Javanese messianic movements had essentially profane and practical goals (according to Sartono), and at least they were not preoccupied with the hereafter, but very much with the present, and did not constitute a flight from the real world. Their syncretistic character, however, makes it hard to establish a clear distinction between them and other types of religious movements.

Many Javanese messianic movements have emerged in a socio-cultural climate where the peasant population had specific grievances against economic exploitation and administrative pressures by the local colonial government, and where a too rapid culture change and the consequent breakdown of tradition have caused general dissatisfaction among them.

In most cases a charismatic leader, already endowed with magical power of healing, and believed to have received a divine revelation or an inner conversion in which a messianic vocation is conveyed, is in a position to assemble a substantial circle of disciples about him.

Javanese messianic movements are usually also nativistic and traditional in nature in that they glorify the original and traditional culture of their ancestors. Since those customs are often considered to have been violated by people with contemporary ideas influenced by Dutch education and foreign culture and also by local civil servants who were under pressure of the Dutch colonial government, the main desire and hope fostered and ritually cultivated in Javanese messianic movements is the revival of the traditional culture of the ancestors and the restoration of the old Javanese kingdom by a Just King, or *Ratu Adil.* There used to be the idea of a coming cataclysm, of which famine, epidemics, crop failures, natural disasters, and the earlier mentioned period of crisis, the *jaman edan,* or "period of madness," are the initial signs.

Those features of Javanese messianic movements are similar to those of the many cargo cults in West Irian, Papua Newguinea and Melanesia, which occurred in the past one hundred years. As we know, many of the cargo cults have erupted into violent anti-establishment, anti-colonial, and anti-foreigners insurrections. In Java it has also turned into violence when the leaders of the movements assumed the role of the *Ratu Adil,* and preached the Islamic holy war, or *jihad,* to overthrow the colonial establishment or local government. Historical accounts of these events are included in the works of Drewes and Sartono Kartodirdjo.[17]

Santri Religious Movements

The Pesantren

There are also movements of Javanese with a *Santri* spiritual orientation, which were often based on a particular Islamic religious school, the *pesantren.* Almost similar to the *Kejawen* spiritual movements, the *Santri* spiritual movements may also be classified into: (1) movements that focus on mysticism, (2) puritanical movements which focus on the return to a pristine, religious society and traditional Islamic religious beliefs and practices, (3) movements which focus on messianic beliefs, and (4) movements which focus on magical practices and occultism.

Mysticism is recognized and institutionalized in Islam, called *tasawwuf.* The mystics are called *shufi,* a term accounting for what has been more generally known *shufism* in Islamic studies (Nibolson 1921; Grunebaum 1961-a; pp. 27-29; Smith 1931). The people who practice *shufism* in Indonesia in geneal, and in Java in particular, are usually organized into mystical movements called *tarekat*[18] under the charismatic leadership of a teacher who is called *mursyid* (Trimingham 1973). By the population of the surrounding area the *tarekat* leader is usually called *kiyahi*.

The mystic teacher may be a person who has gone through a training in a *pesantren* or in another *tarekat*. With a diploma or licence he is entitled to establish a *tarekat pesantren* of his own. However, many mystic teachers and *tarekat* leaders simply inherited their positions from their fathers, who used to be established and renown mystics. They are themselves usually well-trained mystics and licenced teachers, although many are only charismatic leaders without being teachers in the formal sense of the term.

Many famous *tarekat* leaders have a long life history: first they have gone through a thorough training in mystics under renowned teachers in a number of *pesantren* and *tarekat* schools. Subsequently they obtained a long teaching experience in a number of *pesantren* and *tarekat* schools until they felt prepared to establish one of their own (Dhofier 1978). Depending on the educational background and orientation of the teacher-leader, a *tarekat pesantren* belongs to a certain mystical order of which there are several that dominate certain areas of Java. These are, for example, *tarekat* Qadiriyyah, the Naqshabandiyyah, the Syaththariyyah, the Shiddiqiyyah, the Wahidiyyah, the Saziliyyah, and several others. The Qadiriyyah and the Naqshabandiyyah for instance, are old orders that have come to Indonesia in the early 17th century. In Java they are dominant in Banten, the Sundanese area of the Priangan Highlands, and the Javanese Western coastal area of Cirebon (Soebardi 1978). The other orders are more dominant in East Java. The Syaththariyyah is also a very old order, whereas the Shiddiqiyyah and the Wahidiyyah are relatively recent ones, which have many schools along the Brantas River area of Kedhiri and Pare (Modjokuto).

A renowned *tarekat* leader has faithful assistants who serve him devotedly. Several of the assistants live in various areas of Java, and are authorized by the leader to establish branches of the *tarekat*. They are also given the title *badhal* (deputy), and are often also authorized to receive the oath of the *tarekat* from candidates who wished to become members or students of the branch. A centralized administrative organization, however, is usually lacking, and the local branches under the various *badhal* are therefore more or less autonomous. Only the charismatic qualities of the central leader keeps the *tarekat* and its various branches together. The leader requires his deputies to come to the central *tarekat pesantren* at fixed periods, to practice the main *tarekat* rituals with him.

In many cases the solidarity of the students, the adherents, and the laymen followers of a *tarekat pesantren* is intensified by rituals about a sacred tomb in the yard of the *tarekat pesantren* of its legendary founder. This tomb is venerated as a *pepundhen* by the students, adherents, and laymen followers, but also by numerous inhabitants of the surrounding villages who cannot even be categorized as *Santri's*.

Tarekat pesantrens teach their students the branches of Islamic knowledge, i.e. *ilmu'lfiqh* (or Islamic law), *ilmu'lkalam* (theology) and *ilmu 'ttas-sawwuf* (mysticism) like regular *pesantren* schools, but of the students and adherents (*shufi's*) stricter observance of religious duties, blind obedience to the teacher, and the recitation of *dhikir* are demanded in addition.

Dhikir constitutes the most important religious practice of the *tarekat*, and depending on the mystical order to which the *tarekat* belongs, the *dhikir* practiced is either the *chikir jahar* (the loud *dhikir*), the *dhikir kafi* (soft *dhikir*), or a combination of both (Soebardi 1978: pp. 224-226).

According to scholars who have observed *tarekat pesantrens* more closely (Abdurrachman 1978), these schools have unlike the ordinary *pesantrens,* also older students or adherents who are in great distress due to social dislocation or economic insecurity, or because they believed themselves to be lost in an apparently demoralized society. Many of them also seek purification from a sin they thought they had committed in the past, and joined the *tarekat* not so much as to study law or theology, but to find a spiritual solution to their own personal problems.

Students and members of a *tarekat pesantren* do not always have to stay in the compound of the school. They must, however, like the *shufi's* who live in the compound, adopt a rigid and frugal life style, avoid worldliness, practice the *shalat,* and have to fast more frequently than ordinary laymen, in addition to having to attend the courses of progressive training in the *dhikir* ritual in a strict manner. For the *dhikir* ritual they are obliged to clad themselves in the white attire of the *shufi's*.

A famous teacher of a well-established *tarekat* may, however, also have a great number of laymen as his followers; these, however, do not join the *dhikir* rituals. They frequently attend his sermons at the mosque or visit the sacred tomb of the *tarekat's* legendary founder.

Soebardi has studied *tarekat* movements and schools in the Sundanese area of West Java and the Javanese area of Cirebon, and reported that several *tarekat pesantrens* displayed an attitude of exclusiveness and isolation. Its members are often highly suspicious of people outside their group, and reject all socio-cultural changes and innovations (1978). Soebardi and other observers of Javanese *tarekat pesantrens* have also reported, however, that many others were more open towards modern influences (Soebardi 1978; Mursyid 1978; Dhofier 1978; Abdurrachman 1978).

Santri Islamic movements are, as already mentioned, puritanical movements, which focus on the return to pristine Islamic religious beliefs and practices. Concerning the relatonship between the religious leader and his students, adherents, and followers, they are in many respects similar to that of the *tarekat* mystical movements. In terms of the ritual content the *dhikir* is of course lacking in the puritanical Islamic movement.

An example of such a movement is the Budiah Sect, founded in the middle of the 19th century by Haji Mohammad Rifangi of Kalisalak. The history of this sect was studied by Sartono Kartodirdjo (1973: pp. 118-127), and today the sect still seems to have adherents in Pekalongan, in the Western Coastal area, and in the Bagelen area.

Sartono Kartodirdjo also noted the puritanical Islamic movements did not participate in active revolts, although they resented the authroities, repudiated the existing social order, and condemned the presence of alien religions (1973: pp. 112-113). This, however, stands in sharp contrast with the *tarekat* movements which, as the history of Java has shown, very frequently formed a source of revolutionary activities.

Also the *Santri* messianic, or *Imam Mahdi,* movements, have more active revolutionary potentials. This apparently lies in the nature of messianic movements, which preaches the restoration of the traditional order by a Just King, and especialy the *Santri* messianic can easily activate *jihad* Holy War, or *Perang Sabil,*[19] ideas. In the chapter on "Messianic Movements" in his book, *Protest Movements in Rural Java,* Sartono Kartodirdjo described not only the *Kejawen* Javanese *Ratu Adil* movements, but also the same movements by the *Santri's* (1973: pp. 64-105).

Sartono Kartodirdjo also mentioned movements which were concerned with the revolts against the established social order, which were also based on the *jihad* idea, but by using terror, extortion and intimidation of a near-criminal type (1973: pp. 133-139). He described the history of such a movement in the Sundanese area, another one in Banten in the 1920's, and also stories about similar movements in Central and Eastern Java. It is also easy to understand how in this context extensive magical practices rather than the revival of traditional society or of pristine religion became the main concern of the movement. Magic is indeed an important element in Javanese culture.

Notes

1) According to the latest census in 1971, Indonesia has a population of 119,000,000. The next census will be held early 1981.
2) Although most Javanese consider themselves officially and administratively adherers of Islam, the designation *Agama Jawa* for the second syncretistic variant, shows that the adherers consider it to be more basic and familiar to the Javanese way of life. The book *The Religion of Java* (1960) by C. Geertz deserves the merit for having presented the first scientific description of the two religious variants. However, it has used other terms, i.e. *Islam Santri* for the first variant, and *Islam Abangan* for the second. The Javanese word *santri* originally means "student of religion," and Islam Santri therefore means "Islam of the religious students." Abangan means "the reds," and *Islam Abangan* are "Islam of the Reds," meant as a degrading term and may be used in joking relationships, but which may otherwise insult people. More than a century before Geertz's book, a Dutch religious missionary, C. Poensen, has already indicated the existence of the two variants of Javanese Islam.
3) The term comes from *jawi* (=Java), with suffixes *ke*-and-*an*.
4) From the Arabic *batiniyyah*
5) A list of those 100 movements are included in Djumali Kertorahardjo's booklet on *kebatinan* movements in Indonesia (n.d.: pp. 99-102).
6) There is a discrepancy of 11 Central Java organizations in S. de Jong's figures in 1970, based on a list of the *Kejaksaan Tinggi* of Surabaya in 1971, and Prijanti Pakan's figures of 1971, based on sources at the Ministry of Religious Affairs.
7) The representatives of *Hardapusara* who attended the *Kebatinan* conventions in Semarang and Surakarta in 1955 and 1956 were members of the Kudus branch. Kudus is a town in the eastern *Pasisir* (Coastal) area of North Central Java. The movement is listed as such in the BKKI list of 1955 (Djumali Kertorahardjo n.d.: p. 100).
8) He heard: "...voices from deep in his inner self" (Hardjoprakoso 1956: p. 17).
9) There are various studies on this movement. Cf. reports in S. Hardjoprakoso's dissertation (1956), S. de Jong (1973), and H. Hadiwijono (1967).
10) More information on this movement is included in Djumali Kertorahardjo's book (1972: pp. 204-224) and Hadiwijono (1967). Cf. also S. Prodjohoesodo (1965).
11) *Panuntun* in this context means "teacher," whereas the name Gutomo reminds us of Buddha's name Gautama.
12) Pare is the actual name of the town which the MIT team has called Modjokuto.
13) Cf. also C. C. Berg's opinion on this matter (1951: pp. 3-4).
14) The Javanese say: *"Gesang punika namung mampir ngombe."*
15) Some movements use the term *tepekur* for meditation, which is derived from the Arabic *tafakkur*.
16) The oldest is the so-called "older" Dipanegara revolt of 1720, reported by J.

Brandes (1889), and the latest is the Amedkosdi Affair of 1919 (Sartono Kartodirdjo 1973: pp. 101-103).
17) Sartono Kartodirdjo's remarkable dissertation concerns peasant movements in Banten, West Java (1966).
18) Tarekat comes from the Arabic term *thariqa*.
19) *Perang Sabil* is the Javanese term for Holy War.

References

Abdurrachman Soerjomihardjo
>   1962 "Suatu Analisa Tjita-Tjita dan Tindak-Perbuatan Nasional-Revolusi-
>   oner Suwardi Surjaningrat," *Medan Ilmu Pengetahuan,* III.
>   1978 "National Education in a Colonial Society," *Dynamics of Indonesian
>   History,* Haryati Soeoadio, C. A. du Marchie Sarvaas, editor, Amster-
>   dam: North-Holland Publishing Company, pp. 277-306.

Badan
>   1956 *Buku Kenangkenangan Kongres Kebatinan Indonesia ke-I dan ke-II,
>   Semarang dan Surakarta.* Djakarta: Tjahaja Widjaja Kusuma.

Bennett, J. G.
>   1961 *Christian Mysticism and Subud.* London.

Berg, C. C.
>   1951 "Toekomstverwachtingen in het Javaanse Denken," *Schakels,* XLIII:
>   3-8.

Brandes, J.
>   1889 "Iets over de Oudereh Dipanegara in Verband met een Prototype van
>   de Voorspelling van Jayabaya," *Tijdschrift voor Indische Taal–, Land–
>   en Volkenkunde,* XXXII: 268-300.

Dhofier, Zamakhsyari
>   1978 "Mesantren dan Thorigoh," *Dialog,* Edisi Khusus, pp. 9-21.

Djumali Kertorahardjo R. E.
>   n. d. Kertorahardjo R. E., D.

Hadiwijono, H.
>   1967 *Man in the Present Javanese Mysticism.* Baarn, Bosch & Keuning,
>   N. V. (Dissertation, Free University of Amsterdam).

Hadisuwarno
>   1969 *Tjeramah Latihan Kedjiwaan Susila Budhi Dharma.* Surakarta.

Hardjoprakoso, S.
>   1956 *Indonesisch Mensbeeld als Basis Ener Psycho-Therapie.* Leiden.

Honggowongso, S., and Tedjopramono
>   n. d. *Kepercayaan Kepada Tuhan Yang Maha Esa: Pokok-Pokok Ajaran dan
>   Falsafahnya.* Jogyakarta (Unpublished manuscript).

Kartoatmodjo, S.
>   1973 "Educate the Javanese!" ("Geef de Javaan Opvoeding!", A memorial
>   addressed to the Dutch government in January 1903 by Raden Adjeng
>   Kartini). Translated with an introduction by J. Taylor, *Indonesia,* XVII:
>   83-98.
>   1976. "Aliran Kebatinan dan Para Psikologi," *Mimbar Ulama,* I-6: 25-36.

Kartosutedjo K.
  1977 "Kebatinan Menurut Pandangan Orang Awam," *Mawas Diri*, VI-9: 29-31.
Mursyid, Masyþullah
  1978 "Sufisme: Sebuah Ulasan Singkat," *Dialog*, Edisi Khusus, pp. 5-8.
Niels Mulder, J. A.
  1975 *Mysticism and Daily Life in Contemporary Java: A Cultural Analysis of Javanese World View and Ethic as Embodied in Kebatinan and Everyday Experience*. Amsterdam (Doctoral dissertation, University of Amsterdam).
Pakan, Prijanti
  1978 "Pokok-Pokok Masalah Aliran Kebatinan," *Peninjau*, V/2: 93-135.
Prasadia, T.
  n.d."Ilmu Kebatinan dan Psikiatri," *Djiwa*, II-4: 51-60.
Prodjohoesodo, S.
  1965 *Paguyuban Soemarah*. Jogyakarta.
Purwadi
  1970 *Tjeramah ke-III Susila Budhi Dharma*. Surakarta (Unpublished manuscript).
  1972 *Tjeramah ke-IV Susila Budhi Dharma*. Surakarta (Unpublished manuscript).
Said, M.
  1972 *Taman Siswa: Its Principles and Practices*. Jogyakarta:Majelis Luhur Taman Siswa.
  1972-a "Kebatinan," *Basis*, XXI/3: 152-157.
Sartono Kartodirdjo
  1973 *Protest Movements in Rural Java: A Study of Agrarian Unrest in the Nineteenth and Early Twentieth Centuries*. Singapore: Oxford University Press.
Selosoemardjan
  1962 *Social Changes in Jogyakarta*. Ithaca, N. Y.: Cornell University Press.
  1973 "Ilmu Gaib, Kebaktian dan Agama Dalam Kehidupan Masysrakat," *Masalah-Masalah Kerohanian dan Keagamaan*, Jakarta, pp. 24-41.
Soebardi, S.
  1978 "The Pesantren Tarikat of Surialaya in West Java," *Spectrum: Essays Presented to Sutan Takdir Alisjahbana on his Seventieth Birthday*, S. Udin, editor, Jakarta: Dian Rakyat, pp. 215-571.
Veur, P. W. J. van der
  1976 "Freemasonry in Indonesia, 1762-1961," *Proceedings of the Conference on Modern Indonesian History*, Madison: Center for Southeast Asian Studies, University of Wisconsin, pp. 97-118.

13 Games Are Forever: A Preliminary Discussion on Continuity and Change in Manipulative Behavior of the Chinese

CHIEN CHIAO

Introduction

This paper is a part of a larger research project on "Social and Political Strategies in Chinese Culture". Contrary to the stereotype description of the Chinese society as a highly rigid system in which each individual is fixed to a specific status, it contains more alternatives for its members to maneuver and optimize than many other traditional societies. With one of the longest literary tradition in human history, Chinese culture has stored an extremely rich information for such activities. Any person who has long experience in dealing with the Chinese can testify that they are great masters in manipulating social relations for maximum benefits. To study "social and political strategies in Chinese culture" therefore is probably the most efficient way, if not the only way, to reveal the dynamics of the Chinese society and the true face of its social mobility.

Besides the academic one, this project also has a personal goal to fulfill. Though I was born, brought up and completed most of my education in China, still, my seven years of living in a Chinese society in Hong Kong is a rather unique experience. This is the first time I have ever lived in my own society as a "full time" permanently and gainfully employed adult member. My perspective towards Chinese society obtained therefrom is quite different from my previous one. This is in fact comparable to my experience with the American society. As I reflect, my perspective of American society gained later as a faculty member (at Indiana University) was quite different from what I obtained early as a graduate student (at Cornell University). As I reentered my own society in a different capacity, my first and foremost "culture shock" was the intensity of "game playing". True this is rather a common phenomenon in any complex society. But nowhere else have I ever observed such a 'scene" that almost all members of a given organization are engaged in the endless and ever intensifying "game playing" or "politics". Looking from this "vantage point", I have found the political struggles on the Chinese Mainland especially what have been revealed in the "black material" (黑材料) which were published deliberately to expose the wickedness of the persons under attack extremely resembling, though on a much larger scale. I feel that I have been truely a participant observer of the oldest uninterrupted social and political maneuver on earth and among the largest human community which has become much more sophisticated in latter days. I am convinced that this maneuver more than anything else has been the main obstacle to modernization and that I have a moral obligation to make a systematic exposition of it with my training in modern social science.

Some Theoretical Considerations

The main hypothesis of this study is that social and political strategies form a highly sophisticated, extensive and uninterrupted tradition in Chinese culture; what are manifested by the contemporary Chinese, communist or non-communist alike, in their manipulative behavior are basically the continuation of this old tradition. As Xun Lu (魯迅), a famous modern Chinese writer, has commented: "Struggles yet to be over, old patterns will be copied again and again (戰鬥正未有窮期, 老譜將不斷的襲用)".[1] To explore this hypothesis, a two-step research is designed: (1) identification and description of better known strategies, (2) analyses of these strategies. On the basis of these analyses a list of the concepts or behaviors which are essential to these strategies and form the dominant patterns in Chinese social interactions may be derived. This research will be conducted separately on the traditional as well as on the contemporary Chinese material. The results will be lined up together and carefully compared. Understandably, the names of strategies vary greatly from the traditional to the contemporary data. Nonetheless, as long as the basic concepts or behaviors as identified in the second step are largely similar, the hypothesis stands.

"Strategy" is the translation of the Chinese terms *jìcè* 計策, *jìmóu* 計 謀, or simply *jì* 計. It is defined as a socially allowed though not necessarily encouraged scheme with which an individual or a group of individuals try to acquire certain benefits or to avoid disasters. Strategies are "models". Modern views of "model" tend to stress its metaphorical nature. Kaplan (1964:265), for example, has regarded models as "scientific metaphors". He further explains:

> A metaphor, like an aphroism, condenses in a phrase a significant similarity. When the poet writes "the morn, in russet mantle clad, walks o'er the dew of yon high eastern hill," he evokes awareness of a real resemblance, and such awareness may be made to serve the purpose of science. When they do serve in this way, we are likely to conceptualize the situation as involving the use of analogy. The scientist recognizes similarities that have previously escaped us, and systematizes them.

This metaphorical definition of model fits the case of Chinese strategies very well.

In a recent paper of mine "Strategies in Chinese Culture: A Preliminary Discussion" (Chiao 1981) I have identified and briefly discussed 58 traditional Chinese strategies. This list is by no means exhaustive, but, to my knowledge, it includes most of the better-known or "standard" ones. These 58 strategies do not provide any details for operation. They are merely metaphorical idioms. Six of them are composed of three characters, one of them has only one character, all the rest are four character idioms. To be sure, there are books as those cited in my recent papers (Chiao 1980 & 1981) which give individual strategy more or less detailed explanation and successful examples. Unfortunately, most explanations are nothing more than the author's speculation and most examples cited to illustrate the strategies are arbitrarily assigned and often irrelevant. In short, to my knowledge, there is no standard or widely accepted "text" for using the strategies. Nonetheless, they are invaluable in two respects: (1) to provide analogies and associations in constructing details for the operation of the strategies, (2) to identify and describe the ongoing manipulation and to suggest additional steps to be taken.

All the 58 strategies are about various kinds of actions which are expressed in a number of ways: some are historical events such as the Strategy "*Wéi Wèi jiù Zhào* 圍魏救趙) (To besiege Wèi in order to rescue Zhào)"; some are fables like the Strategy "*Lǐ dài táojiāng* 李代桃僵 (The plum-tree dies for the peach tree)"; some are extraordinary behaviors in hypothetical situations, such as the Strategy "*Qì zú bǎo shuài* 棄卒保帥 (To save the king by sacrificing the knights)"; some are dramatic acts like the Strategy "*Xiào lǐ cáng dāo* 笑裏藏刀 (to hide a dagger in a smile)"; and some are simply the key words in the elaborated operations such as the Strategy "*Fǎnjiàn jì* 反間計 (Stratagem of sowing distrust or discord among one's enemies)". Since they are all illustration, figuration, dramatization, or description of various actions, it is possible to strip them down to core or basic actions or behaviors which may be presented in simpler forms.

In my paper "Chinese Strategic Behaviors: A Preliminary List" (Chiao 1980), I have managed to sort out 24 basic behaviors from the 58 strategies and represent them with single characters. I am ready to admit that the procedure I used in the sorting is crude and arbitrary, and the 24 basic behaviors as represented by single characters are just as figurative as the 58 strategies. Nevertheless, in comparison with the latter they have at least the following advantages:

(1) They are more clearly and explicitly defined.
(2) They are not overlapping with each other in their connotations.
(3) They provide a base or framework for meaningful comparison.
(4) They give a series of useful clues to the deeper understanding of the complicated social behavior of the Chinese, especially of their elites who have been constantly and intensively involved in manipulative activities.

The same method is applied in processing contemporary data.

From the contemporary material — mainly interviews of recent immigrants, newspapers and periodicals from Mainland China, I have identified and analyzed 43 strategies. In comparison with the 58 traditional strategies mentioned above, 11 of these 43 strategies are identical in both titles and contents, 18 of them are different in titles but similar in contents, naturally they all fit the 24 basic behaviors deduced from the 58 traditional strategies. The rest 14 of them are different in both titles and contents. Further analysis of these 14 contemporary strategies yields another six basic behaviors which are, though different from the 24 basic behaviors, by no means modern innovations. On the contrary, as we shall see later, they have been popular among the Chinese for ages. In the following, I will give a brief discussion to each of the 30 basic behavior on its manifestation in both traditional and contemporary data.

Thirty Strategies in Context

1. Guān 觀

Guān means to watch or to observe. It is a "play it safe" strategy. In front of a confrontation, it is always safer to watch it from a distance than to get involved as advised by the Strategy *"Gé àn guān huǒ* 隔岸觀火 (To watch a fire from the other side of the river)"*. As a general principle, try to be a spectator instead of a participant so long as possible.

Among the contemporary Chinese, there are people who are rather like what Zedong Mao 毛澤東 (Mao 1937:32) has criticized:

> To hear incorrect views without rebutting them and even to hear counter-revolutionary remarks without reporting them, but instead to take them calmly as if nothing had happened..
>
> To be among the masses and fail to conduct propaganda and agitation or speak at meetings or conduct investigations and inquiries among them, and instead to be indifferent to them and show no concern for their well-being...

During the "Cultural Revolution," this was a favorate strategic behavior for many people who didn't want to get involved in the factional conflicts. The people adhered to this practice were known as *"Xiāoyáo Pai* 逍遙派 (The Unattached Group)"*.

2. Wèn 問

Wèn means to ask or to inquire. When used as a strategic behavior, it refers to a discreet inquiry or investigation of the oponent's situation or intention. The title of the Strategy *"Tóu shí wèn lū* 投石問路 (To ask or to find the way in the dark by throwing a stone)"* figuratively explains this behavior. The Strategy *"Kàn fēng shǐ duò* 看風使舵 (To trim one's sails)"* may be interpreted as a follow-up step to *wèn*.

Both these traditional strategies are very popular among the contemporary Chinese. People who are characterized by this behavior are known as "*biànsèlóng*變色龍 (chameleon)" or "*xiǎopáchóng*小爬蟲 (little reptile)".

3. Dài 待

Dài means to await. It is a more active action than the word suggests. One has to constantly watch the changeful situation and be ready to move when the right moment comes, either premature or delayed motion may forever spoil the chance.

Among the 58 traditional strategies, only the Strategy "*Yǐ yí dài láo*以逸待勞 (To wait at one's ease for an exhausted opponent)" makes *dài* as its core concept, and it is primarily for military. Nonetheless, the concept *dàishí*待時 or in a longer form, *dàishí ér dòng*待時而動 or to wait for the right moment and then take action is a very familiar principle to all ambitious Chinese.

Chinese Communists frequently warn that the "class enemies" are anxiously awaiting the opportunity for *biàntiān* 變天 ("change of heaven" implying the restoration of their rule). People, therefore, should never give up their alert on the "dead tiger".

4. Chèn 趁

Chèn means to take advantage of. It is closely related to *dài*. While *dài* is to alertly wait for the right opportunity, *chèn* is to make sure to grab it when it comes. The Strategy "*Chèn huǒ dàjié* 趁火打刼 (To loot a house while it is on fire)", the Strategy *Shùnshǒu qiān yáng* 順手牽羊 (To lead away a goat in passing)", the Strategy "*Hún shuǐ mō yú* 渾水摸魚 (To take advantage of the murky water to fish)", the Strategy "*Luò jǐng xià shí* 落井下石 (To drop stones on someone who has fallen into a well)", and the Strategy "*Shùnshuǐ tui zhōu* 順水推舟 (To push the boat along with the current)" all emphasize the importance of the *chèn* concept. In general, *chèn* is often used with the word *shí* 時 —— time, or *shì* 勢—— situation. *Chèn shí* 趁時 —— to take advantage of the right time, and *chèn shì* 趁勢 ——to take advantage of the right situation, are believed to be two essential factors of success as indicated in a very popular saying: *shíshì zào yīngxióng* 時勢造英雄——the time and situation produce heroes.

The contemporary equivalents of the Strategy "To lead away a goat in passing" are "*Zhāi táozi* 摘桃子 (Picking up peach)" and "*Yàn guō bámáo* 雁過拔毛 (To pull down some feather of wild geese in passing)". The former usually refers to the cadres who take away the fruit of other people's work; while the latter refers to a more common tactic in which people grab a portion of the thing that goes through his hand.

5. Xū 虛

Xū means lack of substance, hence being sham or feigned. This word is chosen to indicate the kind of action that is not actually and fully carried out. Its main function is either to bluff or to deliberately mislead the opponent.

A number of traditional Chinese strategies have *xū* as their core concepts. Thus, the Strategy *"Xū zhāng shēng shì* 虛張聲勢 (To make a false show of power)" and the Strategy *"Kōngchéng jì* 空城計 (Empty-city stratagem)" are mainly for bluffing. In the Strategy *"Shēng dōng jì xī* 聲東擊西 (To make a feint to the east and attack the west)", the Strategy *"Àn dù Chéncāng* 暗渡陳倉 (To pretend to prepare to advance along one path while secretly going along another)", and the Strategy *"Zhǐ sāng mà huái* 指桑罵槐 (To point at the muberry and abuse the locust)", the first step are all feint which merely serve as a cover for the steps follow. The Strategy *"Mán tiān guò hǎi* 瞞天過海 (To cross the sea by deceiving the heaven)" and the Strategy *"Zéi hǎn zhuō zéi* 賊喊捉賊 (The thief calling 'catch the thief')" are simpler '*xū*' or deceitful actions.

All the traditional strategies mentioned above excepting the "Empty-city stratagem" which is basically a military strategy anyway are to my knowledge popular in contemporary China. Three of them have the equivalents in the contemporary data. The Strategy "The thief calling 'catch the thief'" has appeared several times under the same title. The equivalent of the Strategy "To cross the sea by deceiving the heaven" is *"Dǎzháo hóngqí fǎn hóngqí* 打着紅旗反紅旗 (To oppose red flag with red flag)" which has been a popular accusation since the "Cultural Revolution". Rival factions often accuse each other of playing it. The equivalent of the Strategy "To point at the muberry and abuse the locust" is *Jiè gǔ fěng jīn* 借古諷今 which was a favorate strategy of the "Gang of Four".[2]

6. Huàn 換

Huàn means to alter or to substitute. When it is impossible to remove an unwanted object or to prevent an undesirable matter to happen, one may try to make an alteration or substitution of its substance so that either the object or the matter may become more acceptable.

The Strategy "*Tōu liáng huàn zhù* 偷梁換柱 (To steal the beams and pillars and replace them with rotten timber)", and the Strategy "*Yí huā jiē mù* 移花接木 (To graft one twig on another)" respectively concern substitution and alteration of certain object. The Strategy "*Lǐ dài táojiāng* 李代桃僵 (The plum-tree dies for the peach tree)" illustrated the substitution of a victim in a calamity. The Strategy "*Jiè shī huán hún* 借屍還魂 (A dead person's soul finds reincarnation in another's corpse)" is just the reverse of all the first three strategies. It changes the form, while the other three alter the substance.

Excepting the Strategy "The plum-tree dies for the peach tree", all other strategies just mentioned have frequently appeared in the contemporary data. Xiao-Ping Deng was accused of using the Strategy "A dead person's soul finds reincarnation in another's corpse" to restore the capitalism. The "Gang of Four" on the other hand, have been accused of using the two other strategies in altering Mao's last instructions.

7. Hūn 混

Hùn means to mix, to confuse or to pass off as. The Strategy "*Yúmù hùn zhū* 魚目混珠 (To pass off fish eyes as pearls) suggests the possibility to pass off the sham as the genuine. The Strategy "*Zhāng guān lǐ dài* 張冠李戴 (To put Zhāng's hat on Li's head)" is a scheme to shift either the credits of or blames on one person to another by deliberately confusing their identities.

Both strategies just mentioned appear in contemporary data frequently. They are, however, used in totally different settings. The Strategy "To pass off fish eyes as pearls" is often used in trading where the sham was often sold together with the genuine. The other strategy is favorite for framing an enemy in political struggle.

8. Yū 迂

Yū means to be circuitous. I choose this character to name the basic concept underlying the Strategy "*Wéi Wèi jiù Zhào* 圍魏救趙 (To besiege Wèi in order to rescue Zhào)", the Strategy "*Yuǎnjiāo jìngōng* 遠交近攻

(To befriend distant (states) while attacking those nearby)", and the Strategy "*Pángqiāo cèjī* 旁敲側擊 (To attack by innuendo)". Unlike the characters chosen for other strategic behaviors, it is not borrowed from the titles of the 58 traditional strategies which happen to contain no character suitable for such use.

Yū, as a strategic concept, refers to the action which is not aimed at the primary target in the beginning. Instead, it is carried out on a side often remote target first. The effect herefrom turns around and works on the primary target.

Though there is no particular strategy of the 43 contemporary strategies which has *Yū* as its core concept, its application in political struggle is fairly frequent and highly sophisticated. It is now very clear, the criticism of Wu Han 吳晗 and his play *Hǎi Ruì* 海瑞 was not the purpose by itself, the ultimate target was Shao-Qi Liu but it took quit a few circuitous moves before the action was directly aimed at Liu.

9. Jiè 借

Jiè means to borrow, to make use of or to rely on. It refers to the action in which one wins his goal by making use of a third party. The Strategy "*Jièdāo shārén* 借刀殺人 (To borrow a knife and kill)", and the Strategy "*Jiǎ dào fá Guó* 假道伐虢 (To invade Guó by borrowing a passage (through Yú))", all contain this core concept. Often the opponent's action is turned around and made instrumental in beating him, such as manifested in the Strategy "*Fǎnjiàn jì* 反間計 (Stratagem of sowing distrust or discord among one's enemies)", the Strategy "*Liánhuán jì* 連環計 (A set of interlocking stratagems)", the Strategy "*Jiāng jì jiù jì* 將計就計 (To beat somebody at his own game)". In the case that there are more than one opponents, one of them may be used as an instrument against others such as in the Strategy "*Yī jiàn shuāng diāo* 一箭雙鵰 (To shoot two hawks with one arrow)".

In traditional Chinese marshal art, one of the basic tactics is *jiè lì* 借力 or "borrowing strength". That is to knock down the opponent by making use of his own force as explained by the famous prinicple of *tàijíquán* 太極拳 (shadow boxing), "*Si liǎng bō qiān jīn* 四兩撥千斤 (To turn around a thousand catties with the strength of four *liǎngs* (=200 grams))". In social and political manipulation, *jiè* is also considered as an important and tactful move.

Two popular contemporary strategies have *jiè* as their core concepts. One is known as *zhuōdāo* 捉刀 which means having somebody else to hold the knife for you. In practice, mass are often manipulated to make petitions or demands. The other is known as *Yǐ yí zhì yí* 以夷制夷 which is a borrowing of a diplomatic strategy advocated by bureaucrat of the late Qing Dynasty (1644-1911). As the latter played off one foreign country against another, the contemporary strategist plays off one rival group against another.

10. Jiǎ 假

Jiǎ refers to fictive borrowing such as in the Strategy *"Hú jiǎ hǔ wéi* 孤假虎威 (The fox borrows the tiger's terror)"*. Things involved in such borrowing are usually name, influence, authority, etc. The objective of such borrwoing is to impress or to gain a favor of a third party.

The "Gang of Four" were accused of practicing the similar strategy which is described by a phrase of Xun Lu: *"Lā dàqí zuò hǔpí* 拉大旗做虎皮 (To use the big banner as a tigerskin)"*.[3] The "tiger" in this case obviously refers to Mao.

11. Jià 嫁

Jià originally means to marry off (a daughter, etc.). Its secondary meaning, which is the one used to indicate a strategic motion, is to shift something undesirable like blame or disaster onto somebody else as the Strategy *"Yǐ shì jià huò* 移屍嫁禍 (To shift the misfortune to somebody else by moving the corpse to his place)"* illustrated.

An almost identical strategy with slight difference in title *"Jià huò tārén* 嫁禍他人 (To shift misfortune to another person)"* instead of *Yǐ shì jià huò* is found in the contemporary data.

12. Zuò 作

Zuò basically means to do or to write. But it often means to act or to compose rather than just doing a job straight or writing something factually. Hence it suggests elaboration or exaggeration, as the Strategy *"Xiǎo tí dà zuò* 小題大作 (To make a big issue out of a small problem)"* indicates. Both these behavior and strategy are widely used in contemporary

China. In the political rectification, a common practice known to Chinese Communists is *shànggāng* 上綱, that is, to raise the issue to the higher plane of principle. As a result, a minor error can be inflated to a big crime.

13. Shēng 生

Shēng means to procreate. When used as a strategic action, it often means to fabricate or to make up. The Strategy: *"Wú zhōng shēng yǒu* 無中生有 (To make something out from nothing)" is an elaboration of this idea which originates from Laozi: "All things in the world are procreated by being. All being is procreated by non-being".[4]

No related strategy is included in the contempoary data. This basic concept, however, is frequently used by Chinese Communists. Numerous *yūanyù* 冤獄 (unjust verdicts) have been made up in recent years especially by the "Gang of Four", are mainly the application of this concept.

14. Cáng 藏

Cáng means to hide or to conceal. One may conceal his hostile scheme or agressive intention with a smile as in the Strategy *"Xiào lǐ cáng dāo* 笑裏藏刀 (To hide a dagger in a smile), or a double face as in the Strategy *"Liǎng miàn sān dāo* 兩面三刀 (To be double-faced and attack somebody behind his back)". Sometimes the camouflage may even be a self-inflicted pain as in the Strategy *"Kǔròu jì* 苦肉計 (The ruse of inflicting an injury on oneself to win the confidence of the enemy)".

All these three strategies have appeared in the contemporary data. In addition, a new strategy *"Yángfèng yǐnwéi* 陽奉陰違 (To comply in public but oppose in private)" is also recorded.

15. Mèi 昧

Mèi means to be ignorant as illustrated by the Strategy *"Míngzhī gùmèi* 明知故昧 (To feign ignorance while one knows the situation clearly)". To keep a stolid look which is a kind of *mèi* is a favorite practice of the Chinese. "A person of great wisdom appears dumb" is a popular Chinese idiom. Another common Chinese idiom says: *"Zhuānglóng zuòyǎ, xīn jīng miàn hān* 裝聾作啞心精面敢 (Pretend to be deaf and dumb with a shreweď mind and a naive face)". The Strategy *"Jiǎ chī bù diān* 假痴不癲

(To pretend idiotic though one is not really crazy)" confirms the same principle. The first strategy mentioned above is included in my contemporary data and is a popular one.

16. Diào 調

Diào means to transfer or to dispatch. In actual operation, the opponent or his man is transferred out from a key place or position. The title of the Strategy *"Diào hǔ lí shān* 調虎離山 (To lure the tiger out of the mountain)" is a good figuration of this operation. Its main objective is to create a more favorable situation for the strategist.

The contemporary equivalent of this strategy is *"Wā qiángjiǎo* 控牆角 ". Literally it means to cut the ground from under the corner of a house which also refers to the removal of the opponent or his man from his present position. Once the position is vacant, the strategist fills it with his own man. The strategy is also known as *"Lāchūqú, dǎjìnlai* 拉出去, 打進來 (To drag (their people) out, and fill (our people) in).

17. Chōu 抽

Chōu means to pull out or to take away. As a strategic move, *chōu* is to remove the means either to stop the opponent's progress as the Strategy *"Fǔ dǐ chōu xīn* 釜底抽薪 (To take away the firewood from under the cauldron)" suggests, or to block his access (to success, fame, etc.) as the Strategy *"Shàng wū chōu tī* 上屋抽梯 (To take away the ladder after one has successfully got into the upstair room)" outlines. One of the contemporary strategy which shares this basic idea is *"Jiàkōng fá* 架空法 "which means to raise one to the top with little support at the bottom that is to make him a mere figurehead.

18. Yǐn 引

Yǐn means to draw, to allure or to attract. It is the core concept of the Strategy *"Pāo zhuān yǐn yù* 拋磚引玉 (To cast a brick to attract jade)" in which goods are given away, and of the Strategy *"Měirén jì* 美人計 (Use of a woman to ensnare a man)" in which woman is offered. Goods and woman are two most common kinds of allurement in Chinese society.

Yǐn in fact is based on an ancient social principle as explained by

Laozi: "What will be taken is first bestowed".[5] To give or to make an allurement, however, is a very delicate matter. Unless one has sufficient information and good judgement as to what and how much should be given, and when and how frequent the presentation should be made, his allurement will not help him. Worse yet, it may even hurt him.

Biao Lin was accused to practice the Strategy "Yòu 誘 (To lure)" or "Diàoyú shù 釣魚術 (To fish)" and lured people with high positions, salary and favors.[6] Another contemporary strategy also has yǐn as its core concept but the allurement is oneself: "Yǐn huǒ shāo shēn 引火燒身." It means to draw fire against oneself or to make self criticism in order to attract others to crticize themselves.

19. Jī 激

Jī means to stimulate or to prod, as in the Strategy "Jī jiàng jì 激將計 (To prod somebody into action)". The means of prodding is usually linguistic, such as ridicule, sarcasm, scorn, etc. Though the goal is to get the opponent excited or emotional, the strategist himself must keep cool and cautious and make sure that only the right amount of stimulation be applied. This linguistic game is just as popular at present as in the past.

20. Jǐng 儆

Jǐng means to warn or admonish. The Strategy "Shā jī jǐng hóu 殺雞儆猴 (To kill the chicken to frighten the monkey)" figuratively explains the function of jǐng. In this strategy, action on a person is not really aimed at him but rather sends a message to others. In contemporary China, it is better known as "Shā yī jǐng bǎi 殺一儆百 (To execute one as a warning to a hundred)".

21. Zhì 制

Zhì means to govern or to bring under control. To deal with an opponent brought under control is like to catch a thief in a house whose door has already been bolted as described by the Strategy "Guānmén zhuō zéi 關門捉賊 (To bolt the door and capture the thief)". In order to effectively bring the opponent under control, the Strategy "Xiān fā zhì rén 先發制人 (To gain the initiative by striking first)" points out the advantage of making the first strike. The Strategy "*Fǎn kè wéi zhǔ* 反客爲主 (To reverse the positions of the host and the guest)" stresses the importance of being the master (contrastive to "guest") of the situation. Finally the Strategy "*Qín zéi qín wáng* 擒賊擒王 (To catch bandits, first catch the ringleader)" suggests that to bring a larger number of opponents under control, one has to control their leader first.

Though all four strategies mentioned above have been recorded in the contemporary data, the Strategy "To reverse the positions of the host and the guest" happens to have more entries than others. Besides the title quoted above, it is also known as "*Xuān bīn duó zhǔ* 喧賓奪主 (A presumptuous guest usurps the host's role)". Another entry, "*Fǎnyǎo yī kǒu* 反咬一口 (To trump up a countercharge against one's accuser)" has the similar idea.

22. Bì 避

Bì means to avoid. The Strategy "*Bì zhòng jiù qīng* 避重就輕 (To avoid the important and dwell on the trivial)" points out the essence of this behavior. It is an especially useful scheme in dealing with criticism or accusation —— try to answer only the minor charges but dodge the serious parts. Consequently, it has become a favorite strategy in defending oneself in front of public criticism on Chinese Mainland today.

23. Qì 棄

Qì means to abandon or to give up. A good strategist has to be willing to give up the less important in order to protect or to gain the more important as pointed out by the Strategy "*Qì zú bǎo shuài* 棄卒保帥 (To save the king by abandoning the knights)". The Strategy "*Yù qín gù zòng* 欲擒故縱 (To leave somebody at large first is better for apprehending him later)" employs the same principle. The first strategy is widely mentioned in contemporary Chinese literature not just as a manipulative scheme but also as a moral principle —— to sacrifice the interest of individuals or small groups in order to save that of the larger collective, even the whole nation.

24. Tuō 脫

Tuō means to extricate oneself from or to get rid of. The Strategy "*Jīnchán tuō' qiào* 金蟬脫殼 (Cicada extricates itself from the shell)" is an excellent metaphor for the first meaning of *tuō*. No matter whether the "shell" is put on by others or by oneself, as soon as it becomes a burden, he better gets rid of it. *Tuō* is then a delicate and tactful way to do so. The Strategy "*Zǒu* 走 (To run away)" is more straightforward and simple way of *tuō*.

In various violent political struggles on Chinese Mainland, quite a number of highly sophisticated devices of *tuō* or *zǒu* have been recorded. Basically, they employ either the first strategy, that is, to create a "shell" first and leave it untouched so that nobody would suspect one's intention of escaping, or the Strategy "*Lǐ dài táo jiáng* 李代桃僵 (The plum-tree dies for the peach tree)" to find somebody to take one's place so he can possiblly get himself out of a tough situation.

25. Ren 忍

"*Ren*" means to endure, it is a subtle strategy. One who plans to revolt against the existing institution has to wait for the right chance. Time is therefore an important factor in this strategy since no one can tell when the opportunity comes. Before launching the final blow, one has to withstand every unbearable thing which happens to him. A slight upset may ruin his plan and even endanger his life. This often implies that one has to force himself to take all kinds of humiliation from his enemies before he gets a chance to fight back.

Biao Lin is alleged to have practiced such strategy or the Strategy "*Qū ěr qiú shēn* 屈而求伸 (which literally means to bend in order to stretch further)". He has been described as the true believer of the famous Confucian saying: "lack of forbearance in small matters upsets great plans". Since he considered the seizure of the total power the greatest goal of his life, he always reminded himself not to let any minor persons or matters ruin his major plan.

26. Zuān 鑽

Zuān means to drill. It is often used figuratively to describe the special effort for developing better relations with persons of influence. This or in a longer form *Zuānyíng* 鑽營 has been a basic tactic for climbing up in traditional hierarchy of Chinese bureaucracy. A modern description of this behavior is *"Wú kǒng bù rù* 無孔不入 (To seize every opportunity to develop personal relations)".

27. Lā 拉

Lā means to pull or draw. When used as a manipulative behavior, it refers to pulling some person or persons to one's side by building closer ties with them. It has been an old tactic in constructing one's social network. In contemporary China, two strategies are directly related to this idea: *"Lā jiāoqing* 拉交情" which means to form ties with a specific person, and *"Lā shāntóu* 拉山頭" which means to form a faction.

28. Tuī 推

Tuī means to push. It pictures a polite way to turn down a request, evade a responsibility or a commitment. The key point of this operation is to push or shift it to somebody else. Its main purpose is not to offend anybody while leave oneself clear out of any involvement. Since *tuī* is a basic movement in *tàijíquán* 太極拳 (shadow boxing), practicing *tuī* strategic action is often referred to as *dǎ tàijíquán* 打太極拳 which is a well-known strategy among the Chinese, communist or non-communist.

29. Tuō 拖

Tuō means to pull, drag or stall. Here it indicates a tactic to avoid making a decision by delaying or dragging it on indefinitely. As time goes by, the issue may gradually lose its urgency to the point that it no longer demands a decision. Such strategy is well described by a common saying: *"Dàshì huà xiǎo, xiǎoshì huà liǎo* 大事化小，小事化了 (To turn big problems into small problems and small problems into no problem at all)". Such is a characteristic behavior of Chinese bureaucrats past and present.

30. Kōng 空

Kōng means empty or void. This concept is advocated by Zong-Wu Li (1939:23) as one of the six principles for a bureaucrat to guard his position. According to Li, the *kōng* principle applies both in words and action. When a bureaucrat puts something in writing, either commenting on others' documents or making his own statements, he makes them as empty and vague as possible. When he is engaged in a task, he always leaves plenty of leeways so that he can detach himself quickly from it as soon as it turns to be a liability to him.

Biao Lin's alleged "*Sān bù zhǔyì* 三不主義 (Three Nots Principle)" which includes not to take responsibility, not to make suggestions and not to offend people[7], also bears the *kōng* idea.

Conclusion

As we go through these 30 basic concepts, the picture is quite clear. Each is deeply rooted in the past and flourished at present. They are the characteristics of the Chinese manipulative behavior today as they were in history. They form a highly complicated system or as a writer puts it, "a thick and tight network. All principles of Marx-Leninism or policies of the (Chinese Communist) Party, once they run into it, they stop to work as if they were petrified by electricity." (Liu 1979:35)

Notes

1) This sentence has been frequently quoted. One example, *Guangming Ribao* 光明日報 (Guangming Daily), 19 October 1976.
2) For details see Chiao 1977.
3) See *The New Evening Post* (Hong Kong), 19 October 1976.
4) Translation by Lin (1977) with the author's modification.
5) Translation by the author.
6) See *Renmin Ribao* 人民日報 (People's Daily), 27 June 1975.
7) See *Renmin Ribao*, 8 April 1974.

References

Chiao, Chien

    1977 "Use of History as a Political Strategy by the 'Gang of Four'," In *The Gang of Four: First Essays after the Fall,* Steve S. K. Chin, ed., Hong Kong: Centre of Asian Studies, The University of Hong Kong.

    1980 "Chinese Strategic Behaviors: A Preliminary List," *Proceedings of the International Conference on Sinology held in Taipei, Aug. 15-17, 1980,* Taipei: Academia Sinica.

    1981 "A Preliminary Investigation of the Strategies in Chinese Culture," In *Ethnic Groups, Society and Culture of China: Essays in Honor of Professor Ruey Yih-Fu's Eightieth Birthday,* Yih-Yuan Li and Chien Chiao, eds., Taipei: Shihhuo Publishing Co.

Kaplan, Abraham

    1964 *The Conduct of Inquiry.* San Francisco: Chandler Publishing Co.

Li, Zhong-Wu 李宗吾

    1939 *Hòu Hēi Xué* 厚黑學 (How to Have Thick Skin and Black Heart?). Hong Kong: Dazong Publisher (1962).

Lin, Paul J. (trans.)

    1977 *A Translation of Lao Tzu's Tao Te Ching and Wang Pi's Commentary.* Michigan Papers in Chinese Studies.

Liu, Bin-Yan 劉賓雁

    1979 *"Rén yāo zhī jiān* 人妖之間*,"* *Renmin Wenxue* 人民文學, September Issue, Reprinted in *The Seventies Magazine,* No. 119(December 1979), pp. 22-38.

Mao, Ze-Dong

    1937 "Combat Liberalism," In *Selected Works of Mao Tse-Tung,* Peking: Foreign Languages Press, 1967, Vol II, pp. 31-33.

14 Continuity and Change in the Japanese Personality[1)]

TAKAO SOFUE

Introduction

Since about 1970, one of the most common items of jargon used frequently in Japan is *danzetsu* (discontinuity), which refers to the rift between younger and older generations. Discontinuity is a popular subject for dicussion in newspapers, weekly magazines and books, and is also a frequent topic in management seminars.

Members of old generations often deplore the fact that they cannot understand youngsters and feel both irritated and lonely after long disputes with the young about respect for the Emperor and other topics. "The Japanese have changed a lot!" is a phrase commonly used when older people make critical remarks about youngsters. At the same time, however, it has been evidently observed that the basic character of the Japanese has not changed and that they behave and think as they did before and during the World War II. Because of these two sharply contrasting views the problem of continuity and change in the Japanese personality has become an important topic for study by social scientists.

In this paper I shall first introduce and discuss the results of some recent quantitative studies on the topic of discontinuity, and then present my own observations on the subject.

Some Quantitative Studies

It is perhaps most appropriate to begin by discussing the results of a

long-term project undertaken by the Research Committee on the Study of
the Japanese National Character of the National Institute of Statistical
Mathematics (Hayashi, *et al.* 1970; Hayashi 1974). This study originated
in a nation-wide survey conducted in 1953, and followed-up by similar
quinquennial surveys in 1958, 1963, 1968, 1973 and 1978 (The 1978
data is still in the process of analysis, no results are yet available). Each
survey was done interviewing directly 3,000-4,000 subjects aged twenty
years and over, who were selected by stratified, random sampling.

In each survey, the questionnaire used contained about fifty items,
and some of them are overlapping. Table 1 shows the questions on which
opinions changed appreciably (20% or more) in the 15 years between
1958 and 1973. On the other hand, there were many other questions on
which opinions hardly changed at all. Questions indicating the most remarkable continuity during the period are listed in Table 2. Among them
the results of Question 2.5 are unique. The proportion of the "Follow
nature" attitude decreased constantly from 1953 through 1968, but suddenly increased in 1973. Clearly this is related to the problem of "environmental pollution," which has aroused the general public since around
1970.

Table 1
Questions on which opinions have changed appreciably (20 % or more)
(Results of the project of the Research Committee on the Study of
the Japanese National Character, Institute of Statistical Mathematics)

%		1953	1958	1963	1968	1973
Q. (#4.10) "If you have no children, do you think it necessary to adopt a child in order to continue the family line, even if there is no blood relationship? Or do you think this is not important?"	Yes, would adopt	73	63	51	43	36
Q. (#4.5) "In bringing up children of primary school age, some people think that one should teach them that	Agree	65	—	60	57	41

money is the most important
thing. Do you agree with
this or not?"

Q. (#3.9)*
"Some Prime Ministers,
when they take office, pay
a visit to the Imperial
Shrine at Ise. What do
you think about this
practice?"

Better to go	50	33	28	28	21

Q. (#8.1)
"Some people say that if
we get good political
leaders, the best way to
improve the country is for
the people to leave every—
thing to them, rather than
for the people to discuss
things among themselves.
Do you agree with this or
disagree?"

Agree	43	35	29	30	23

Q. (#7.1)
"Some people say that
with the development of
science and technology,
life becomes more con—
venient, but at the same
time human feelings are
diminished. Do you agree
or disagree with this
opinion?"

Agree	30	33	37	40	50

Q. (#6.2)
"If you could be born
again, would you rather
be a man or a woman?"

Prefer being a woman — (opinion of women)	27	36	48	50

---

*The Imperial Shrine at Ise, dedicated to Amaterasu, the ancestor goddess of the Impe-
rial Family of Japan, is the most important shrine for Japanese Shintoism. Shintoism,
however, was a doctrine to support Japanese imperialism and especially Japan's invasion
of China, Korea and other countries. Consequently, Shinto shrines were legally separated from the State after the defeat in the World War II. But some Prime Ministers visit
the Imperial Shrine at Ise, and this has been criticized by intellectuals as a step toward a
revived imperialism.

Table. 2
Questions on which opinions have hardly changed
(Result of the project of the Research Committee on the Study of
the Japanese National Character, Institute of Statistical Mathematics)

Q. (#5.6)
"Suppose you are working in a firm where there are two types of department chief.
Which of these two would you prefer to work under?:
  A. A man who always sticks to work rules and never demands any unreasonable
    work, but on the other hand, never does anything for you personally in matters not
    connected with the work; or
  B. A man who sometimes demands extra work in spite of rules against it, but on the
    other hand, looks after you personally in matters not connected with the work.

	1953	1958	1963	1968	1973
Type B (Paternalistic)	85	77	82	84	81

Q. (#5.1d)
"If you are asked to choose two out of this list that are important, which of two would
you point out?:
  (a) Filial piety, to be dutiful to one's parents
  (b) Repaying indebtedness
  (c) Respecting individual rights
  (d) Respecting freedom

	1953	1958	1963	1968	1973
Filial piety	—	—	61	61	63
Repaying indebtedness	—	—	43	45	43
Respecting rights	—	—	48	44	45
Respecting freedom	—	—	40	46	43

Q. (#2.1)
"If you think something is right, do you
think you should go ahead and do it even
if it iscontrary to usual custom, or do you
think you are less apt to make a mistake
if you follow custom?"

	1953	1958	1963	1968	1973
Go ahead	41	41	40	42	36

Q. (#2.5)
"Here are three opinions about man and
nature. Which one of these do you think
is closest to the truth?:

	1953	1958	1963	1968	1973
Follow nature	27	20	19	19	31

  (a) In order to be happy, man must
    follow nature.
  (b) In order to be happy, man must
    make use of nature.
  (c) In order to be happy, man must
    conquer nature.

Summarizing the statistical analyses of the responses to all questions, Chikio Hayashi, Chairman of the Research Committee, concluded that there had been very little substantial change in the fundamental Japanese way of thinking. He emphasized in particular that this trend of continuity is most remarkable in the basic patterns of human relations, whereas traditional Japanese social ideas have been receding gradually and have tended to be replaced by non-traditional, rational and positive ideas.

Among other studies analyzing change and continuity is the work of Taiji Hayasaka, a social psychologist. In 1969, he distributed a survey questionnaire among 138 employees of a company in Tokyo. The subjects were asked their opinions ("agree" or "disagree") on 30 sentences (Part I) and 30 traditional proverbs (Part II). Dividing the subjects into Group A (20-24 years-of-age), Group B (25-39 years-of-age) and Group C (40-60 years and older), Hayasaka discovered that there was no significant difference between Group A and Group B in their opinions about customs, with the exception of following 5 items:

(1) "Never forget to make a present every year to a family who saved your parents long ago;"
(2) "You should obey your parents' orders, even if they are somewhat unreasonable;"
(3) "Relatives should be united together strongly, with the head family in the center;"
(4) "The president of a firm is like a head of a family;"
(5) "Since harmony is most important within a firm, it is better not to voice any opposing opinions."

When Group A was compared with Group C, however, significant differences emerged in 19 items. In Part II of the questionnaire (questions about proverbs) significant differences between Group A and Group B existed in only 8 items, whereas those between Group A and Group C occurred in 11 items. After reviewing his data and other related studies, Hayasaka concluded that the rifts between generation were not particularly remarkable as had been generally thought, and that people tend to exaggerate such discontinuities.

Anthropological Observations

The preceding section summarized the results of two major studies, both of which indicate a clear continuity in Japanese psychological trends. However, such quantitative studies suffer from limitations. True, the questions used in both studies were carefully selected and elaborate, but still we must look at the difference between "actual patterns of behaviors" and "ideal patterns of expected behaviors." In the case of the questions 8.1, for example, about "leaving everything to political leaders," the number of responses agreeing with this idea decreased rapidly between 1953 and 1973. However, to what extent the people may *actually* resist despotic leaders is another problem. Another example is the question about two types of department chief. Although the result indicates the constant preference of paternalism, another recent study shows that present-day Japanese youngsters dislike "too paternalistic" chiefs and teachers and they hate to have their private life overly interfered-in by their superiors (Matsubara 1971:109-111). My own observations endorse this recent tendency, and many similar examples exist.

To supplement the discussion of quantitative analyses, I will go on to present some of my own anthropological observations on the topic of discontinuity.

Predominant Continuity and Few Changes

Although the studies discussed above attest to changes in Japanese psychological traits it is doubtful to what extent the core of Japanese personality or national character has changed.

Since Ruth Benedict's classic book, *The Chrysanthemum and the Sword,* published in 1946, just after the world War II, a tremendous number of studies on Japanese psychology and behavior have been conducted by both Japanese and Western (mostly from the U.S.A.) social scientists. A few of the many works available are those by Beardsley (1965), Caudill and Schooler (1969), Caudill and Weinstein (1969), DeVos (1960), Lebra (1976), Norbeck and DeVos (1956), Reischauer (1977) and Vogel (1965), all Americans, and Minami (1953), Nakane (1967, 1970) and Sofue (1970, 1973, 1979) by Japanese. A survey of these studies reveal the same basic characteristic of Japanese personality. For example, the American anthropologist, John W. Connor (1977:9-10), contrasts Japanese and Americans as indicated in Table 3. He concludes that these contrasting characteristics can be summarized as follows:

> Japanese: Emphasis on collectivity, duty and obligation, hierarchy, deference and dependence
> American: Emphasis on individualism, equality, rights and priviledges, self-reliance and self-assertion

Table 3
Japanese and American Characteristics (Connor 1977:9-10)

Japanese	American
1. Reliance on the group	1. Individualism
2. Children trained to be docile, obedient and dependent	2. Children trained to be independent
3. Mother-son bond	3. Husband-wife bond
4. Emphasis on hierarchy	4. Emphasis on equality
5. Emphasis on duty	5. Emphasis on rights
6. Dependency need	6. Independence; fear of dependence
7. Passivity (non-aggressiveness)	7. Aggressiveness or active mastery
8. Submissive attitude toward authority	8. Grudging acceptance of those in authority
9. Emphasis on collaterality	9. Emphasis on individual autonomy
10. Achievement of goals set by others	10. Achievement of individual goals
11. Emphasis on ascribed status	11. Emphasis on achieved status
12. Compulsive obedience to rules and controls	12. Resentment and dislike of rules and controls
13. Obligation to the family	13. Obligation to oneself
14. Emphasis on self-effacement	14. Emphasis on self-assertiveness
15. Restriction of personal relations to a small group	15. Openness and accessibility to others
16. A sense of responsibility to others	16. Responsibility to oneself
17. Deference and politeness	17. Tendency to mark of play down the superiority of others
18. A sense of fatalism	18. A sense of optimism
19. Success through self-discipline	19. Success through pragmatism and the exploitation of opportunities
20. Emphasis on compromise, precise rules of conduct, and situational ethic	20. Emphasis on righteousness, generalized rules of conduct, and a universal ethic

In the similar way, the Japanese social scientist, K. Yoshimori, contrasts Japanese and West Europeans. Table 4 is a partial summary of his conclusion (Yoshimori 1979:21).

Table 4
Japanese and West European Characteristics
(adapted from Yoshimori 1979:21)

	West European	Japanese
Way of Thinking	analytical	intuitive
Cognitive Way	logical	emotional
View of Nature	control of nature	harmony with nature
View of Fate	defiance to fate	obediance to fate
Norm of Behaviors	individually defined	defined by group
Planning	long-term	short-term
Interpersonal Relationships	competition, criticism, direct	compromise, harmony, indirect(suggestive)

These two discussions seem to coincide with those by many other scholars in Japan and the West, and I am in general agreement with them. Considering the traits of the Japanese listed in Table 3 and 4, I conclude tentatively that they have hardly changed since before the World War II. At the same time, however, some exceptions must be pointed out, as discussed below.

Changing Vertical Relationships

Items 4 ("Emphasis on hierarchy"), 8 ("Submissive attitude toward authority") and 17 ("Deference and politeness to superiors") in Connor's work recognize the importance of vertical relationships among Japanese. In *Japanese Society* (1970), anthropologist Chie Nakane also stresses this point, defining Japanese society as a "vertical society." The Japanese edition of her work, published in 1967, was widely read among the general public, and as a result, the expression *tate shakai* or "vertical society" has since become part of the popular Japanese vocabulary. But, Nakane's work has also been criticized in Japan, for she emphasizes vertical relationships to such an extent that she ignores the importance placed by Japanese on horizontal relationships. On the whole, however, Japanese are obviously more sensitive to vertical relationships than either Americans or West Europeans.

The values of hierarchy and subordination were institutionalized during the Feudal Age (1603-1868), borrowing from Chinese Confucian concepts. Scholars agree that the Japanese Government developed a structure requiring the extreme submission of those considered inferior to those considered superior; consequently inferiors had to do whatever the Government or superiors wished. Item 12, "Compulsive obedience to rules and controls," was born out of this historical circumstances, although the word "compulsive" is a little too strong. Item 18, "a sense of fatalism" ("obedience to fate" in Yoshimori's list) should also be related to the above. I would also like to stress here that reverence for authority has long been a factor in encouraging the adoption of overseas culture, especially that of the West. Japan was able to modernize because every effort was made to learn from the dominant group, i.e., from the Western powers that have been viewed as superior authorities since the Meiji Restoration in 1868 (Sha 1976:108).

At this point, however, it should be emphasized that there is obviously a gap between the generations in terms of their sensitivity to vertical relationships and related traits discussed above. This value has diminished in importance among young people, especially since the middle of 1960s. The extremely radical students' revolt by new-leftist groups at almost all universities in Japan toward the end of 1960s is an obvious result of this change. At the same time, however, it may be said that these students' movements greatly accelerated the pace of change.

Interpersonal relationships, for instance, among members of high-school and college sports clubs are gradually replaced by more horizontal and democratic relationships. Honorific terms among young people are generally replaced by simpler and direct expressions, a fact constantly lamented by the older generation. The traditional way of greeting by bowing politely has now been simplified and reduced to a waving of hands, and the like.

In this context I might add that from the pre-War period until around 1960 the most frequent symptom of neurosis among young Japanese was a fear of blushing, i.e., a fear that one might blush before one's superiors. That this symptom has disappeared since about 1960 has been explained by Japanese psychiatrists as the result of a rapid decline in sensitivity to vertical relationships.

Heterosexual Relationships in Transition

The most remarkable change among the post-War younger generations has taken place in their heterosexual relationships. Interpersonal relationships between the opposite sexes were greatly influenced by Confucian
ethics during the Feudal Age. Women were supposed to be submissive
and obedient to men; wives were supposed to obey their husbands. Thus
the man-woman relationship became most strongly "vertical." This trend
became much weaker after the World War II, but still remained until
recently. Among youngsters born after World War II (in other words, those
less than 35-years-of-age as of 1980) heterosexual relationships are much
different. Their marriages are mostly "love marriages" rather than arranged
marriages (my personal observation is that "love marriage" today may
account for about 80 % of all marriages in large cities). After marriage,
relations among husband and wife are mostly horizontal, such as in helping each other with daily chores. A few years ago scholars coined the term
to describe a non-traditional type of married couple *"tomodachi fufu"*
(tomodachi=friend and *fufu*=married couple), since the husband and wife
regard each other as a friendly "partner." "New family" (English words
being used directly) is another .term used for this kind of family.

In 1969, students' revolts occurred at most Japanese universities and
students barricaded themselves for a few months within campuses, until
finally they were evicted by police. During these periods of occupation
young men and women shared the same building, and, obviously stimulated by this, the number of young, unmarried couples living together has
suddenly increased in large cities since around that time. A word *dosei*, to
"live together," subsequently entered popular use.

The status of village women has also changed considerably. Most
conspicuous recently is that young, village housewives speak-up and participate actively in public meetings, although in the 1950s they were still
timid and silent, especially in the presence of their mothers-in-law (Inagaki
1980:223).

Some Changes in Collateral Relationships

As is already mentioned, Japanese society stresses vertical relationships. In addition, it should be noted also that they emphasize "col-

laterality," as indicated, for instance, in item 9 of Connor's list. This collateral relationship, however, occurs only among those who know each other personally, and no personal relationship exists among those not known to each other. This leads to the perception that Japanese are very kind to acquaintances but brusque to people whom they do not know. One might characterize them as partisan or cliquish, and this may be related to item 15 ("Restriction of personal relation to a small group") in Connor's list. However, a strong sense of group solidarity is not necessarily small in scale, and can be extended to the whole nation; the sense of being "we Japanese" gives a collective identity to the people as a whole vis-à-vis the outside world. This generates strong cooperation among Japanese, but impedes international communication and cooperation.

But that tendency, too, seems to be gradually changing among younger people, who, on the whole, are more open and then to have much better international communications owing to their wider experience overseas. These youngsters and young housewives are increasingly active in citizens' movements aimed at the improvement of conditions of daily life, the abatement of environmental pollution, and similar activities.

Passivity, Emphasis on Compromise and Group-Orientation

The first trait Connor lists to define the Japanese is "reliance on the group." He also refers to collectivity again at the beginning of his final summary. Connor also stresses that "Children are trained to be docile, obedient, and dependent," as noted in item 2. These traits were pointed out in Yoshimori's list and have been discussed by many other scholars. However, were one to seek a more fundamental psychological characteristic leading to this tendency, "emphasis on compromise," which appears at the end of Connor's list, could be selected. In this connection the following scheme of interpersonal relationship, proposed by psychologist Y. Kataguchi, would be useful:

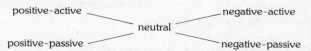

"Positive-active" means that "the subject is positive to the other, but, at the same time, neither passive nor submissive to the other; in other words, he expresses love or friendliness toward the other." By contrast, in the positive-passive type of relationship the subject is submissive toward, or dependent on, the other. The negative-active relationship is where the subject expresses aggression toward, or hatred or criticism of, the other. Finally, the negative-passive type is where there is an avoidance, or a tendency to escape from the other person. Positive-passive and negative-passive types are extremely common among Japanese. Connor expresses this as "passivity" in item 7, and refers to a similar characteristic in item 14, "emphasis on self-effacement."

Takeo Doi, a psychiatrist, presents the concept of *amae* as the key to understanding Japanese psychology (Doi 1962, 1963, 1971). *Amae,* meaning "to depend and presume upon the other's benevolence," has been used repeatedly to express Japanese interpersonal relationships. Doi believes that the child forms an *amae* relationship with the mother early in life and this ultimately leads to a so-called "mother-complex" (See item 3 of Connor's list). This relationship is maintained into adulthood and emerges as a very strong dependency needs (See item 6 of Connor's list).

When we analyze dependency, passivity and compromise in their most elemental forms, we find that they arise from weakness in self-assertion, lack of self-confidence, and uncertainty about oneself. As a result, what might be described as sensitivity to the eyes of others, or "other-directedness," emerges. All these seem to be the most fundamental characteristics of the Japanese personality and my observation is that they have not changed, even among today's younger generations.

I mentioned earlier the fear of blushing as a symptom of neurosis among young Japanese, until about 1960. Another very common symptom from pre-War days was fear of eye-to-eye confrontation ("*shisen-k-yofusho*" as it is called by Japanese psychiatrists) — a very strong fear of being seen by other persons. According to studies conducted by psychiatrists, this symptom is found only among Japanese, and is thought to be attributable to Japanese hypersensitivity to the eyes of others (Kasahara 1972, 1974). It should be noted here that this symptom remains unchanged even today, which might indicate the continuity of hypersensitivity among present-day younger Japanese.

Changing Achievement Aspiration

As several scholars have stated (Caudill & DeVos 1956; DeVos 1973) strong "achievement aspiration" should also be considered as an important basic trait of Japanese work ethics.

There is no agreement among scholars as to how this trait originated. Some scholars hold that Japan's intensive agricultural system strengthened the farmers' will to work hard, but the strongest factor was probably the Chinese Confucianism stressed by the Feudal Government of the Edo Period (1603-1868). It should be added that another strong influence was provided by *Shingaku*, "practical ethics" preached by Baigan Ishida, a philosopher of the early 18th century. He believed that industry, economy, honesty and dedication were the ways to riches and success, and his teachings were gradually adopted by ordinary citizens and farmers, both men and women. His ideas were widespread in the 1780s, when famine and poverty were rife.

The Edo Period was characterized by an extremely strict class system, but, from the late eighteenth century until the Meiji Restoration (1868), it had become possible to improve one's social status by education. Even a poor farmer could become a rich merchant through education, and, by becoming a scholar he could even be appointed to an important government post. Thus farmers and merchants alike tried to provide their children with an education. In 1868, just before the Meiji Restoration, 43 % of all boys and 10 % of all girls in Japan (about 86 % of boys and 30 % of girls in Tokyo) are believed to have been receiving education (reading, writing and arithmetic). This rate was higher than that of the United Kingdom at the time. Immediately after the Restoration a nation-wide system of obligatory education was introduced, and by 1875 54 % of all boys and 19 % of all girls were attending school (Sha 1976: 94-110, 138-144). This high rate of school attendance facilitated Japan's modernization, and the tradition of "success through self-discipline," noted in Connor's item 19, arose. This trend was increasingly emphasized by the Meiji Government as part of the *fukoku kyohei* (wealthy nation and strong army) policies, after the 1895 victory in the Sino-Japanese War, and was gradually connected with the militarism and imperialism that lasted until 1945. It should also be noted that the teaching of the nineteenth century agriculturalist, Sontoku Ninomiya on industriousness and frugality, formed an important part of the curriculum in the nation's elementary schools from around this time until 1945.

So far I have discussed the origin and nature of achievement aspiration in Japan. However, this trend has obviously become weaker among younger Japanese, since around the mid-1960s. Influenced by the West, the importance of enjoying leisure time and recreation has come to be emphasized among younger Japanese, and changing work ethics seem to be a cause of irritated disputes between the older and the younger generations.

View of Nature

Finally I would like to refer to the Japanese view of nature, which is completely neglected in Connor's discussion. The sociologist, Florence Kluckhohn (1953), categorized the ethnic groups of the world according to their attitude toward nature: 1) man subjugated to nature; 2) man in nature; 3) man over nature. The first category contend that man must always be obedient to nature; the third, that man must work to change nature and control it. The second one characteristically regards "all natural forces and man himself as one harmonious whole, one is but an extension of the other and both are needed to make the whole."

The Japanese attitude toward nature most appropriately belongs to the second of these types. "Harmony with nature," as is written by Yoshimori, would be an adequate description, too. It is an attitude frequently expressed in traditional Japanese fine arts and one which especially characteristic of Japanese architecture and landscape gardening. Traditional design does not feature paintings throughout the interior of a building; instead it uses natural colors as much as possible. Items are arranged so that if a window is opened, one can see a garden which has been designed to show nature. Thus there is a continuity between the interior living space and the outside. It can be noted also that, in writing *haiku* (poem), one is supposed to make reference to the season.

Traditional Japanese foods are also markedly different from those of neighboring China and Korea. Many foods are not processed, a typical example being raw fish. Fish is eaten raw in Korea, too, but it does not occupy such an important place in the diet; while the Chinese have no such custom at all. The Japanese custom is possibly related to the fact that, in contrast to China and Korea, the use of animal meat and fat was relatively limited. It should also be connected with a fundamental Japanese view of nature; this is also reflected in the way Japanese arrange foodstuffs on the table on formal occasions as aesthetically as possible.

Thus one of the Japanese characteristics is the concept of "man in nature," a trait which obviously has helped them produce a variety of distinctive art forms. Conversely, the desire to control nature and the inclination to observe nature (especially, birds, plants, stars) have not taken root among the Japanese. Consequently, there has been no real development of a scientific tradition which attempts to understand natural phenomena through observation, a tendency that retarded the growth of natural science and scientific techniques in Japan.

In Japan it appears that the traditional view of nature will endure. Although, paradoxically, it is true that the general orientation of Japanese society today is already toward "man over nature," as a consequence of rapid industrialization and urbanization, each Japanese as an individual still seems to retain the traditional "man in nature" orientation. At the same time, however, it can be anticipated that today's youngsters, who have had very few contacts with nature (plants, trees and insects, etc.), may have a very different view of nature when they reach adulthood.

Notes

1) Sections of this paper have been discussed elsewhere (Sofue 1973, 1976, 1980)

References

Beardsley, R. K.
  1965 "Personality Psychology," in *Twelve Doors to Japan,* ed. by J. W. Hall & R. K. Beardsley, New York: McGraw-Hill.
Benedict, R.
  1946 *The Chrysanthemum and the Sword.* Boston: Mifflin.
Caudill, W. &G. DeVos
  1956 "Achievement, Culture and Personality: The Case of the Japanese Americans," *American Anthropolgist* 58:1102-26.
Caudill, W. & C. Schooler
  1969 "Symptom Patterns and Background Characteristic of Japanese Psychiatric Patients," in *Mental Health Research in Asia and the Pacific* (vol. 1), ed. by W. Caudill & T. Y. Lin, Honolulu: East-West Center Press.
Caudill, W. & H. Weinstein
  1969 "Maternal Care and Infant Behavior in Japan and America," *Psychiatry* 32:12-43.
Connor, J. W.
  1977 *Tradition and Change in Three Generations of Japanese Americans.* Chicago: Nelson-Hall.
DeVos, G.
  1960 "The Relation of Guilt to Achievement and Arranged Marriage among the Japanese," *Psychiatry* 23:287-301.
DeVos, G. (ed.)
  1973 *Socialization for Achievement: Essays on the Cultural Psychology of the Japanese.* Berkeley and Los Angels: University of California Press.
Doi, T.
  1962 "*Amae:* A Key Concept for Understanding Japanese Personality Structure," in *Japanese Culture,* ed. by R. J. Smith & R. K. Beardsley, Chicago: Aldine.
  1963 "Some Thoughts on Helplessness and the Desire to Be Loved," *Psychiatry* 26:266-272.
  1971 *Amae no Kozo* (Structure of *Amae*). Tokyo:Kobundo.
Hayasaka, T.
  1971 *Gendai no Wakamonotachi* (The Contemporary Youth in Japan). Tokyo: Nihon Keizai Shimbunsha.
Hayashi, C.
  1974 "Nihonjin no Kokoro wa Kawattaka?" (Has the Japanese Mind

Changed?), in *Nihonjin Kenkyu I* (Study of the Japanese: Part I), ed. by Nihonjin Kenkyukai, Tokyo: Shiseido.

Hayashi, C. et al.
1970 *Daini Nihonjin no Kokuminsei* (A Study of Japanese National Character: Part 2). Tokyo: Shiseido.

Inagaki, F.
1980 "Nihonjin to Oshaberi" (Verbal communications among the Japanese), *NHK Hoso Bunka Kenkyujo Nempo* (Annual Report of the Research Institute at the Japan Broadcasting Corporation) 25: 222-234.

Kasahara, Y.(ed.)
1972 *Seishi Kyofu, Taishu Kyofu* (Fear of Eye-to-Eye Confrontation and Fear of Bodily Odor). Tokyo: Igaku Shoin.
1974 "Fear of Eye-to-Eye Confrontation among Neurotic Patients in Japan," in *Japanese Culture and Behavior,* eds. by T. S. Lebra & W. P. Lebra, Honolulu: University Press of Hawaii.

Kluckhohn, F.
1953 "Dominant and Variant Value Orientations," in *Personality in Nature, Society and Culture,* eds. by C. Kluckhohn, & H. A. Murray, Cambridge: Harvard University Press.

Lebra, T. S.
1976 *Japanese Patterns of Behavior.* Honolulu: University Press of Hawaii.

Matsubara, J.
1971 *Gendai no Seinen* (Contemporary Japanese Youth). Tokyo: Chuo Koronsha.

Nakane, C.
1967 *Tate Shakai no Ningen Kankei* (Human Relations in a Vertical Society). Tokyo: Kodansha.
1970 *Japanese Society.* Berkeley and Los Angels: University of California Press.

Norbeck, E. & G. DeVos.
1961 "Japan" in *Psychological Anthropology,* ed. by F. L. K. Hsu, Homewood, Illinois: Dorsey.

Reischauer, E. O.
1977 *The Japanese.* Cambridge: Harvard University Press.

Sha, S.
1976 *Nihon Kindai Nihyakunen no Kozo* (Structure of the Past Two Hundred Years of Japan). Tokyo: Kodansha.

Sofue, T.
1970 (ed.) *Nihonjin: Sono Kozo Bunseki* (The Japanese: Readings in Culture and Personality). Tokyo: Shibundo.
1973 (ed.) *Nihonjin wa Do Kawattaka?* (How have the Japanese Changed?).

Tokyo: Shibundo.

1976 "Psychological Problems of Japanese Urbanization," in *Responses to Change: Society, Culture and Personality,* ed. by G. DeVos, New York: Nostrand.

1979 "Aspects of the Personality of Japanese, Americans, Italians and Eskimos: Comparisons Using the Sentence Completion Test," *Journal of Psychological Anthropology* 2: 11-52.

1980 "Ishiki to Kokuminsei ni Okeru Jizoku to Henka" (Continuity and Change in the Japanese Psychological Attitude and National Character), *Shakai Shinrigaku Nempo* (Annual Review of Social Psychology) 21: 51-73.

Vogel, E. F.

1965 *Japan's New Middle Class.* Berkeley and Los Angels: University of California Press.

Yoshimori, K.

Seio Kigyo no Hasso to Kodo (Principles and Behaviors of the West European Business Enterprises). Tokyo: Daiamondo.

15　Buddhist Approaches in Anthropology : An Understanding of Margaret Mead

SHIN-PYO KANG

Whenever there is the study of man, there is anthropology. Anthropology is nothing but 'the study of man.' What is the 'anthropological' tradition in East Asian society and culture? The study of man is the basic concern of all men all over the world and all the time. Each society and culture has its own concept of man in its own way. According to its own cultural traditions I think that it may be defined religiously, familially, politically, or economically. In fact, the religious definition would be the most outstanding pivotal point in the effort of definition. For example, Confucianism and Buddhism are the defining religions in East-Asian cultural tradtiion. In my opinion, these two great religious traditions are two sides of one culture; namely praxis and theory.

The basic interest of the two religions is in man. They try to answer 'how to live' and 'what is man.' Confucianism is concerned with man's social life, and Buddhism with man's understanding of himself. The binary set of 'how to live' and 'what is man' is, of course, in complementary relationship (Kang 1974). Without an understanding of 'what is man' there would be no proper prescription for how man is to live; and without proper behavioral practice, there would be no possibility of knowing the true nature of man. Wei-summa(爲甚磨 why is it) and shi-summa(是甚磨 what is it) are the binary set of basic concern in Chinese. Traditional Korean understand Confucianism and Buddhism as matters of outer and inner worlds and life spaces. Then it follows that out and inner life worlds of man are the matters of praxis and theory.

As generally understood, Buddhism is "not a religion in the generally accepted sense of the word, and it would be more accurate to describe it as an ethico-philosophy to be practised by each follower" (Saddhatissa 1970:9). In other word, it is more related with philosophical system of man's 'knowledge of the highest stage' (ibid). The philosophical system could be viewed as a sort of anthropological traditions among Asian minds. What I would like to discuss in this paper is the possible existence of anthropological traditions, as a systematic search of 'what is man,' in East Asian society though not so solid academic discipline as Euro-American society, and an understanding of an American anthropologist, Margaret Mead, in terms of the Buddhist tradition, which could tell a possible convergence of the two East and West traditions of anthropology.

Given the remarkable position of Margaret Mead in contemporary anthropology, it is necessary to reevaluate and reanalyze her work (*American Anthropologist,* special issue on Margaret Mead, Vol. 82, No. 2, June 1980). Mead struggled with the essential problem of anthropology, what is man's nature, through her field work rather than by theoretical studies. Her behavior in this regard can be seen as quite similar to that of a Buddhist monk (Mahayana rather than Hinayana). If in this manner there is a complementary relation between the interests of anthropology and those of a Buddhist monk, we can look for Asian cultural traditions as they are reflected in the monk's daily life and thought. That is, if we compare Margaret Mead's method of approach and the monk's spiritual discipline (cultivation of self), we can reevaluate Mead. The main purpose of this study is to make clear the "anthropological" method in East Asian cultural tradition.

My first premise is that anthroplogy and Buddhism have the same basic root problem. That is because of the complementary relationship between Buddhism's deep study of human nature and anthropology's concern with the essential problem of man. However, in what follows it will be seen that Buddhism and anthropology are not exactly the same. Nevertheless anthropology's method of reaching its objectives through field work (Mead 1972, 1977) and the monks seeking after 'enlightenment' through self-imposed rule-obeying hardships are closely related. Let us illustrate with a few concrete examples.

First of all the process of Buddhist seeking after truth and anthropological field work are related. It is an established principle that the anthropologist must spent at least one year in a different environment living in a different culture. When he enters into a different culture sphere, he must live in totally different life-space where the food, climate, physical ecology and language are all strange. Since this is not pleasant, he has various emotional difficulties. We can regard the undertaking of anthropological field work and entering the priesthood as similar kinds of behavior amounting to the same thing. Literally, entering priesthood is expressed by "departing from home"(出家). Isn't there a close connection between Mead's spending 9 months in Samoa and entering the priesthood? Margaret Mead through her field work existence could find the spirit of 'staring at wall for 10 years of meditation'(面壁十年).

Secondly there is the problem of relating the *Koan* (公案, 話頭) to anthropological problematic hypotheses. In anthropological field work one starts with certain problematic hypotheses; the Buddhist seeks truth by concentrating on a *Koan*. They are similar in the manner of seeking to solve fundamental uncertainties. In going to Samoa Mead wanted to find out whether the emotional disturbance of adolescent girls (in America) was due to physiological or cultural causes (Mead 1928). Of course, the anthropological hypotheses and the Buddhist monk's *Koan* are not exactly the same. However, there is a correlation between them with regard to the main focus of interest.

Third, there is the problem of relating Culture and Personality to Buddhist thought. There is in fact a thread of connection between Culture and Personality and Buddhist self reflection. In other words there is a close relation between the conception of personality in anthropology and the examination of self (understanding of self in "chain-relationship" 因緣) in Buddhism. Mead showed clearly in her work, *Sex and Temperament in Three Primitive Societies* (1935) the relation between temperament and culture. It is inevitable that culture modifies the personality of those who live in its environment. If there are people with temperaments that are not tolerated by the culture, they will either be expelled from society, or be forced to live in abject humiliation. Mead in her work on the three New Guinea tribes (the Arapesh, the Mundugumor, and the Tchambuli) clearly showed the contrast between her temperament and American culture as well as what her own temperament actually was. Out of this emerged a definition of culture itself.

Finally there is the question of what are the results of field work. To generalize, field work makes clear the explanatory principle of culture and society. Mead goes one step further and utilized the results of her field work in order to make a practical contribution to society. Mead's performance appears to be similar to that of the Mahayana Boddhisattva (覺者) who gives helps (布施). One can conclude that Mead in her awakened self knowledge was not unlike the Boddhisattva who lives freely on this earthship.

References

Saddhatissa, H.
>   1970 *Buddhist Ethic; Essence of Buddhism.* London: George Allen and
>   Unwin

Kang, Shin-Pyo.
>   1974 "The Structural Principle of Chinese World View," In *The Uncon-
>   sciousness in Culture; Structuralism of Levi-Strauss in Perspective,* ed.
>   by Ino Rossi, New York: Dutton

Mead, Margaret
>   1928 *Coming of Age in Samoa*
>   1935 *Sex and Temperament in Three Primitive Societies*
>   1972 *Blackberry Winter.* New York: William Morrow
>   1977 *Letters From the Field.* New York: Harper

INDEX

Aborigines
    Malay, *see Orang asli*
    Taiwanese, 3–4,89,93–98,
      172–178
Achievement aspiration, 10,270–71
Actual pattern, of behavior, 264
Adaptation
    cultural, 23
    ecological, 26
Age grade system, in the *Puyuma*, 172
Agriculture
    cash crop, 55
    dry, 24
    subsistence, 55
Ancestor worship
    in China(Taiwan), 7,169–70,172,
      178–79
    in Japan, 7,170–72,178
    in Korea, 7,118,123,167–68,
      172,178–79,188–90
    in the *Puyuma*, 7,172–78
Animism
    in Indonesia, 66
    in Korea, 7,195
Anthropology
    applied, 154
    in Asian countries, 1–6
    and Buddhism, 11,278–80
    in Indonesia, 3,45–78
    in Korea, 4,117–35
    linguistic, 34,134
    in Malaysia, 2–3,29–41
    medical, 6,134
    in the Philippines, 2,15–28
    philosophical, 135
    and sinology, 105–15
    in Thailand, 4–5,143,153–55
    urban, 134, *see also* Urbanization,
      Slum
Archaeology
    in the Philippines, 2,15–19,21–22
    in Thailand, 5,145–53

Baharon, A.B.R., 35–36,38–39
Band, organization, 26–27
Belief system
    Korean, 8,194–96
    Thai, 155
Banjamin, Geoffrey, 33–35
Beyer, H.O., 16,19–20,22,25
Buddhism
    in East Asia, 11,277
    in Indonesia, 222–23
    in Java, 223–24
    in Japan, 171
    in Korea, 118,192–93,195
    in the *Puyuma*, 173–74
    in Thailand, *see Meru*

Carey, Iskander, 33,35,37
Cargo cult, 232
Charismatic leader, 231–33
Chen, Chi–Lu, 1,3–4
Chia, see Family, Chinese

Chiao, Chien, 4,9–10,181,243–44
Chieftainship, 39
Cho, Oak–La, 7–8
Christianity
    in Indonesia, 222
    in Korea, 8,193
    in the Puyuma, 173–74
Class consciousness, 8,210,214–15, 217
Cœdès, George, 145–46,207–208
Confucianism
    in China(Taiwan), 169–70, 172,179
    in East Asia, 277
    in Indonesia, 222
    in Korea, 7,125,167–68,172, 178–79,185,188–89,195
Connor, J.W., 265, 269–71
Conspicuous consumption, 40
Council of elders, 27
Cultural complex, 26
Cultural lag, 5,155
Cultural trait, 26,89–90
Culture
    Austronesian, 90–91
    Chinese 9,91,105–106, 108,241–42
    Indonesian, 45–47,51
    Indonesian primitive, 66
    Japanese, 10, see also Personality, Japanese
    Javanese, 225, 232, 236
    Korean, 117–118,135
    of the orang asli, 3
    of Pacific Islands, 126
    Philippine, 15,19–20,22,28
    Philippine prehistoric, 22,25–26
    of the Taiwan aborigines, 90, 94,98–99
    Thai, 5,8,139–142,152–54
Culture change

    in Indonesia, 9,46,59,62,231
    in the Philippines, 2–3, 20–21
    in Taiwan, 98–99
    in Thailand, 8,216

Datu, organization, 28
Descent
    ambilineal, 173,177
    patrilineal, 7,168,170,172
Development
    agricultural, 100
    community, 49,59,63,156
    indigenous, 26
    national, 56,59,154
    project, 2,3,6
    regional, 156
    rural, 21
    socio-economic, 8
Diffusionism, 25,118

Ecological niche, 26
Ecology
    problems of, 64
    cultural, 6, 134
Endicott, K.M., 32–33,37–38,40–41
Ethnic diversity, 57–58
Ethnic group, 3,19,59,66,221,223
Ethnicity, 3
Ethnic problem, 3
Ethno-cultural origin, 2,3,6
Ethnographic study
    in Indonesia, 61
    in the Philippines, 19–21
Ethnohistory
    of China, 98
    of Korean kinship, 134
Endogamy, village, 173
Evolutionism, 66
Exogamy, 122
Expolitation
    of the orang asli, 3,35–37,40

in Java, 231

Family
    big, 109
    Chinese, 4,108–115
    cycle, 122
    division of Chinese, 109–15
    federal, 109,114
    Japanese, 7,112,170–72
    Korean, 4,120–22
    nuclear, 109
    patriarchal, 121
    Philippine, 21
    planning, 62
    stem, 109,121,170
    structure, 62
    of the Taiwan aborigines, 95
Fen-chia, see Family, division of
    Chinese
Fertility, cultural aspect of, 57,62
Folk arts
    Korean, 126–27,130
    Taiwanese, 98
Folk belief
    Korean, 118–20,131
    Taiwanese, 98
Folk custom, Korean, 119,124–27
Folk literature
    Korean, 130
    Taiwanese, 98
Folklore
    Javanese, 223
    Korean, 1,4,118
    Taiwanese, 98
Folk religion, Korean, 7,119,
    131–134,185–88
Freedman, Maurice, 106–108,
    169,180–81
Functionalism, 66,95
Funeral rite
    in Thailand, *see Meru*

see also Rite of passage

Geertz, Clifford, 50,61,236
Geomancy, 131,190
Great tradition, 105–107

Held, G.J., 46–47,51,66–67
Hinduism
    and Buddhism in Thailand,
        203,205,207,216–17
    in Indonesia, 222
    in Java, 223–24
Historical study
    and anthropology in China,
        107–108
    in Thailand, 5,150–53
Household
    in Chinese family, 112–114
    composition of, 62
Human type, 23–24

Ideal pattern, of behavior, 264
Ie, see Family, Japanese
Islam
    in Indonesia, 221–22
    Javanese, 223–24, *see also*
        Religious movement, Javanese
Integration
    level of sociocultural, 26–28
    national, 59
Inter-ethnic relation, 59–61
Inter-racial relation, 59

Jocano, Landa, 1–2,21

Kang, Shin-Pyo, 11,277
Kindred
    organization 27
    in the *Puyuma,* 173
Kingroup, unilineal, 66
Kinship

ideology, 6
Indonesian, 50,66
Korean, 4,120,122–23
Puyuma, 7,173–78
and social organization, 22
terminology, 123
Koentjaraningrat, 1,3,9,45,47,50,62
Kroeber, A.L., 20,90

Land–tenure, 54–55
Language community, in Indonesia,
221
Leadership
in Indonesia, 52,63
in *orang asli,* 39
Lee, Kwang-Kyu, 1,4,180,196
Lineage
Korean, 4,120,122–23
Puyuma, 7
Little tradition, 105–106

Manipulative behavior, *see* Strategy
Marginality, 185
Marriage
cross-cousin, 66
ghost, 122
system in Korea, 122
Material culture
Korean, 1,4,118–20,127–29
Philippine, 19
of the Taiwan aborigines, 96
Matriarchate, 111
Mead, Margaret, 11,278–80
Medicineman, 27
Memorial tablet, *see* Ancestor worship
Meru, 8,201–18 *passim*
origin and symbolic meaning of,
203–10
shape of, 202
sociopolitical change and, 210–14
and village society, 214–16

Method
comparative, 121
ethnohistorical, 118,134
qualitative, 57–59
quantitative, 58–59
statistical, 121
Middleman, 35
Migration
of the Chinese, 91
of the Filipinos, 2,23–25
of the Taiwan aborigines, 89–90
Minority group, 1–3,26,29,93,135
Model
believed-in traditional, 106
conscious, 106
immediate, 106
metaphorical definition of, 243
Modernization, 6,271
Mother-in-law complex, 122
Multiple burial, 126
Mythology, Korean, 117–19,129

Nakane, Chie, 108,181,264–65
National character, 264
National identity, 2,16,21
Nationalism
in Indonesia, 47
in Japan, 179
in the Philippines, 16
in Thailand, 150
Niida, Noboru, 109–11
Nutrition, sociocultural aspect of, 63

Oedipus complex, 127
Oral tradition, Korean, 1,
118–20,129–30
Orang asli, 2–3,29–41 *passim*

Patron-client relationship, 37
Personality
culture and, 279

Japanese, 10,259–273
Political conflict, 40
Political participation, of the *orang asli*, 38–39
Political structure, 3,40
Polygyny, 122
Population
    change, 21
    increase, 59,62
Praxis, and theory, 277
Puyuma, 7,172–78

Racism, 150
Rank, 39
Religious movement
    Javanese, 9,61,225–36
    kebatinan, 9,225–31
    messianic, 9,231–32
    santri, 9,232–36
Residence
    uxorilocal, 173–74,176
    virilocal, 174,178
Retirement field, 114
Rice-terracing, 24
Rite of passage, 119–120, 125,201–202

Salleh, Hood, 1–3,33
Sharecropping, in Indonesia, 53
Shamanism
    Korean, 4,7,117–20, 132–34,187–190–92
    Siberian, 133
Shifting cultivation, in Korea, 124
Shiga, Shuzo, 111–14
Sinology, 4,105–115, *passim*
Slum, ethnography of, 21,124
Social class, 8,27,106,112,271
Social mobility, 8,10,241
Social organization, type of, 26–28
Social stratification, 63,195
Social structure, 19,98

Sociology
    in Indonesia, 45–78
    in Thailand, 143,154
Sofue, Takao, 10,264,273
Strategy, of the Chinese, 241–258 *passim*
Structuralism, 6,134
Suenari, Michio, 4,6–7,180–81
Symbolism, 6,8,134

Taoism, in Korea, 118,195
Technology transfer, 21

Urbanization, 21,51,62,124,273

Vallibhotama, Srisakra, 2,4–5, 8,149,155,205
Value
    concept of, 3
    conflict of, 37
    economic, 40
    orientation, 19,22,50,57,62–63
    political, 39
    social, 41
Village
    compact, 27
    composite, 27
    lineage, 123
    study, 4,105,120,123–24

Wang, Sung–Hsing, 4,181
Ward, organization, 27
Ward, B.E., 105–106
Warrior, organization, 27–28
Wat, 201–18 *passim*
Woman study
    in Indonesia, 62
    in Korea, 122

Yoshimori, K., 266,269,272